SHAPING THE SUPERINTENDENCY

A Reexamination of Callahan and *The Cult of Efficiency*

SHAPING THE SUPERINTENDENCY

A Reexamination of Callahan and *The Cult of Efficiency*

WILLIAM EDWARD EATON
Editor

Teachers College, Columbia University
New York and London

Published by Teachers College Press, 1234 Amsterdam Avenue
New York, NY 10027

Library of Congress Cataloging-in-Publication Data

Shaping the superintendency : a reexamination of Callahan and The cult
   of efficiency / William Edward Eaton, editor.
      p.   cm.
      Includes bibliographical references.

      1. Callahan, Raymond E., 1921–   Education and the cult of
   efficiency.   2. Education—United States—History.   3. School
   management and organization—United States.   4. School
   superintendents—United States.   I. Eaton, William Edward, 1943–
   LA216.C283S53   1990
   370'.973—dc20   89-38171
                                                                          CIP

ISBN 0-8077-2985-X

Printed on acid-free paper

Manufactured in the United States of America

96 95 94 93 92 91 90 89   8 7 6 5 4 3 2 1

Contents

Preface   vii
Acknowledgements   xi

1. "The Emperor's New Clothes": Raymond Callahan and
   Education and the Cult of Efficiency
     Eugene F. Provenzo, Jr.   1

2. The Vulnerability of School Superintendents:
   The Thesis Reconsidered
     William Edward Eaton   11

3. Footnotes on Callahan's Teachers College
     Robert J. Schaefer   36

4. Raymond Callahan and *The Cult of Efficiency*:
   About the Writing of History of Education
     H. Warren Button   67

5. One Road to Historical Inquiry: Extending One's
   Repertory of Qualitative Methods
     Louis M. Smith   79

6. Reforming Education American Style
     Frank W. Lutz   110

7. Callahan's Contribution in the Context of American
   Realignment Politics
     Laurence Iannaccone   135

8. The Violation of People at Work in Schools
   Arthur G. Wirth   165

References   183
About the Contributors   195
Index   199

Preface

This book began as a conversation between several of us who had been students and colleagues of Raymond Callahan. Callahan was just planning his retirement from Washington University, and we were discussing that fact as we stood in the lobby of a San Francisco hotel in between sessions of an annual meeting of the American Educational Research Association. From the three or four of us that were in that particular group, the idea of putting together a series of essays that would commemorate the 1962 publication of Callahan's *Education and the Cult of Efficiency: A Study of the Social Forces That Have Shaped the Administration of Public Schools* spread to several other people who logically needed to be involved, and expanded to other ideas about methodology and education that were expressive of the current thought and work of the participants. It turned out that our group of authors included four former students of Callahan and four former colleagues.

Arthur G. Wirth and Louis M. Smith worked as colleagues of Raymond Callahan for over 30 years at Washington University's Graduate Institute of Education. The three were quartered in a small corridor that contained only six offices. This proximity contributed to close association over the years. As one would expect, there was the usual banter about handball games to be played, the welfare of their children and wives, and the latest scuttlebutt concerning some university or department issue. But the conversations did not end there. There was a deep and abiding respect among the three, and a scholarly paper or book could not be written without sharing the core ideas from inception to completion with one another.

Much of the credit for creating this exciting environment belongs to Robert J. Schaefer. Brought from Harvard in 1955 to be a departmental chair, Schaefer created the Graduate Institute of Education and became its first Director. He conceived the idea (based upon a direction already determined by Harvard), sold the plan to the central administration, and handpicked the new faculty. Within a relatively short time span, the department moved from no reputation to national recognition. Schaefer left St. Louis in 1963 to become the Dean of Teachers College, Columbia University.

Laurence Iannaccone was one of the young, bright stars brought by Schaefer to the Graduate Institute. His contributions to the emerging field of the politics of education were aided by his association with Raymond Callahan and the other faculty that were being assembled. Brought from his graduate studies at Teachers College, Columbia in 1959, Iannaccone stayed but a short time at Washington University before leaving to accept a professorship at the Claremont Graduate School in 1964.

Warren Button has the distinction of being both a colleague and a student of Callahan. At one time, both were graduate students in the Department of History at Washington University. While Button went to teach in the public schools, Callahan, taking advantage of the GI Bill of Rights entitlements that he had earned in the United States Navy, went to work on his doctorate at Teachers College, Columbia University. Callahan returned to accept a faculty appointment in 1952. Later, Warren Button became a graduate student and worked closely with Callahan in the creation of *Education and the Cult of Efficiency.*

Frank Lutz came to the Graduate Institute of Education to study school administration. Here he came under the influence of both Iannaccone and Callahan. Lutz had entered with the thought of returning to a career as a practicing school administrator. But the ideas and theories that were flowing freely were inspiring, and to be anything other than a scholar soon became out of the question.

Eugene Provenzo's graduate student days at the Graduate Institute of Education came toward the end of Callahan's productive career. Provenzo enjoyed the rare opportunity of working with a well-established scholar who still had "fire" in his belly.

I entered the Graduate Institute between the time of Button and Provenzo. This was at the economic zenith of the operation, when National Defense Education Act Title IV fellowships were plentiful and when the Graduate Institute was riding the crest of a Training Teacher Trainers (triple T) grant. Like Button before me and Provenzo who followed, I found Raymond Callahan to be an outstanding doctoral advisor. He was readily accessible, infinitely patient, and a careful listener to the personal problems and research dilemmas that inevitably plague graduate students.

The authors of this collection are well acquainted with Raymond E. Callahan's *Education and the Cult of Efficiency*. The book was an attempt to look objectively at the historical development of American public education at the turn of the century. Callahan delineated the major historical forces of the era, identified the major players, depicted actual administrative settings, and measured public opinion by reviewing the popular magazines of the period. His major focus was the effort to discover the canons of administrative theory that were shaping the position of school superintendent. What he found was that the impact of the big business ethic, specifically scientific management, upon the minds of school leaders was so profound that it had gone beyond the normal bounds of influence to become a cult. This cult of efficiency dominated administrative thinking and administrative theory for several decades to follow. Even today, we find remnants of enthusiasm for its tenets.

The danger in this, thought Callahan, was more than an overconcern for simple practicality. The danger lay in the tendency to establish a mechanistic view of schools that threatened to cheapen the idea of human development into a process/product analysis.

The field of education owes Raymond Callahan tribute for bringing this to our attention. *Education and the Cult of Efficiency* deserves a reading and frequent rereading so that the lessons it offers remain clear in our minds.

Acknowledgements

The authors of this book are grateful to Teachers College Press for agreeing to publish this manuscript. The people at the press were very easy to work with throughout the process.

The authors would also like to thank the several publishers who graciously allowed the use of sections of printed matter that come under their copyright protection. The publishers who were so cooperative included: The University of Chicago Press, which allowed us permission to quote extensively from Raymond Callahan's *Education and the Cult of Efficiency* and Thomas Kuhn's *The Structure of Scientific Revolutions*; J. H. Hexter, who permitted us to quote from *The History Primer*; Routledge and Kegan Paul for permission to use sections of Lawrence Stone's *The Past and the Present*; and The University of North Dakota's Center for Teaching and Learning for permission to quote from the study of S. Freedman, J. Jackson, and K. Boles entitled *The Effect of Teaching on Teachers*.

Special thanks are extended to the National Society of Professors of Education and to Teachers College *Record* for allowing the use of the chapter by Arthur G. Wirth. The chapter began as a draft for this Festschrift, developed into the Charles DeGarmo Lecture before the National Society of Professors of Education, and was then published in an edited version by the *Record* (Summer, 1989).

Finally, the editor of this book would like to thank his wife, Judy, and the secretaries of the Department of Educational Administration and Higher Education at Southern Illinois University at Carbondale— Ms. Teri Stobbs, Ms. Patty Glover, and Mrs. Debbie Mibb—who typed, printed, proofread, and covered for him while he tried to dodge his administrative responsibilities in order to meet the demands of manuscript production.

SHAPING THE SUPERINTENDENCY

A Reexamination of Callahan
and *The Cult of Efficiency*

1 "The Emperor's New Clothes":
Raymond Callahan and
Education and the Cult of Efficiency

EUGENE F. PROVENZO, JR.

Over 25 years after its publication, Raymond E. Callahan's *Education and the Cult of Efficiency* (1962) remains one of the most widely cited and influential books in the field of American educational history. In the following essay, an attempt is made to examine the significance of Callahan's work and its role in the historiography of American educational history.

The Genesis of *The Cult*

Callahan began the research for *Education and the Cult of Efficiency* in 1957. A former graduate student of the educational sociologist George S. Counts—to whom the book is dedicated—Callahan saw his research as being particularly relevant to the historical period in which he was writing. In the preface to the book, for example, he presents his main thesis, arguing that

> I am now convinced that very much of what has happened in American education since 1900 can be explained on the basis of the extreme vulnerability of our schoolmen to public criticism and pressure and that this vulnerability is built into the pattern of local support and control. This has been true in the past and, unless changes are made, will continue to be true in the future. Thus it was predictable in 1957 that school administrators would respond quickly to the criticism which followed the launching of the first Russian satellite and would begin to place great emphasis upon science and mathematics. It was also very predictable that they would welcome and quickly adopt James B. Conant's recommendations for change in the high schools,

1

for, with his great stature in the country, his suggestions were made to
order for defense. (p. viii)

Clearly, Callahan's work was a response to issues that faced educators in
the late 1950s and early 1960s. His findings led him to believe that it was
time to begin to "take a hard and realistic look at our patterns of local
support and control. These arrangements are supposed to protect us from
the tyranny of an all-powerful central government and to provide the
opportunity for local initiative and experimentation" (p. ix).

The Success of *The Cult*

Callahan's emphasis on the relevance of his work to contemporary
issues in education may, at least in part, explain the book's extraordinary
popularity. Its arguments clearly struck a chord that was meaningful to a
wide range of educators beyond just the field of educational history. In an
academic field where the average sales of a book may be 2,000 to 3,000
copies, Callahan's *Education and the Cult of Efficiency* sold tens of
thousands of copies. During its first ten years it went through six printings.

Besides achieving a wide readership, *Education and the Cult of
Efficiency* has also become a widely cited book. A review of the *Social
Science Citation Index* for the years from 1970 to 1985 puts into quantifi-
able terms how influential the book has been. During that period the
book was cited a total of 212 times in articles alone, ranging from a low of
6 citations in 1973 to a high of 24 in 1975; by 1985 it was still being cited
12 times, and none of these figures include the book's widespread citation
in other books.

The initial response to *Education and the Cult of Efficiency*, while
positive, did not give any hint of what would become its overwhelming
popularity. *Book Review Digest* for 1963 includes a total of nine journals
or magazines that reviewed the book. An occasional review can be found
in 1964 and 1965. In general, the response to the book seems to have been
typical for an academic book of its type. J. W. Stein, in the *Library
Journal* (1963), for example, explained that Callahan had "written an
important critical work for educational collections in many libraries"
(p. 3445). While writing a favorable review, N. H. Cartwright (1963) in
The Mississippi Valley Historical Review, described what he believed
were significant limitations of the book:

The book deserves to be read not only by those whom it indicts, but by all those concerned with the improvement of our schools. It should be read, however, for what it is and with due regard for what it is not. For all of the subtitle, the book is not a study of the social forces that have shaped the administration of the public schools. It is a study of only one of those forces. And even that is incomplete. It does not give adequate recognition to the fact that school superintendents are required to be business administrators. . . . The book should be taken for what it is, a useful caricature. As such, it emphasizes a particular feature which might be missed in the examination of a portrait. But it is no substitute for the portrait. (p. 722)

In retrospect, however, the real significance of the book is pointed to by a reviewer in the *Saturday Review* (P. W., 1962) who, after identifying Callahan, described the unique character of its content.

Callahan is a professor of education at Washington University in St. Louis and a student of George Counts of Columbia's Teachers College. . . . For a long time educators with such a background were on the defensive and reluctant to admit that anything had gone wrong with our great experiment of universal education. The fact that some of them are now willing to join in the critical reassessment may herald a new day in educational thought. (p. 60)

The Contribution of *The Cult*

Callahan's work represented the first full-length documentary study in what was to evolve into a major new thrust in American educational history. Although other distinguished works were being published in the early 1960s, such as Lawrence A. Cremin's *The Transformation of the School: Progressivism in American Education, 1876–1957* (1961), which won the Bancroft Award in History, it was Callahan's work which was the first to challenge the overly optimistic and traditional interpretation of "the public school triumphant" characterized by the early twentieth century educational historian Ellwood P. Cubberley.

According to Cubberley (1919), the growth and development of the public school system in the United States was part of an inevitable historical development:

> To be familiar with recent developments, to be able to view present-day educational problems in light of their historical evolution and their political and social bearings, and to see educational service in its proper setting as a great national institution evolved by democracy to help solve its perplexing problems, the writer holds to be of fundamental importance to the beginning student of education. (p. viii)

For Cubberley, the historical development of the United States and its public schools was part of a larger faith in America's destiny—a destiny closely linked to a belief in progress. This historical imperative—the acceptance of the inevitability of progress—was the assumption that drove the interpretation of the history of American education until the early 1960s.

Callahan was by no means the first historian to attack Cubberley's interpretation of the development of the American public schools. As Bernard Bailyn explained in his bibliographical study, *Education in the Forming of American Society: Needs and Opportunities for Study* (1960), Cubberley's work represented a highly limited and circumscribed interpretation of the history of American education, in which he had fallen into the trap of interpreting the past as "simply the present writ small" (p. 9). In other words, that the roots of our present culture, and in the case of Cubberley, our educational system, have simply been a logical extension or continuation of our European heritage and early Colonial experience.

Lester J. Cappon, in the introduction to Bailyn's work, maintained that while the history of American education had received a great deal of attention from scholars, it was a history that was viewed largely from the narrow perspective of formal instruction:

> The history of American education offers great opportunities for restudy, but not because it has been neglected or because it was strewn with technical abstractions during the early period. Instead, it has suffered at the hands of specialists who, with the development of public education at heart, sought historical arguments to strengthen their "cause." If there was a story of the past worth writing, it was viewed from the narrow concept of formal instruction. If schooling was institutionalized in the schoolhouse of the nineteenth century, its antecedent must be lurking in a comparable building of and curriculum of the colonial period. If the public school became the norm, its

origin must be discoverable in an inferior institution of an earlier generation. (in Bailyn, 1960, pp. vi–vii)

Cappon goes on to explain that an "unhistorical approach to the past, with its resulting anachronisms, has colored many of the works in the history of American education" (p. vii). Bailyn's work suggests to Cappon that there are abundant sources available for the writing and rewriting of American educational history.

The recognition of the need to rewrite the history of American education represents what is perhaps the most important contribution made by Bailyn (1960). For him, historian/educators like Cubberley had "with great virtuosity" drawn up "what became the patristic literature of a powerful ecclesia" (p. 8). In doing so, they became totally isolated from "the major influences and shaping minds of twentieth century historiography" (p. 9). According to Bailyn,

> The number of books and articles on the schools and colleges of the colonial period, on methods of teaching, on the curriculum, school books, and teachers is astonishingly large; and since at least the end of the nineteenth century the lines of interpretation and the framework of ideas have been unmistakable. And yet, for all of this, the role of education in American history is obscure. We have almost no historical leverage on the problems of American education. The facts, or at least a great quantity of them, are there, but they lie inert; they form no significant pattern. (p. 4)

American educational history had become almost exclusively limited to the history of formal instruction.

Bailyn's *Education in the Forming of American Society* ultimately argued that education was properly defined as the sum of all of those things intended to enculturate child, youth, and adult. Thus the history of American education included not only the institution of the school, but also the home, the church, newspapers, and so on. Schools were a small part of the total pattern and process. As argued in an earlier publication with my coauthor H. Warren Button (1983),

> Bailyn's advice was in some ways awkward to accept. It entailed a complete redefinition of a subfield of history. More exactly, it abol-

ished the accepted definition. History of education was cultural history and social history; all of history but "with the politics left out." It
was a prospect that opened bright possibilities for educational historians. It was also life in a ganzfeld, a world without cues and direction.
(pp. xiv–xv)

Bailyn had proposed a new conceptual mapping of the field—an alternative geography. What he had not done, however, was actually explore any
of the traditional regions of the field using the new conceptual approaches that he had outlined.

Callahan's accomplishment was that he was the first to explore the
traditional regions of educational history using the new conceptual
schemes outlined by Bailyn. This is not to say that he was necessarily
following Bailyn's lead. In fact, Callahan had been working on *Education
and the Cult of Efficiency* for at least three years prior to the publication
of Bailyn's work. What Callahan did do was take a traditional area of
educational history—school administration and more specifically the
history of the school superintendency—and debunk the myths surrounding it that had been created by individuals such as Cubberley.

Callahan cites the work of Cubberley in great detail throughout
Education and the Cult of Efficiency. When citing Cubberley speaking
before a general session of the 1915 meeting of the National Education
Association, Callahan clearly points to the role which Cubberley was
playing in creating a totally new professional model for the school
superintendent. Callahan (1962) quotes Cubberley to the effect that

> The recent attempts to survey and measure school systems and to
> determine the efficiency of instruction along scientific lines have alike
> served to develop a scientific method for attacking administrative
> problems which promises to compel us soon to rewrite the whole
> history of our school administration in terms of these new units and
> scales of measuring educational progress and determining educa-
> tional efficiency. All of these developments point unmistakably in the
> direction of the evolution of a profession of school administration as
> distinct from the work of teaching on the one hand and politics on the
> other. (p. 217)

Callahan points to the fact that Cubberley, in his textbook *Public
School Administration* (1916), began his chapter on "The Superintendent
of Schools" with the subtitle "A New Profession." For Cubberley, the

development of the school superintendency in the United States was part of a preordained process—one involving greater efficiency and social improvement. Callahan once again cites Cubberley who claims that

> School supervision represents a new profession, and one which in time will play a very important part in the development of American life. In pecuniary, social, professional, and personal rewards it ranks with the other learned professions, while the call for city school superintendents of the right type is today greater than the call for lawyers, doctors, or ministers. (p. 218)

Callahan, through meticulous research and reasoning, demonstrated in *Education and the Cult of Efficiency* that a much more complex model of the superintendency was at work than that described by Cubberley. According to Callahan, beginning in the early decades of this century a "cult of efficiency" began to be practiced in school administration. Business ideology based on the efficiency models of the time-motion study expert Frederick Taylor were applied, with often disastrous results, to education. Models of industrial efficiency were applied to classroom settings and the work of students and teachers. School superintendents, subject to the pressures of efficiency and their own vulnerability, capitulated to the demands of business.

One may take for granted that Callahan's was an innovative, perhaps even brilliant thesis. He demonstrated his ideas through a series of carefully reasoned and thoroughly documented arguments. Yet, even taking all of this into account, one is compelled to ask why the book had such an overwhelming impact on the field of educational history. Part of the answer may come from the fact that Callahan had developed an outstanding book at precisely the right time in terms of the development of the field. Callahan's research clearly demonstrated what other historians such as Bernard Bailyn were already pointing to—that the traditional interpretation of American educational history that predominated (the "Cubberlerian" point of view of the public school triumphant) was no longer adequate. Callahan was rather like the child who observed that not only were "the Emperor's new clothes" not magnificent, they did not exist at all. Callahan established through impeccable documentation that what Bailyn referred to as "the patristic literature of a powerful academic ecclesia" (p. 8) was essentially false. The historical evidence clearly demonstrated not only the weakness and vulnerability of the superintendency, but the limitations of the schools both in the past, and therefore by inference, in the present.

The publication of *Education and the Cult of Efficiency* represented the opening of an intellectual floodgate. In a certain sense, once the limitations of the schools and their administration—their complex function and extreme vulnerability—were demonstrated, they could never again be looked upon in the uncritical light of Cubberley and his followers. Callahan had quite literally shown that the Emperor was without his clothes.

The Cult and the
Shifting Historical Paradigm

What Callahan had accomplished can be explained in part by looking at the work of the historian of science Thomas Kuhn. In the now classic work *The Structure of Scientific Revolutions* (1964), Kuhn explains that in the early stages of development in any field of science such as physics or biology, researchers confront the same range of phenomena, but not the same particular phenomena. In describing these phenomena there is a wide range of interpretation concerning what is actually being observed.

Following the initial stages of a field's development, however, these differences in interpretation cease. What typically occurs is that a theory emerges in the form of what Kuhn describes as a "paradigm." A successful paradigm provides the most complete explanation available of the phenomena that a particular field of scientific inquiry is concerned with.

"To be accepted as a paradigm, a theory must seem better than its competitors, but it need not, and in fact never does explain all the facts with which it can be confronted" (Kuhn, 1970, p. 17). Thus Einstein's *Theory of Relativity* represents a classic example of the emergence of a new scientific paradigm—one that critically redefined the traditional understanding of Newtonian physics. Einstein's theories led to the redefinition of the existing scientific paradigm and provided the basis for the development of a new science. The extraordinary shifts in commitment from an old paradigm to a new paradigm are what Kuhn describes as "scientific revolutions."

The introduction of a new paradigm implies a redefinition of the field and its traditional knowledge, one that "requires the reconstruction of prior theory and the reevaluation of prior fact" (Kuhn, 1970, p. 7).

History, for Kuhn, becomes a means of inquiry. As he explains: "History, if viewed as a repository for more than anecdote or chronology, could produce a decisive transformation in the image of science by which we are now possessed" (p. 1).

By going back and examining how discoveries were actually made, a very different image emerges of how new scientific knowledge is created than what is typically described in most textbooks. Conflicts between researchers, false starts, and misinterpretations all determine the rate at which a field develops. The road to a unified research consensus becomes extraordinarily difficult to achieve.

What Callahan achieved in *Education and the Cult of Efficiency* was the demonstration of a new paradigm. His work, which came precisely at the right time and moment in the development of the field of American educational history, demonstrated the limitations of Cubberley's overly simplified interpretation of the public school triumphant. In this sense, Callahan, more than any other single historian, gave birth to what has subsequently been described as the Revisionist movement in American educational history. *Education and the Cult of Efficiency* was the first in a series of books that have redefined the field. Following Bailyn's suggestion, historians such as Lawrence Cremin not only questioned the traditional Cubberlerian interpretations of the public school triumphant, but suggested new sources and conceptual models that could be used to interpret the course of American educational history.

More radical historians were to follow. Michael B. Katz, in works such as *The Irony of Early School Reform* (1968) and *Class Bureaucracy and Schools: The Illusion of Educational Change in America* (1971), raised issues of class and social structure that were largely inconceivable if one were limited to the interpretive model presented by Cubberley. Other historians with similar arguments represent the historiography of the field over the past couple of decades.

The Prescription of *The Cult*

The widespread acceptance of Callahan's *Education and the Cult of Efficiency* should finally be understood in the context of the era in which it was written. Callahan, although a historian, had been trained primarily by a sociologist. He inevitably came to the field of educational history as something of an outsider looking in. From George S. Counts it is logical to assume that Callahan learned much of his critical and utilitarian perspective. *Education and the Cult of Efficiency* was published in the year of the Cuban missile crisis, at the height of the Kennedy Administration. He clearly saw his work as one that was important to the formulation of social policy. In the final chapter of the book, based upon his findings, he called for "bold and vigorous leadership from the education profession and from prominent persons in public life, including the President of the United States. We must realize the seriousness of the situation and approach the question as we would any other national problem" (p. 261).

Using his historical research as the basis for his arguments, Callahan asked his readers to realize that "the introduction into education of concepts and practices from fields such as business and industry can be a serious error. Efficiency and economy—important as they are—must be considered in the light of the quality of education that is being provided" (p. 263). In a certain sense, *Education and the Cult of Efficiency* was not only a case study of the history of the school superintendency, but a prescription for the creation of new models of schooling, and for new ways of understanding and interpreting the history of American education.

2 The Vulnerability of School Superintendents:
The Thesis Reconsidered

WILLIAM EDWARD EATON

Those who turn to Raymond Callahan's *Education and the Cult of Efficiency* (1962) for a quick review of what the "vulnerability thesis" is and what it entails are in for a bit of a shock. There is no chapter with that title; there are no labeled charts or graphs depicting the idea; indeed, the term cannot even be found in the index except as the following subentry: "Administrators: vulnerability and insecurity of, 52–54." Even within this meager two-page discussion, most of which is quotations from other sources, there is no mention that this is a major thesis. One has to go to the preface to see the thesis specifically stated:

> I am now convinced that very much of what has happened in American education since 1900 can be explained on the basis of the extreme vulnerability of our schoolmen to public criticism and pressure and that this vulnerability is built into our pattern of local support and control. This has been true in the past and, unless changes are made, will continue to be true in the future. (p. viii)

There is no shortened explanation as to what the thesis is, because the entire book is an explication of the vulnerability concept.

Callahan began his study of school administrators in an effort to trace the influence of American business leaders and business values upon the school. His attitude toward business was critical, and he got the idea that American education had suffered from undue interference from commercial quarters from his major professor at Teachers College, Columbia University—George S. Counts. *Education and the Cult of Efficiency* is dedicated to Counts. For Counts, though, the concept was ideological. Counts viewed American society in terms of the "haves and have-nots" and concluded that "democratic socialism" would provide

11

the only solution to this dangerous political and economic social division. Callahan was not similarly doctrinaire. He proceeded to look for historical evidence in tracing the influence of business upon the educational community.

Following the publication of *The Cult*, Callahan and H. Warren Button published a chapter entitled, "Historical Change of the Role of the Man in the Organization: 1865–1950" that was included in the 1964 Yearbook of the National Society for the Study of Education. Button had assisted Callahan in the research for *The Cult* and was now collecting information about school superintendents for his dissertation, which Callahan directed. The following quotation from *The American School Board Journal* caught the attention of both men early in their review of sources:

> No recent year has seen such wholesale changes in superintendencies and other high school positions as the present year—1913. In the Middle-West there has been a perfect storm of unrest culminating in wholesale resignations, dismissals and new appointments. (Callahan & Button, 1964, p. 80)

It was this quotation and other data of a similar sort that set Callahan's mind to work in an effort to explain such dramatic turnover.

The Formative Period of the American Superintendency

Vulnerability of school superintendents—and this is whom Callahan is talking about when he talks about "schoolmen"—began with the movement to centralize school management by the appointment of an agent to the board of education. Throughout the seventeenth and eighteenth centuries, elected boards of education effectively handled the decision-making processes. School enrollment was low, classrooms were often borrowed or rented, and there were no budgets for supplies, textbooks, or anything else beyond the pitiful wage of the teacher. By the midpoint of the nineteenth century, circumstances had changed. Rapid increases in the population combined with evangelical efforts on behalf of universal schooling by persons such as Horace Mann and Henry Barnard had led to the formation of school districts that had legal standing as corporate and political entities, that levied and disbursed taxes, that held land and buildings, that met payrolls of several teachers, and required pedagogical and managerial leadership. These activities, being beyond the capacity of part-time and uncompensated elected officials to attend to, gave rise to the need for school executives. The very first superintendents were appointed before the Civil War, but the real increase came after 1870. In 1870 there were but 29 persons who held the title superintendent (Cubberley, 1922, p. 58).

The shaping of the American school superintendency took place in the meeting halls of the National Education Association's Department of Superintendence and in the rough and tumble of the real world of schools before 1900. The early superintendents were interested in practical affairs because they had to be. This was a time of increasing enrollments, school construction, frenzied finance, and the molding of the educational bureaucracy. But the superintendents were also sensitive to the need to be educational philosophers and statesmen.

During the formative period of the superintendency, 1875-1900, the Department of Superintendence debated the emerging role of the superintendency. At least three different models of the superintendent were available to them: (1) the school inspector, (2) the business manager, and (3) the combined position of the general superintendent.

The school inspector was a European model well known to the American schoolmen. The federal systems of both Prussia and France employed school inspectors. The inspectors regularly visited all the schools in their jurisdiction, supervised instruction, took leadership in minor curricular adjustments, and offered pedagogical advice. They did not manage money or facilities; they did not hire teachers.

The business manager was an agent of the board of education responsible for obtaining contracts, supervising building construction, and overseeing the fiscal authority of the board. It was not expected that this person would be knowledgeable about pedagogical matters.

The combination role fused these other two offices. In 1884, R. W. Stephenson, the Superintendent of Schools of Columbus, Ohio, argued for the combination role:

> When a board of education under its general control commits the entire management to one officer, he is called the Superintendent of Schools; but when his powers and duties are limited to the selection of teachers, their assignment to grades, the organization of schools, clas-

sification of pupils, arrangement of the course of study, oversight of methods of discipline and teaching, and all that pertains to the conduct of the schools, that the supreme purpose for which they have been established may be attained, he is called the Superintendent of Public Instruction. In some cities and towns the superintendent is nothing more than the business agent of the board. His duties are limited to writing and inspecting contracts, faithfully reporting to the board all failure of teachers to keep the pupils under proper control, seeing that all employees of the board give full time, and in the case of failure see that the proper deduction of salaries is made, and keep himself informed of any rising danger of decapitation of any member of the board for whatever cause, keeping his finger on the public pulse of ward politicians and reporting the same at the earliest moment. (NEA *Proceedings*, 1884, pp. 283-284)

Having outlined these three models, Stephenson supported the general superintendent form. He acknowledged, however, that for "this work a superintendent is not fitted by his training and experience as a teacher. For this reason few men, every way competent to manage the department of instruction, are well qualified to direct wisely and economically the business affairs of a system of schools" (p. 286). The combination role would require someone "as the manager of finance, shrewd, economical, and liberal; as the superintendent of instruction, scholarly, judicious, systematic, and comprehensive, and as a politician, discreet, active, fearless, and patriotic" (p. 292). Interestingly, he used the same paper to call for greater efficiency in school administration, but warned against superintendents who were "machine men, who treat children as a mechanic would a pile of boards he runs through a planer. Their systems are iron-clad—children are dealt with in masses—individualities are ignored" (p. 291).

William H. Maxwell, Superintendent in Brooklyn, and later in New York City, argued before the Department of Superintendence in 1890 for the school inspector model. There would be, under his plan, state control of education, a uniform course of study, and a standardized way of dealing with school matters. A board of education would continue to exist, but as the agent of the state in matters of selecting school sites, superintending construction, and in disbursement of monies. Under this proposed system, the city superintendent would work for the state even though appointed by the local board. He should, thought Maxwell, be

appointed for life, as a Supreme Court Justice (p. 459). The superintendent would become, then, an inspector.

The discussion that Maxwell's address generated was longer and
more interesting than the address itself. H. S. Tarbell, of Providence,
Rhode Island, objected on the grounds that local control of education
was firmly entrenched. Aaron Gove, of Denver, thought that the business
functions belonged with the superintendent. Acknowledging that "it has
been said that 'the personal dangers to the superintendent are, that he
may become a business man,'" Gove felt that the greater "personal and
public danger with the superintendent is that he be incompetent intelligently to participate in the business affairs of the corporation, whose
executive officer he is or should be" (p. 462). Eventually, the model of the
combination of instructional supervisor and business manager held sway.
Being either one or the other was judged to be too limiting and impractical. This new superintendent was now doubly vulnerable; he would be
judged as educator *and* business manager.

The Vulnerability of the Superintendent

The research that produced *Education and the Cult of Efficiency*
(1962) persuaded Callahan that school superintendents were not only
susceptible to the threats of business interests, but to other social forces as
well. Many other forces could, and indeed would, materialize. This was due
to the nature of the job. Administrators were unprotected by tenure and
subject to the whim of the public. In many respects they were like elected
officials in this regard, but without the support of central committees or
without the means to placate hostile camps with patronage or pork barrel
legislation. Unlike politicians, they were appointed and reappointed by
school boards who were ordinarily elected by an extremely small number
of voters. Research demonstrates that such low voter turnout in school
board elections allows great possibility for single issue candidates, for
personal vendettas, and for mischief of every imaginable kind.

Vulnerability to Macro-issues

Vulnerability has both a "national" and a "local" dimension. Or, to
put it another way, there are macro-issues and micro-issues. *Education*

and the Cult of Efficiency is a historical case study of a macro-issue, the influence of the business ethic on the nation's schools. Other macro-issues that have greatly affected the schools during other time periods have been the declining resource base of the 1930s, the crowding and substandard nature of school facilities in the 1940s, the desegregation movement of the 1950s, the increase of civil rights for students in the 1960s, and the impact of drugs and the requirements of making special provisions for handicapped children in the 1970s. All of these issues generated their share of blue-ribbon commissions, pronouncements by self-styled experts, changes in state-mandated curricula, and sensational newspaper coverage. The local superintendent had to respond. His vulnerability to these macro-issues was directly proportional to his mental agility in convincing his board or the general public that he was aware of the issue and was working hard to shape the local response. The local response had to follow the local belief structure while being couched in the rhetoric established at the national level. Larry Cuban's (1976) historical case studies of school superintendents in the 1960s and 1970s ably demonstrates this process. But vulnerability also has the dimension of micro-issue.

Vulnerability to Micro-issues

Callahan's vulnerability thesis is based upon the observation that local school administrators are under pressure because of local control and support. The school superintendent is responsible to an elected, or in a few cases appointed, school board who reflect parochial viewpoints, the constraints of archaic local taxing patterns, and the ambiguities of community power structures. These realities often prevent the superintendent from the full exercise of professional judgment. Favoritism and nepotism in hiring and promotion, the award of food and materials contracts to local businesses, and even routine decisions as to whether a scholastic athlete should be disciplined may become issues that threaten the job of the superintendent. Or, as David Tyack (1964), phrased it:

> A schoolman's daily routine consisted—like that of a police chief's or surgeon's—in part of other people's emergencies, and the risks of mistake were great. But there was little effective way of sharing these risks within an understanding group of peers. So long as there was no agreed-upon canon of expertise in practice, and so long as laymen

were the omnipresent judges, life for the superintendent could be an endless accusation of malpractice. (p. 278)

Intraorganizational and Extraorganizational Factors

The vulnerability of the superintendent can also be analyzed in terms of whether or not the conflicts experienced are intraorganizational or extraorganizational. These are terms developed by Ziegler, Kehoe, and Reisman (1985) in their comparative study of school superintendents and city managers. By intraorganizational, they mean conflict that is generated within the bureaucracy as opposed to that coming from outside forces. Disgruntled teachers or an insubordinate principal would be examples of intraorganizational, while extraorganizational conflict could be illustrated by confrontational public groups angered over a school closing or a racial incident. They reported that the superintendents they interviewed, approximately 50 in their sample, indicated that the greatest source of problems was intraorganizational in nature. In either case, of course, the eventual conflict centers between the superintendent and the board of education.

Is Vulnerability Brought to the Job?

In the same work, Ziegler, Kehoe, and Reisman speculate as to whether the vulnerability of school superintendents is more perceived than real. They conclude that it is more perceived by comparing the nature of controversy faced by superintendents and city managers. School superintendents seem to have little stomach for conflict, and the authors postulate that this attitude is related to the nature of their training. Citing March and Simon (1958) and other textbooks, they claim that superintendent training programs teach students that conflict is bad, and that disagreement is unhealthy. They also claim that superintendents believe that "losing" such conflicts even 5 percent of the time is too often (p. 49). The conclusion, based upon limited evidence, is that superintendents bring vulnerability to the job.

This is an interesting idea, certainly worthy of further study, but not supported longitudinally. Superintendent training programs are things of the present and not of the past. Statistics on rapid superintendent turnover precede such programs by a number of years.

Vulnerability as Generalization and Thesis

In talking about the vulnerability thesis, we need to keep in mind that there are two aspects, the specific historical context of 1910 to 1930 and the more general assertion that vulnerability causes job turnover independent of time. The first instance is a historical generalization based upon data. The second instance is an example of a historical thesis.

Vulnerability as Generalization

Raymond Callahan's vulnerability generalization is specifically predicated upon at least three assumptions: (1) the influence of business and the business ethic upon the educational enterprise in the early twentieth century was likely to be pernicious and self-serving; (2) education would have been better if boards of education appointed "educational statesmen" of scholarly bent rather than managers; and (3) the superintendent's vulnerability increased over time because antagonisms were cumulative. The specificity of these claims, as stated in *Education and the Cult of Efficiency*, was for the period 1910 to 1930. Each of these points requires further discussion.

That business's influence was more likely to be pernicious to schools than beneficial was actually framed within rather narrow chronological limits. Callahan's claim is based upon events in business development between 1910 and 1930 and not in the era before or since. It was within that specific time frame that Taylorism, the cost accounting mentality, and "efficiency before all else" reached their zenith. *Education and the Cult of Efficiency* makes, I believe, a persuasive case that these ideas penetrated the fabric of American education and extracted a toll upon operations by reducing children to widgets and by converting the superintendent from an educational leader to a resource manager.

Profound social change is often reflected in metaphor, and, indeed, the era that Raymond Callahan described was no exception. For education it meant the virtual abandonment of the romantic nineteenth-century view of the school as a "garden." The extended metaphor depicted the child as a tender seedling, the teacher as a loving gardener, the curriculum as nutrient, and the final process as the transformation of the seedling into a blossoming, hardy plant. Henceforth, the school was a factory, the child was raw material, the teacher was an assembly line worker, the curriculum was the production process, and the final result was a marketable product wanted by a consumer economy.

Callahan wanted superintendents to be educational statesmen. By this he meant persons who took the long view of history, persons who accepted the belief that there was a sacred quality to childhood, persons who were by their very nature more philosophical, more reflective than reactive. His research had led him to examine the life and work of leading school superintendents. His personal favorite was William Maxwell, superintendent in Brooklyn, and then, following consolidation of the boroughs, New York City. Callahan also liked Andrew Draper, who moved from a superintendency to the Presidency of the University of Illinois. The ideal, though, would have been William Torrey Harris. It was Harris who superintended the St. Louis schools, who had retreated to Concord to become a full-time philosopher. But Harris had retired before the efficiency movement began. Least liked by Callahan were Frank Spaulding, Franklin Bobbitt, and Ellwood P. Cubberley, who became the villains of the piece. Callahan blamed them for not offering greater resistance to what he conceived as inimical forces.

The idea that vulnerability increases over time is not specifically developed in *The Cult*, but it is implied. The forces that can undermine the effectiveness of a superintendent are several and are cumulative. Decisions by school board members or pressures brought by teacher organizations or citizens' groups are often the result of a pattern of disagreement or frustration built up over time. The superintendent, thus, becomes accountable for all decisions made, both past and present, and even for those policies which he might personally disagree with, but is forced to administer because of board of education policy. This pattern leads to inevitable destruction.

Vulnerability as Thesis

The vulnerability thesis, which goes beyond 1910–1930 and is discussed as a predictive model, is predicated upon three assumptions: (1) the nature of the superintendency makes the holder vulnerable, (2) vulnerability is cumulative and thus increases over time, and (3) vulnerability leads to rapid turnover.

Consider the line graph shown in Figure 2.1 where the horizontal axis represents years of service from beginning to an unspecified time and

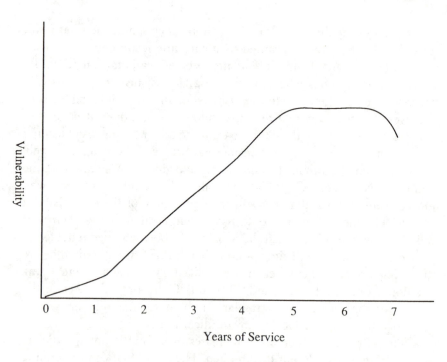

Figure 2.1   THE VULNERABILITY CURVE

where the vertical axis rises from no vulnerability (at the point of employment) to some degree of great vulnerability. The superintendent's vulnerability curve begins at the bisection of the axes and edges upward and to the right. This movement is related to the contract cycle. At the beginning, the superintendent is chosen and supported by a school board that is presumed to be completely or at least nearly unanimous in their support. Again, presumably, some period of "honeymoon" ensues between the board and their superintendent. But as time passes the opportunities for disaffection increase as the superintendent matches his ideas and operational methods with the preconceptions of individual board members. By the end of the second or third year, depending upon both the length of the contract and the scheduled board election, the first critical plateau is reached. The superintendent may now find a split board. The peak of vulnerability comes at the fourth to sixth year, again depending upon the contract and election cycle. At the peak, the superintendent's contract may not be renewed. This pattern is the basis of the Callahan thesis.

Reaction to the Vulnerability Thesis

Education and the Cult of Efficiency (Callahan, 1962) struck a responsive chord among educational scholars and practicing school superintendents. To begin with, it was a well-written book. Callahan wrote in a straightforward and uncomplicated manner and demonstrated great skill in marshalling mountains of data without overwhelming the reader. The book was also coincidentally well timed, as Provenzo has pointed out in Chapter 1. The American Historical Association had been concerned with the quality of historical research in education and had appointed a subcommittee to study the problem in the mid-1950s. Most of the committee's findings appeared in Bernard Bailyn's 1960 book entitled *Education in the Forming of American Society*. The book contained a stinging criticism of the work of educational historians and called for the need for critical scholarship in the field. Lawrence A. Cremin, who served on the subcommittee, responded with his highly regarded *Transformation of the School* in 1961, and Callahan's *Cult* appeared the following year. The book also helped to fill a void in the literature of a careful descriptive study of American schools in the early twentieth century.

The vulnerability thesis was well received by school administrators because it documented what was already a commonsense belief. Willard Waller, writing in his *Sociology of Teaching* in 1932, had said:

> We may say that the superintendent has a typical life history in the community. This typical life history repeats itself again and again in the life of one executive, and in the community with different executives. The life history seems to be about as follows: When the new executive takes charge of the school system, he has the support of nearly the entire community. . . . The board is usually with him to a man. This undivided support is his until some incident occurs which brings him into conflict with an individual or an organized group in the community. It is not long before such an incident occurs. . . . The essential weakness of his position is that it gives him an opportunity to

make many more enemies than friends. Opportunities for becoming unpopular, to the point, almost, of infamy, are numerous, but opportunities for gaining friends are few.

... At the end of his first year, the superintendent has made some enemies, but the majority of the community, let us say, is still satisfied with the manner in which he is conducting the school. He has made some bitter enemies, as, apparently, he unavoidably must. ... The superintendent has by now acquired certain enemies on the school board and they serve in the community as further radiant points of antagonism toward him. But the important fact, and the inexorable tragedy of the superintendent's life is that in the second year he usually makes a few more enemies, but he rarely has an opportunity to restore the balance by making friends of those who have previously been inimical to him. ... Let us say that the superintendent has given the community a satisfactory school and that he is able at the end of the second year to win the fight. But if he does win at the end of the second year, he stands a greater chance of losing at the end of the third, for his position is continuously weakened. He makes more enemies than friends. And he makes decided enemies, if not bitter enemies, and only lukewarm friends. (quoted in Carlson, 1972, pp. 137–138)

Book reviews of *The Cult* provide a couple of points of discussion. Lloyd Jorgenson, writing in *School Review* (1964), applauded Callahan's painstaking research and recommended the book to "regular" historians, educational historians, and educationists. Jorgenson's objections centered around the book's commitment to proving the vulnerability thesis:

It is safe to say that most readers will consider this a highly significant piece of work, quite apart from the validity of the vulnerability thesis. Even granting that local control has been a fruitful source of mischief in American education, some would question the adequacy of this thesis as an all-embracing explanation of the weaknesses of American school administration. It comes uncomfortably close to being a single-causation theory, and the fate of single-causation theories in historical work has not been a happy one. (p. 234).

Jorgenson's charge is a serious one which will be dealt with later in this chapter.

A principal strength of Raymond Callahan's *Education and the Cult of Efficiency* was the effort at laying some of the blame of school failure at the feet of schoolmen. The literature of the field of educational history, prior to this time, was characterized by the defensive posture maintained by the writers. They were more than willing to ascribe all shortcomings to uncontrollable outside forces. Ellwood P. Cubberley's writings in education provide a classic example. Cubberley cast the history of American education into an epic similar to Norse mythology where the victories of American public education were won at terrible cost on the field of honor and the enemies quickly regrouped to plan the next assault.

Contemporary reactions to the vulnerability thesis have come from historians, educational philosophers, administrative theorists, and administrative practitioners.

The reaction to the vulnerability thesis by historians is such that it would be fair to characterize it as mixed. Part of the problem goes back to the objection raised by Jorgenson in *School Review* (1964): historians have a trained conscious prejudice against single-cause theories and, actually, against theses in general. The development of the contemporary historical paradigm came only after long warfare with historical determinists who espoused a variety of single-cause theories ranging from religion to Marxism. Part of the current inflexibility on the part of historians comes from the fact that the war is not over and the issue remains sensitive.

Most historians are trained in their craft to make very limited claims as a result of their scholarship. They do make generalizations dependent upon time, place, and circumstance, but hesitate to go beyond that. A historical thesis is different from a historical generalization in that it claims to break the bounds of time, and, to a far lesser extent, place and circumstance. The word "thesis" that trails vulnerability in the phrase vulnerability thesis, therefore, creates discomfort.

Educational historians are more generous to the vulnerability generalization of the period 1910–1930. *Education and the Cult of Efficiency* is considered a valuable contribution to the field of historical endeavor. Having said this, it should be pointed out that educational historians, like regular historians, come in every hue and shade and that those who profess strong ideological dispositions react in different ways to the work of Callahan. Marxists have found some comfort in noting the bourgeois nature of the efficiency movement. Revisionists have found less to applaud. They believe that Callahan did not go far enough in condemning the schoolmen. Still others would view Callahan's work as unnecessarily critical of the schoolmen.

Though the number of educational philosophers who have noted the work of Callahan has been small, those who have noted it have been supportive. Carmine Yengo, writing in the *Harvard Educational Review* (1964), posited:

> In delineating this relationship between scientific management and the changes undergone by American public education in the first half of the twentieth century, Dr. Callahan has performed a scholarly service which the field of education has sorely needed since Dr. Merle Curti first glimpsed the same relationship in 1935. (p. 34).

Administrative theorists have paid the most attention to Callahan's vulnerability thesis. The field of administrative theory is dominated by the paradigm of political science and is couched in the language of political construct. Power, being the central construct of political science, can be analyzed within the bureaucratic setting of the school system. Typical of such an approach would be *Governing American Schools: Political Interaction in Local School Districts* by Ziegler, Jennings, and Peak (1974). The authors, in the third part of their book, look at conflict and cooperation between boards and superintendents, taking the position that the superintendent and the board are engaged in a contest for influence.

The idea and reality of vulnerability has been supported by practicing school administrators. In an article entitled "Urban Superintendents: Vulnerable Experts," Larry Cuban (1974), then superintendent at Arlington, Virginia, described the perils of the urban superintendency:

> In 1953, for the 25 largest school systems, the average incumbent superintendent served six and a half years; a decade later current tenure slipped to five and a half years; and in 1973 it was just over four years.
>
> Consider turnover rates. Between 1960 and 1969 only two large urban school systems held onto their top schoolman. Between 1970 and 1973, of the 25 largest school systems, 23 (92%) appointed new superintendents.
>
> Around him [the superintendent] swirls a perpetual cross-fire of expectations, requests, and demands from board members, middle-level bureaucrats, principals, teachers, students, and civic groups. Yet he sits atop this complex, often disorganized system exercising little control over what happens. For example, different board members

may enter and exit. Inflation rates rise while financial resources are inflexible. Principals may ignore or sabotage mandated programs.

Impossible demands are placed upon the superintendent's time and energy. One candidate for an urban superintendency was told by a finger-shaking member of the search committee, "We want you available to us seven days a week, 24 hours a day." (p. 280)

An interview with Mark Shedd, just after he was ousted as Superintendent in Philadelphia in 1972, produced the following bittersweet conjecture:

In the last analysis, with most decisions you make, you're damned if you do and damned if you don't. These days it's a no-win game, so you might as well make up your mind to do what you think is right and let the chips fall where they may. (quoted in Blumberg, 1985, p. 7)

Practicing school administrators who know about the vulnerability thesis seem to accept it as true and reasonable. Those unfamiliar with the concept are no less insistent that they lead a precarious professional life.

Education and the Cult of Efficiency, and the vulnerability thesis which it espouses, is still a widely read and oft-cited book. The fact that it is still in print twenty-five years later is adequate evidence to support the former contention, and Provenzo in Chapter 1 gave evidence to support the latter.

But it is fair to ask more detailed questions about the vulnerability issue, using contemporary data and theory. The focal point is the superintendent of schools.

The Thesis Reconsidered

Contemporary Data

A great deal is known about the people who occupy the American school superintendency, and this has been true since the 1920s. The American Association of School Administrators (AASA) studied its membership in 1922, 1932, 1951, 1959, and 1971. In 1958, Neal Gross, Ward S. Mason, and Alexander W. McEachern published their *Explorations in Role Analysis: Studies of the School Superintendency Role,* which studied over 100 superintendents and 500 board of education members in the Commonwealth of Massachusetts. Countless doctoral dissertations have looked at the superintendency as well.

Current data on the American superintendent of schools appears in the fall 1986 issue of *Spectrum* entitled, "Characteristics of Public School Superintendents." Superintendents work a 54.6 hour work week, they have 9.7 years of experience as a superintendent, 64 percent are satisfied with their work, 95 percent are male, 37 percent hold the doctoral degree, and 50 percent of them think that their salaries are adequate. The latter reaction is understandable given a national average salary of $60,700. It is this level of salary that represents the most dramatic change in the longitudinal data on superintendents. Comparing the AASA data of 1971 with those of the Educational Research Service (ERS) data of 1985, one finds salaries moving from an average of $17,433 to that of $60,707. Perhaps the advent of collective bargaining was responsible for the change. As teacher pay increased, boards of education kept the superintendent's ratio of pay to teachers at a 2.5 to 3.0 differential.

The average age of the superintendents has increased a little over the last 60 years, but so has the average age of the population in general. Educational levels have notably increased because of changes in the certification requirements of the states and because of the competitive nature of the job of superintendent. The incentive of good pay has apparently caused interested applicants to want to be able to present themselves as both experienced and well-educated. The doctoral degree, for example, is seldom required for the position of superintendent. Having the degree is believed to give one an advantage over those applicants who do not possess the degree, but have similar work experience. The one factor that has changed the least, even given demographic changes in our nation that would have led to other conclusions, is that a large number of persons who occupy the superintendent's position were born and reared in rural areas or small towns. In 1971 the figure was an astounding 86 percent!

Contemporary studies of the superintendency reinforce Callahan's concept of vulnerability. A study of West Virginia superintendents undertaken by Martin and Zichefoose (AASA, 1980) showed that the "failure rate"—defined as superintendents who were fired or resigned to move to a "lesser" position—was over 90 percent. "The superintendent is a political animal whose fight for existence is nearly always doomed to failure," say Martin and Zichefoose.

To enhance the chances of survival they recommended more training in business management:

> Businessmen dominate boards. . . . Businessmen expect superintendents to have the business acumen and financial ability to make management decisions about a multi-million dollar enterprise that will permit the organization to operate in the most economical and efficient way possible. . . .
>
> In order to increase the probability of success, superintendent programs must be infused with massive doses of business management, political science, sociology and communication skills. (pp. 3 & 5)

The data on West Virginia superintendents support the vulnerability thesis. The comments of the authors also introduce a point of great concern for Callahan—the influence of the business ethic in the training of superintendents. Believing in the efficacy of business methods, boards of education require superintendents to be familiar with such procedures. Superintendents, or superintendents-to-be, realizing such board expectations, require that their training programs contain such elements. They feel that they already know something about curriculum, instruction, and general education as a consequence of having been a teacher. What is wanted is information about finance, management, and school law. This is reflected in the surveys of AASA. When asked to rank the graduate courses considered to be of most value to them, superintendents responded by saying that courses in school finance, personnel administration, public relations, management, law, supervision, and data processing were most important. Professors of educational administration, anxious to preserve enrollments, design such courses, and all parties become locked into the cycle. Robert Schaefer alludes to such a cycle in Chapter 3 of this book.

Courses considered least important had to do with psychology, sociology, curriculum, and teaching methods. But one should be a little wary of such responses because graduate training in administration comes early in one's professional career. It might be true that superintendents who possess the survival skills gleaned from the subject matter of finance and law would then appreciate advanced knowledge of curriculum, instruction, arts, social science, and the humanities, but their "formal" training has been completed.

Change Increases Vulnerability

The forces and movements that make the superintendency difficult change over time. From 1900 to 1930, the period analyzed by Callahan, efficiency was often at the root of the problem. In the 1930s the Great Depression required financial wizardry to keep many school districts solvent. In the 1940s superintendents had to plan for severe crowding in the nation's classrooms. In the 1950s the massive school building programs created difficulties for the superintendent who could not plan and execute brick and mortar operations. In the 1960s the major problems were civil rights, desegregation, and busing. In the 1970s school discipline, drugs, special education, accountability, and shrinking enrollments that led to reductions in the teaching force and the closing of schools were central issues. In the 1980s the emphasis has shifted to curriculum and student achievement. Overlapping these issues has been the constant problem of establishing workable and reasonable relationships with increasingly strident teacher organizations.

This fact of change helps to explain some of the vulnerability of superintendents. The successful superintendent of the 1960s who possessed the skills necessary to control and appease angry citizens on such emotional issues as desegregation and busing may not have possessed the skills needed for the 1970s. Larry Cuban's (1976) study of four urban superintendencies describes that reality very well. New eras demand new skills, and last year's successes do not guarantee continuing success.

Reasons for Superintendent Turnover

Turnover among school superintendents has been studied from several angles. Richard Carlson (1972) divided superintendents into two groups: "place-bound" and "career-oriented." Though Carlson's definition is more sophisticated, a simple explanation of the idea is that the latter plans for the job in terms of training and then makes career moves strategically, hoping to end up in a prestigious position, while the former more or less falls into the job. Several subsequent studies have accepted Carlson's terminology and have collected data that support Carlson's contentions that the career-bound superintendent moves with greater frequency. Though of value to the field and interesting in concept, Carlson's findings do not directly relate to vulnerability. Most of what Carlson describes is voluntary turnover.

The reasons for *involuntary* turnover among superintendents are much more difficult to ascertain. There is a natural and understandable reluctance for superintendents who have been fired to want to document the reasons for some researcher. Both individual superintendents and boards of education go to unusual lengths to make dismissals look like voluntary turnover. This they do in an effort to mask certain local problem situations and as a result of agreements with superintendents who exact pledges to make dismissal look like voluntary turnover in exchange for their quietly leaving before the contract period expires. Involuntary turnover includes such factors as district consolidation, death or serious illness, and dismissal. It is this last factor, dismissal, that is at the heart of the vulnerability thesis. Alas, it is the most difficult factor to document.

Martin Burlingame's study (1977) of turnover among superintendents in Illinois between 1960 and 1976 is as good a study as we have, both because it systematically collected data from a sample of 100 superintendents, and because it thoroughly reviewed similar studies conducted elsewhere. Burlingame's data supported the data collected in other states, to wit:

1. Small districts have the highest rate of superintendent turnover. The tenure of those superintendents is short.
2. Small districts usually employ individuals as superintendents who have had either no prior experience as superintendents or who have a pattern of serving as superintendents in small districts for short time periods—usually less than three years.
3. Roughly one superintendent of every five (20 percent) is new to his or her district each fall. Small district superintendents are disproportionately represented in this category. (p. 6)

Burlingame's review of the other studies concluded that true vertical mobility among superintendents was small. Most superintendents sought new positions in districts that paid more money but had approximately the same number of pupils and teachers. This represents horizontal mobility. Burlingame's findings for the state of Illinois paralleled the national literature. He even found that mobility was not only horizontal in terms of the size of the district, but also had a geographic aspect: Superintendents in suburban areas stayed in the suburbs, downstate superintendents stayed downstate, and so forth. The data, however, cast little light on the issue of dismissal.

My observation is that certain districts are more likely to repeat the pattern of dismissal. This could be due to a number of causes:

1. The local situation has reached the degree of "impossible" (angry citizens, severe financial conditions, uncontrollable teacher unions, and so forth).
2. Once dismissal procedures are instituted by a board they find they have less reluctance to repeat them, (known among the practitioners as "the shark has the smell of blood").
3. A new superintendent who replaces a dismissed predecessor is subject to more scrutiny.
4. The membership of the board has usurped the power normally given to the professional administrator and refuses to return it.

Even this list of possible reasons is far from exhaustive. Specific studies which attempt to get at the last factor need to be conducted. It would be my hypothesis that boards of education comprised of persons who have never worked in a setting that required the separation of policy development from administrative action might not understand the need for this separation. Farmers, housewives, small business owners, and self-employed individuals would have no experience with such separation of function. Superintendent training programs, on the other hand, place a heavy emphasis upon the separation of such functions.

Laurence Iannaccone and Frank Lutz's *Politics, Power and Policy: The Governing of Local School Districts* (1970) uses a political model to describe one dimension of vulnerability. They view the stability of the board as a critical issue. A stable board tends to develop stability between itself and the superintendent. Changes in the board bring the conditions for instability and set the stage for dismissal. This would not create vulnerability since vulnerability is already there in latent form. It would, however, serve as a catalyst to speed up the reaction in human chemistry.

Possible Refinements to the Thesis

It is my contention that Raymond Callahan's vulnerability thesis goes a long way in explaining the actual situation of school superintendents. With the refinements that will be suggested here, it could become an even more powerful explanatory thesis.

Effect of School District Size

Analyzing the American superintendency as though it were a monolithic entity would be a mistake; the size of school districts varies immensely. The general superintendent in New York City who is responsible for over 40,000 teachers and who oversees so many schools that he or she could not visit them all in a single school year has a fundamentally different job than the superintendent who manages a single building with six teachers. The American Association of School Administrators, in its longitudinal studies of the superintendent, realizes this and has divided the superintendency into four groups. Group A includes those superintendencies with pupil enrollment of 25,000 or more. Group B ranges from 3,000 to 24,999, Group C is 300 to 2,999, and Group D is under 300. The later studies done by the AASA further refine this division by breaking Group A into three subgroups: superintendent with 100,000 or more students, those with 50,000 to 99,999, and those with 25,000 to 49,999.

If Callahan was aware of these divisions and used them in forming his vulnerability thesis, it is not apparent in the sources that he cited. When one actively takes such divisions into account, certain refinements are possible.

The American superintendent's first job is typically in a Group C district (300 to 2,999 students). This provides the greatest opportunity for a young man (or rarely, woman) to enter the position. The pay is lower, though still greater than that of the corresponding teacher or principal in the district, and the managerial responsibilities are small. Entering the first superintendency represents a significant career shift. The job is shaped by the expectations of the school board. As noted earlier, the school board, consisting of lay persons with little knowledge of contemporary educational thought, do understand something about the importance of fiscal management, building maintenance, and the threat of lawsuits. Since these areas attract the greatest interest of board members, they write job descriptions that reflect that concern. This places the beginning superintendent into the dilemma of having to learn quickly and demonstrate expertise in areas previously unknown to him. This in

turn shapes expectations about further graduate training in school administration on the part of the new superintendent.

Studies that have looked at involuntary turnover have been mostly
case studies documented in large city settings corresponding to AASA's
Group A. Most of the case studies thinly veil particular situations of past
or current activity in New York City, Los Angeles, or Chicago. Yet the
data tell us that the greatest turnover among superintendents takes place
in Group C settings, which are the settings we know the least about. In
part, the problem is a result of administrative theorists who have formulated the language of analysis. The concepts and constructs have been
derived from urban and suburban school districts. In many cases, there
are no parallels in rural or small town situations.

It should be understood that the form and content of vulnerability
varies from district to district and can also be related to the size of the
district or community served. Politics in small communities tend to be
informal and covert. In large cities the politics tend to become formal
and overt. Actions in small communities may result from the lack of a
countervailing force. If the small community has but a single church or a
single car dealership, then the superintendent had better consider his
religious tenets and automobile preferences. In a larger community, the
existence of a dozen churches and a dozen dealerships negates the
problem. Small town superintendents also speak with some frequency
about encountering "first families," individual irate parents, unchange-
able traditions, and the aggressive determination to remain firmly in the
nineteenth century. Big city superintendents complain of unfriendly
newspapers, partisan politics, and the necessity of jumping on every new
educational bandwagon that comes down the street. There are, then,
differences in type of vulnerability, and subsequent investigations might
show one kind to be more dangerous than another. Callahan, though, did
not develop this idea. Most of his historical data were drawn from case
studies of big city superintendents.

The Idea of Cultivation

There is an antidote to the cumulative nature of vulnerability. What
Professor Callahan came to realize was that the astute superintendent did
not sit idly by and let this negative scenario mechanically unfold without
attempting to influence its course. This is achieved by "cultivating"
school board members. Meeting with them personally in both social and

professional settings, seeking advice when it is not really needed, and encouraging supporting board members to have their friends, or at least those of like mind, to stand for election to the board, are examples. This process of cultivation serves as the counterweight to the natural force of increasing vulnerability. Where this is successfully done, the curve moves down the vertical axis over time. Though it may never reach the point achieved at the beginning, it can provide a superintendent with an extremely long tenure of service. Callahan saw this and often remarked, in his classes, of the long career of Aaron Gove in Denver who served as superintendent from 1874 until 1904.

Cultivating a board of education is a process that has been known about for some time. Again looking at Ellwood P. Cubberley's 1922 revision of *Public School Administration*, we find a section called "Educating a Board." Here, Cubberley asked an unnamed superintendent "who had held his position for nearly a quarter of a century, and who was noted for his ability to carry his board of education with him, what was the secret of his fine control" (p. 146). The superintendent replied,

> "I spend much time in familiarizing my board with the needs of the schools, and the reasons for the recommendations I desire to make. Sometimes this is done by taking board members with me for a day in the schools, sometimes it is done over a dinner table." (p. 146)

This cultivation idea, if employed, can introduce a corollary to the vulnerability thesis.

The Development of Professionalism

Vulnerability has also been counteracted by professionalism. By professionalism I mean the concerted effort, over time, toward creating a distinct occupational role and then setting about to persuade others that the "ideal" role that one espouses is a standard everyone should accept. This involves both actual skills and preferred behaviors. Professionalism usually implies a certain exchange. In exchange for systematic training and endorsement of a code of ethics, the professional demands autonomy in the process of exercising judgment over practice. The best analogies come from the fields of law and medicine, and the whole idea of bringing similar arrangements to education has been best developed by Myron Lieberman in his book, *Education as a Profession*, which was published in 1956.

Most of the effort in establishing professionalism, be it myth or reality, is undertaken by associations. The associations establish standards of licensure and write conduct codes and then develop strategies for indoctrinating the general public into accepting autonomy as a quid pro quo. This process has been happening in American education for both teachers and administrators for over a hundred years. The successes or failures of the process are directly related to the degree to which the public accepts the exchange. For administrators, the "public" refers mainly to the specific composition of the local school board. The effort has been made to educate school boards into understanding the difference between policy and its administration. The general rules and guidelines which constitute policy are offered as the province of the board. The manner and means of carrying out policy are defined as administration. The superintendent wants a free hand at administering board policy without having a board of education peering constantly over his or her shoulder. This accomplished, often at great effort, the superintendent makes subtle encroachment into policy by attempting to influence policy formulation by controlling the board's agenda.

Such professionalism works as a counter to vulnerability to the degree that it is successful. If a superintendent can educate the board appropriately, certain issues that might increase vulnerability can be neutralized by the doctrine of professionalism. As examples, consider two situations. In situation one the superintendent is faced with a decision that, due to its inherent nature, will satisfy one group while angering another. The astute superintendent will search for existing policy upon which to make a decision which he or she can then hide behind. If no such policy exists, the superintendent will go to the board and lay out a hypothetical situation, which is actually real, and then seek the formation of a policy to hide behind. In either case the policy becomes a shield. Policy manuals are very popular with practicing superintendents.

In situation two, the superintendent attempts to institute an innovation. Innovations of any kind are fraught with danger. The prudent superintendent avoids them. But when faced with an unrelenting demand for innovation, the wise superintendent reviews the educational literature, looking for successes elsewhere. The superintendent then implements the change, using the experience of another community as the blueprint. Failure or problems that arise from the innovation can then be explained away as a failure in the professional knowledge base and not as failures of local leadership.

Conclusion

In summary, it appears clear to me that the vulnerability of school superintendents has been demonstrated both by data on turnover and by the anecdotal record of superintendents themselves. Callahan should be credited with singling out this phenomenon and naming it. The case he makes for the business ethic being a major "macro-issue" in the era 1910–1930 is also persuasive. What is needed, however, are studies which attempt to control a number of variables that have been identified.

The primary difficulty will lie in gathering accurate data on which superintendents have actually had their employment terminated. As pointed out earlier, there is a certain determination on the part of boards of education to make "involuntary" dismissal look "voluntary." Assuming that this can be done, it would then be useful to look at such variables as size of district; orientation of the superintendent, using Carlson's career-oriented or place-bound; cause of the dismissal (macro-issue vs. micro-issue, intraorganizational vs. extraorganizational); the nature of the board itself, using some of the concepts developed by Lutz, Iannaccone, Ziegler, and others who work in the area of the politics of education; the predispositions of superintendents which are a result of formal training; and the role of professionalism. Such studies would be a significant addition to the literature of educational administration.

3 Footnotes on Callahan's Teachers College

ROBERT J. SCHAEFER

If a leisurely traveler meandered down the Wabash River south from Vincennes toward Evansville, he would pass through the village of New Harmony. Unless he were particularly observant of roadside plaques, or an avid amateur historian, the brief encounter would seem in no way memorable. New Harmony appears identical to hundreds of other rural hamlets in southern Indiana—small, slow-moving, bypassed, and somnolent. There is scant vestige of the exciting social experiments which once flourished there. Neither the German communitarian settlement under George Rapp, nor the socialist community founded by the English philanthropist, Robert Dale Owen, have left much of a visible trace. The absence of artifacts, however, should not obscure New Harmony's significance both to utopian socialism and to Marx's later formulation of scientific socialism.

In comparable fashion, if a casual traveler strolled through the offices and classrooms of Teachers College (TC), Columbia University, he or she could not easily discern that some of Raymond Callahan's arch villains and most idolized heroes once flourished there. As an organic institution whose existence transcends the lives of individuals who constitute its ranks in particular historical periods, the College retains few clues about the personalities of former professors, whether heroic or villainous. Similarly, the details of faculty debates, irrespective of how passionate they may have been, are obscured, even transmuted, in the officially bland minutes of faculty meetings. There are no roadside plaques on 120th Street. Nor are there historical tablets in the corridors to remind the visitor of the intellectual and emotional investments once made in arguments about the appropriate preparation of school administrators. But just as the communal experiments at New Harmony affected the later development of socialist thought, one suspects that early training programs in school administration, which Callahan deemed capitulation to a pervasive business ideology, exert a continuing influence on the life of the College. My "Footnotes on Callahan's Teachers College" are essentially an effort to explore such a suspicion. The inquiry will be guided by a series of issues implicitly or explicitly raised by Callahan (1962) in *Education and the Cult of Efficiency*.

Clearly, Callahan's concerns were far broader than the mere in-house life of a single institution. His focus, as the subtitle of his book indicates, was the *Social Forces That Have Shaped the Administration of the Public Schools*. Its grand theme was the vulnerability of school superintendents, and its summative conclusion was that events and forces affecting education between 1910 and 1930 constituted an American tragedy. Even when his investigations demanded analysis of the role of universities in the drama, Callahan dedicated approximately equal time, and equal denunciation, to developments at Chicago, Stanford, and Harvard as he devoted to Columbia. My footnotes, then, are admittedly partial, and like a movie version of a great book, pay little heed to the author's original intentions.

Conflicting Perspectives on the Influence of Training

At no point in his *Education and the Cult of Efficiency* does Callahan systematically develop or defend the thesis that university preparation in school administration determines how administrators actually behave on the job. In common with most of us who spend their professional lives in training others for educational roles, he simply assumes that what professors do, or fail to do, is crucially important. He marshalls overwhelming evidence, of course, that early studies in administration emphasized technical, often seemingly trivial, aspects of the job. He demonstrates convincingly that courses in school economies, pupil accounting, personnel, and plant management predominated to the disadvantage of possibly broader inquiry into the purposes of education, the needs of society, the facilitation of the teaching-learning process, or the role of schools in a democracy. He avers, somewhat poignantly, that if only early professors in administration had had the wisdom, or perhaps the moral strength, to resist invidious business ideology, we would not so universally conceive of schools as factories, pupils as products, teachers as labor force, and superintendents, not as educational statesmen, but as Chief Executive Officers. "If America," he concludes, "had had a tradition of graduate training in administration—genuinely educational, intellectual, and scholarly, if not scientific—such a tradition might have served as a brake or restraining force" (p. 245).

In describing early preparatory programs so carefully, and criticizing them so vigorously, Callahan affirms his assumption that what is taught in large degree determines job performance. Many of us, pedagogically optimistic, share this assumption; certainly, as will be demonstrated later, contemporaneous professors and most students at Teachers College believed enthusiastically in the significance of their studies. The point, however, is that not all observers of the period hold a comparable faith in the influence of training. Some, indeed, assume that training is largely irrelevant.

A number of critics have argued, somewhat persuasively, that university programs in educational administration are inherently ineffectual. They remind us that an overwhelming majority of aspiring, and often practicing, administrators undertake graduate training on a strictly part-time basis while carrying emotionally draining full-time jobs. How can attitudes be changed, fresh conceptualizations understood, or new skills mastered if one's primary energies must necessarily be devoted to the "here and now" demands of school work? Others point to the all-too-familiar credentialing syndrome—the state-mandated requirement to enroll in prescribed courses irrespective of prior experience, perceived relevance, or consensus within the university or profession about what such studies might profitably entail. Still other skeptics bemoan the lack of high admission and/or scholarly standards in most university schools of education, the press upon professors by students to respond to on-the-job particulars, or, more important, our inability to persuade students that programs in administration possess a constantly enlarging, elegantly coherent body of theory and knowledge that is crucial to successful performance.

David Tyack and Robert Cummings (1977) summarize such arguments as follows:

> Under certain conditions specialized training might have considerable impact on the subsequent careers of graduates. One way is the transmission of particular skills or knowledge clearly needed in a distinct occupation—for example, in electrical engineering. Another way professional programs have an effect is to ration entry into an occupation as medical schools do with their restrictive admission and

limited output. A third model of influence might be to provide intense socialization in the distinct norms of a group—for example, at West Point or a Jesuit seminary.

Graduate training in educational administration fits none of these models very well. There is intense argument and considerable diversity in practice concerning the skills or knowledge necessary for superintendents. Unlike medical schools, programs in educational administration have generally not been selective in admission nor has certification seriously narrowed the pool of candidates eligible for positions. . . . Furthermore, the way in which most administrators have pursued their professional training—sporadically in summer or evening courses over a number of years—makes it unlikely that graduate work alone provided the intense socialization needed to produce major changes in occupational behavior. (p. 58)

The Social Origins Tradition

There is strong tradition in both sociology and history, as well as in the study of education, that the social origins of groups and individuals— their class, sex, religion, ethnicity, and geographical backgrounds—are highly predictive of later behavior. This explanatory mode is probably too familiar to require documentation; Charles Beard's *Economic Interpretation of the Constitution* (1941) comes readily to mind, as do the social class studies of W. Lloyd Warner and his co-workers (e.g., Warner & Lunt, 1941, 1942; Warner, Meaker, & Eells, 1960). Recall the innumerable studies in education in the 1950s which, accepting Warner's rather static formulation of the concept of class, sought to locate teachers in the hierarchy, and more pervasively, to identify difficulties in teaching, and in testing, based upon class differences between pupil and teacher, or between test maker and test taker. Research on teaching effectiveness has long attempted to demonstrate relationships between the social characteristics of teachers and their "capability" in the classroom. Research so formulated had encountered grave conceptual and methodological difficulties, and little success, though this should not obscure the general plausibility of assuming that social characteristics somehow affect performance.

In their studies of leadership in American schools through 1954, Tyack and Cummings (1977) explicitly reject Callahan's assumption that training in administration is significantly related to job performance. Their claim is that while the superintendent's job has been radically altered by changes in the internal and external organization of school systems, the personal and social characteristics of superintendents have been relatively uniform and have probably been crucial determinants in their selection and performance. They conclude that "formal training in educational administration has had marginal impact on the character of educational leadership" (p. 50).

In somewhat comparable fashion, Richard Carlson's studies (1962, 1972) of executive succession and of the careers of superintendents lead him to express considerable skepticism about the importance of professional training. Instead, he emphasizes personality orientations—"place-bound" and "career-bound"—and, in more recent years, the importance of religion, sex, ethnicity, and other nonprofessional variables.

Tangentially, if somewhat ironically, since he was one of Callahan's most revered mentors at Teachers College, George Counts' classic study of *The Social Composition of Boards of Education* (1927) tended to reinforce a comparable point of view. Recall that Counts saw the business orientation, generally conservative views, ordinarily male gender, and Anglo-Saxon ethnicity of school board members affecting their tendency to hire superintendents of similar background and perspective. His findings made a positive response to his later question, *Dare the School Build a New Social Order?* (1932) considerably less likely.

Cultural and Intellectual Factors as Historical Determinants

To categorize intellectual and cultural aspects of historical development under "conflicting perspectives," as if they are in any way antithetical to Callahan's view, is, on the face of it, absurd. His *Cult of Efficiency* is a major contribution to social and cultural history. His relentless pursuit of the impact of Taylorism on American thought parallels Richard Hofstadter's study of *Social Darwinism* (1959). In equal fashion, his interpretive themes are wholly compatible with Merle Curti's *Social Ideas of American Educators* (1935), a universally recognized classic in intellectual history. Both saw the pervasive influence of business rhetoric and the capitalist system on educational development.

Callahan's perspective, however, is at variance with intellectual historians who have chosen to examine other ideas and other cultural movements as major determinants of educational change. Consider, for example, Lawrence Cremin's *The Transformation of the School* (1961), subtitled *Progressivism in American Education, 1876–1957.* Both books examine essentially the same period (Cremin covered a somewhat longer time span), both were highly lauded immediately upon publication and in the years since, both were widely heralded as stellar examples of what serious scholarship in the history of education could produce, and both are still extensively cited. It is difficult to imagine that two books so similar in these ways could be so different in style, in emphases, and, indeed, in interpretive mode.

Cremin (1961) provides a convenient summary of his work in his Preface. He asks, rhetorically, "What was this progressive education movement that in two generations worked a transforming influence on American education?" (p. xx). In response he explains:

> Actually, progressive education began as part of a vast humanitarian effort to apply the promise of American life—the ideal of government by, of, and for the people—to the puzzling new urban-industrial civilization that came into being during the latter half of the nineteenth century. The word "progressive" provides the clue to what it really was: the educational phase of American Progressivism writ large. In effect, progressive education began as Progressivism in education: a many-sided effort to use the schools to improve the lives of individuals. (p. xx)

The index to the *Cult of Efficiency* contains no reference to Progressive Education as such; Progressivism as a political-social movement is noted briefly in the Preface. The index to *The Transformation of the School*, in like manner, includes no reference to "scientific management" or to "efficiency," and Taylorism is noted only in a brief footnote. Even when both authors deal with the same phenomenon (e.g., The Gary Plan and Platoon Schools), their interpretations are markedly dissimilar. Cremin saw the Gary Plan as an example, par excellence, of progressive education and essentially as "an effort to apply to an urban school system Dewey's idea of education as 'an embryonic community life'" (p. 155). Callahan judged the Gary Plan, particularly as it was described and packaged for general use in American schools, as a quintessential example of the "efficiency expert at work" and of the "factory system" applied to the schools. He duly noted that Superintendent William A. Wirt, the originator of the Gary Plan, had been a student of Dewey at Chicago and that he called his system a "work-study-play school." He emphasizes, however, that both Wirt and his followers—those who attempted to market and popularize platoon schools—stressed the system's presumed economy, efficient use of school plant, and maximum (possibly over-maximum) utilization of teaching personnel.

That Cremin had read a prepublication version of *The Cult* is confirmed by the abovementioned footnote. In it, he cites several studies pertinent to the Gary Plan's proposed application in New York City and concludes, "Finally, the Gary Plan is discussed as the quintessence of 'Taylorism'—or business efficiency imposed on the schools—in a recent manuscript by Raymond Callahan of Washington University" (p. 158n). Callahan was undoubtedly aware of the general thrust of the *Transformation*, but probably did not have an opportunity to examine Cremin's volume as a whole. The work on *The Cult*, although not published until 1962, was completed before the *Transformation* was issued in 1961 by Alfred A. Knopf. The stark contrasts between the two volumes quite possibly explain *The Cult*'s publication by the University of Chicago Press rather than by Alfred A. Knopf, which had published Callahan's earlier text, *An Introduction to Education in American Society* (1956), and which, by conventional contractual arrangements, held prior rights to his subsequent work. Knopf may well have decided that it could not, without embarrassment, offer two such conflicting views of historical reality.

The Sociology of Work Tradition: The Job Makes the Man

In an important sense, arbitrarily listing the sociology of work tradition as a "conflicting perspective" to frames of reference held by Callahan, is a gross contradiction. After all, his "vulnerability thesis" itself clearly arises from the social circumstances of the superintendent's work. He sees American patterns of local control and support of schools and the occupationally imposed requirement to face "a knife poised at their financial jugular vein each year" (p. iii) as basic contributors to job insecurity and the lack of professional autonomy among administrators.

The justification for labeling the formative influence of the job itself as a conflicting perspective is primarily a matter of emphasis. Callahan sees vulnerability as one, albeit crucial, fact of administrative life caused by built-in aspects of the job; he does not conceive of the schoolman's work as affecting, more pervasively, his habits of thought, his social relationships, his language patterns, and, indeed, his very person. Many social theorists who might be identified as representative of the sociology of work tradition examine the influence of occupations in this more inclusive fashion.

Thorstein Veblen was perhaps the best known proponent of such views. Robert MacIver, in his *Society: A Textbook of Sociology* (1937), describes Veblen's thought:

> His guiding principle, reiterated insistently in his various writings, may be stated as follows: In human life the great agencies of habituation and mental discipline are those inherent in the kind of work by which men live and particularly in the kind of technique which that work involves. Here, above all, must be sought the influences which shape men's thoughts, their relations with one another, their culture and institutions of control. (p. 453)

A half-century after Veblen first enunciated this view, Pitirim Sorokin (1947) contended:

> When the same occupational operations are performed from day to day for many years, they effectively modify the mental, moral, social, physiological, and anatomical properties of their members in accordance with the nature and requirements of the occupational work. Each occupation tends thus to remake its members in its own image. And the longer an individual stays in the same occupation the deeper is the transformation. (p. 211)

As might be readily predicted, most contemporary researchers, pursuing comparable themes, have chosen to study organizations—governmental and corporate—and professions other than education. *Men and Women of the Corporation* (Kanter, 1977) is an excellent recent example. Written earlier, William Whyte's *Organization Man* (1956) provides a popular account of the impact of the corporation upon the lives of individuals whom it employs. *Up the Organization* (Townsen, 1970), ostensibly written as a handbook for those struggling to preserve their personal authenticity despite the organization, is less plausible in the advice it offers than in the insights it affords about the formative power of the corporation. *Boys in White* (Becker, Geer, Hughes, & Strauss, 1961) is a highly readable analysis of the professionalization process in a medical school; it deals not at all with curriculum or formal training, but with how students are socialized into the field. Robert Merton, G. K. Reader, and Patricia Kendall's *The Student Physician: Introductory Studies in the Sociology of Medical Education* (1957) is an equally convincing, perhaps more technically elegant, account of this process. Henry Mintzberg's *The Nature of Managerial Work* (1973), a particularly pertinent example, examines the distinguishing characteristics of managerial tasks, irrespective of the occupational setting in which an administrator may work. Based upon his own empirical data, but incorporating findings by several other organizational sociologists, Mintzberg discovered striking commonalities imposed by the job itself. Among the manager-subjects he intensively studied was a superintendent of schools.

The Job of School Teaching

Among representatives of the sociology of work tradition who have been interested in education, Willard Waller (1961) is perhaps most readily recalled. No adult who has spent any time in the schools could fail to be stimulated and enlightened by the illumination he brings to the setting. Using detailed observational reports in diverse schools, and innumerable interviews with teachers of varying age, experience, and background, he examines his data through familiar lenses—sociological concepts of dominance, role, status, and power. The signal contribution of his *The Sociology of Teaching* (1961) is that it teaches us how to look at the school as a social institution. Reading it, one begins to understand what happens to and among the human beings who constitute the school. As Waller points out, teachers are neither standardized instructing machines nor randomly unique personalities, but whole human beings interlocked in a network of human relationships. It is this network, and the individual relations and roles of the people within it, that determines the outcomes of education and the occupational similarities which teachers share.

While Waller's writing is universally heralded as a seminal contribution to educational literature, it does not appear to have spawned innumerable offspring. Dan Lortie's *Schoolteacher* (1975) and his earlier analyses, using conceptions of craft, profession, and bureaucracy as heuristic models and examining teaching under a variety of conditions, are perhaps most frequently cited as in the Waller tradition. Kevin Ryan's *Don't Smile Until Christmas* (1970), focusing modestly on the experiences of first-year teachers and written in an easy, almost conversational style, clearly owes a conceptual debt to Waller (1961). Phillip Jackson's

Life in Classrooms (1968) provides a warm and lively account of what it is like to be a teacher, but it emphasizes the instructional strategies of teachers and the dilemmas inherent in their craft rather than the molding power of their occupational settings. Rivaling Waller in richness of observational and interview detail, Louis Smith and William Geoffrey's fascinating ethnographic studies of an urban classroom (1968) and Smith and his coauthors' study of innovative schools (Smith & Keith, 1971; Smith, Prunty, Dwyer, & Kleine, 1983) are more comprehensive in scope and clearly emerge from a wider range of intellectual antecedents than the sociology of work tradition.

I remain personally convinced that there is a relative dearth of educational research dealing with the myriad ways the school affects the language, habits of thought and action, and attitudes of adults who work within its walls. The laments I keened in *The School as a Center of Inquiry* (1967) still seem largely justified.

The Job of the School Administrator

While I have never attempted either a qualitative or quantitative assessment of the relevant literature, my impression is that much more is known about the occupational life—in Veblen's or Sorokin's terms—of school administrators. Certainly, organizational sociology with its analyses of administrative behavior in situ has grown tremendously; its insights, by extrapolation, enhance our understanding of managers in schools. Certainly, too, there has been in the last twenty-five years a veritable explosion—some still judge it less a bang than a whimper—in the serious study of school administration. There are literally hundreds of studies on the tasks superintendents confront, their exercise of power, their decision-making and leadership styles, their social and cultural backgrounds, their training, their salaries and status, their mobility, the organizational climates in which they function, and their reactions to innumerable, if often ephemeral, pedagogical and social issues. Whatever the degree of current knowledge about the educative influence of the administrator's job, however, the sociology of work tradition can be readily seen as a viable, possibly productive point of view.

My intent, obviously, in discussing these arbitrarily deemed conflicting perspectives is to attempt to shed reflected light on *The Cult* and the conceptions on which it stands. None of the listed alternatives is irreconcilably opposed to Callahan's intellectual frames of reference. As a graduate student at Teachers College, he could not have avoided awareness of the influence of progressive education on American life. As a social and cultural historian, he might easily have anticipated Tyack and Cummings' (1977) emphasis upon the social backgrounds of superintendents as a major determinant of administrative behavior. Finally, Waller's comments about the transiency and insecurity of school executives are strikingly congruent with the vulnerability thesis. The point remains, hopefully, that explorations of other *Realms of Meaning,* as Philip Phenix (1964) stated in his inquiry into curriculum, enhance one's understanding and appreciation of Callahan's thought.

Early Training Programs In Educational Administration at Teachers College

Callahan judged early studies in educational administration to be disproportionately responsive to business ideology, overly technical, often trivial, and, above all, lacking in any vision of educational purpose in an industrialized, democratic society. He describes, with conscious evenhandedness, programs and their chief spokesmen at several universities— Franklin Bobbitt at Chicago, Elwood Cubberley at Stanford, Edward Elliot at Wisconsin, Paul Hanus (in large degree through his field associate at nearby Newton, Massachusetts, Superintendent Frank Spaulding) at Harvard, and George Strayer at Columbia. However, it is apparent implicitly in *The Cult* and explicitly in his "The Changing Conceptions of the Superintendency in Public Education 1865–1964" (1967) that he considered Teachers College to be the most culpable offender.

> In the 1920's the person who contributed the most to the establishment and extension of the business-managerial conception was George Strayer, the leader in educational administration at the institution which awarded more advanced degrees in administration than all the other graduate schools in the country between 1910 and 1930.
> Strayer believed, along with Spaulding and his Dean at Teachers College, James E. Russell, that professional training should provide the student with the specific skills he needed to do the job. And this emphasis upon the specific and immediate tasks was carried to the

doctoral dissertation as Strayer contended that 'there is no detail of the work of the administrator that may not properly become the subject of intense investigation by those who are candidates for the doctor's degree in the professional school.' The result was an emphasis upon the techniques and mechanics of administration. (1967, pp. 13–14)

The comments which follow are by no means intended as an effort to refute Callahan's basic conclusions about administrative studies. His views are too well developed, too fully documented, and indeed, too closely congruent with my personal judgments to warrant any full-scale challenge. Nonetheless, from an internal perspective, his characterizations sometimes seem overdrawn and, to a degree, abstracted from their full historical context. At some points, on the other hand, his interpretations might have been even more persuasive had he chosen to embed them in a fuller, more nuance-filled account of Teachers College's particular institutional experience. These footnotes, then, are offered both as minor directional corrections to Callahan's headings, and as internally experienced asides which, to some small extent, make his conclusions more plausible and more convincing.

The Administrator-Philosopher-Scholar-Statesman

Partly because he genuinely admired their scholarship and their intellectual style, and partly because they provided a conveniently stark contrast to technical managers, Callahan frequently cites William Torrey Harris, superintendent in St. Louis and later United States Commissioner of Education, and William H. Maxwell, superintendent in Brooklyn and later in New York City as a whole. He notes that Harris was trained in the classical tradition at Yale and that he wrote engagingly on a wide variety of topics—"A man," he points out, "who was widely acclaimed as a leader in philosophy as well as education." Callahan recounts Harris's view of the task of the superintendent:

"The efficient superintendent sets into working order three educative influences to support the one great work of education in the school system: namely, an educative influence in wise measures and correct insight, for the members of the school board; second, an educative influence resulting in insights into methods, and a growth in personal self-control, and besides these a culture in literature and art and science, for the teachers; thirdly, for the community, an enlightened public opinion which knows what the schools are actually doing and can intelligently explain merits and defects, and tell what changes are desirable for onward progress." (1967, p. 33)

In *The Cult*, Maxwell's views are often used as counterpoint to the banality of a Bobbitt or the brashness of a Spaulding. In his *Changing Conceptions of the Superintendency in Public Education* (1964), Callahan provides a summarizing description:

> Maxwell was president of the Department of Superintendence, a member of the Conference on English of the Committee of Ten, Chairman of the Committee of Fifteen and for many years associate editor of the *Educational Review*—one of the finest educational journals ever published in this country.
>
> Nicholas Murray Butler, who worked closely with him for years, after listing the academic honors Maxwell had won as an undergraduate and graduate student states that "he never abated his scholarly habits, and his extensive reading, study and writing contributed as much as his distinguished public career toward winning the honorary degrees of doctor of laws granted by Columbia University in 1901." Equally important, Maxwell thought the most important qualification for teaching was scholarship. As he put it, "Ignorance is at the root of most of our bad teaching." (p. 34)

It is more than mildly ironic that Nicholas Murray Butler and James Earl Russell, the two men most responsible for the emergence of Teachers College as the largest and possibly most culpable producer of "superintendents as business managers," held views remarkably consonant with those espoused by Harris and Maxwell. Butler's role in the establishment of TC as an integral, but independent, part of Columbia University has been nicely summarized by Lawrence Cremin in a brief article, "The Shaping of Teachers College" (1967).

In 1897, after James Earl Russell had reluctantly agreed to assume administrative responsibility for Teachers College, Butler was instrumental in working out an agreement that recognized TC as Columbia's faculty of education, and provided TC students and staff full access to the resources (courses, libraries, and so forth) of the university. The agreement further specified that TC would maintain its own trustees, seek its own endowment, and remain financially independent. The Columbia trustees doubtless feared that the struggling young college might prove a burden and, hence, prudently insisted upon fiscal separation.

Nicholas Murray Butler is universally recognized as one of the most powerful and highly respected educators of the twentieth century. One may regret his fabled authoritarianism, or question his often conservative stance on social issues, but there have been few doubts expressed about the caliber of his intellect or the depth of his scholarship. Certainly, no one could imagine that he labored so diligently and over so long a period to establish Teachers College, Columbia University, merely to train educational technicians.

Having occupied for some twelve years the spacious, high-ceilinged office once used by James Earl Russell, and having relatively easy access to much of his correspondence, his memoranda to the faculty, his published writings, and his annual reports to the trustees, I gradually developed a deep respect and real fondness for the man. Many years earlier, at Harvard, I had been assigned a small, but lovely, arch-windowed office once used by William James. In both settings, I am afraid, I devoted more than anyone's duly allotted daydreaming time to musing about the character and work of my predecessors. My firm impression of Dean Russell was of a person of deep commitments, of wide-ranging, sometimes esoteric, but never superficial intellectual interests, who was capable of seeing humor in even the most difficult circumstances and, above all, unerring in his judgments of academic authenticity.

It was somewhat shocking upon reading *The Cult* to discover that Dean Russell was mentioned only twice—once because he used Cubberley as his assistant in an early course in school administration and another time because he had appointed Professor Strayer to the faculty and had supported him in his insistence that the doctoral dissertation in educational administration could properly and appropriately deal with the smallest detail of administrative practice. *The Cult* offers no appraisal of Russell's qualities, nor is there any suggestion, of course, that Russell contributed to the efficiency mania. My regret is only that Callahan, if he had included Russell within his purview, would have found a congenial colleague, one whose views he could both share and admire.

Early in his 30-year career as Dean, Russell had formed a clear idea of the proper professional training of educators, one that embraced broad liberal education, sound scholarship in the academic discipline to be taught (or, in the preparation of school personnel other than teachers, as a basis for personal intellectual style), systematic pedagogical or technical studies, and sustained practice in teaching or in other educational specialties. And he had worked out a clear conception of the kind of professional school that could provide such training, one that would rely on other divisions of the University for general and specialized academic education, and that would itself sponsor teaching and research in the history and philosophy of education, in educational psychology and child development, and in the theory and practice of teaching. Is such a vision not compatible with the views espoused by Harris and Maxwell?

Courses Versus Programs in Educational Administration

Russell's conception of the kind of program appropriate to graduate professional study was certainly realized at Teachers College through 1915. Fundamentally, there were simply not enough courses in administration—even if one accepts Callahan's characterization of their worth—to constitute a program of studies or even to dominate the course enrollments actually pursued by prospective and practicing administrators. It is important to recall, also, that in the early twentieth century, decanal preferences were not likely to be taken lightly by faculty members not yet aware of their collective potential or convinced that administrators could be safely ignored.

Russell's capabilities as a recruiter of able and often charismatically persuasive professors cannot be denied. Armed with his vision of professional training, Russell patiently searched the country for the men and women who could make it real, recruiting in a decade and a half a galaxy of stars that included Edward L. Thorndike, Paul Monroe, John A. MacVannel, Frank McMurry, Julius Sachs, David Eugene Smith, Gonzalez Lodge, Henry Johnson, Arthur Wesley Dow, and Patty Smith Hill. As Lawrence Cremin (1967) observed, "The brilliance of this faculty has often been remarked upon; Russell's taste was surely superior" (p. 7). But even more important from the point of view of candidates in administration were the breadth and balance of this faculty. There were humanists and scientists, scholars and artists, theorists and activists, traditionalists and modernists, the tough-minded and the tender-minded—to all Russell afforded encouragement and free rein. Consciously pursuing a policy of diversity, he deliberately sought professors as specific counterbalances; for example, a William Bagley as opposed to William Kilpatrick and other "progressives," or a Patty Hill whose views on early childhood education differed radically from those espoused by the long-established head of the kindergarten, Susan A. Blow.

That students were indeed exposed to diverse and competing ideas is readily documented by examining old transcripts and student folders still stored in the Office of the Registrar. And my most vivid recollection, as dean, of attending alumni meetings across the country, is the frequency with which former students recalled or inquired about professors from fields other than their personal specialization. My point, of course, is that before 1915, if Professor Strayer and his immediate colleagues in administration were able to create technically minded business managers, they had to accomplish such magic with only fractional control of the curriculum.

The Study of Practice as a Source of Professional Knowledge

Recalling, anecdotally, his first year as Dean of Teachers College, Russell (1937) reveals his conviction that the study of practice itself can be one source of professional knowledge. He reminisces:

> I was especially anxious to make a bid for advanced students. A course in school supervision and school management was on the program. Occupied as I was—not to say disqualified for obvious reasons—I made bold to approach Superintendent Gilbert of Newark with the argument that inasmuch as he had written a little book on school management he was the man to help us out. Asked what I had in mind, I told him that such a course should be aimed at prospective school principals. He wanted to know how much time would be allotted to the course. I said to have graduate credit it should run at least two hours throughout the year. His hands went up in astonishment, "Why," he proclaimed, "I can tell all I know in six weeks." My rejoinder was that I wasn't as much concerned with what he could tell as with what the students should learn. "Why not have them investigate what the schools are doing," I asked, "and how school systems are being managed?" "Do you propose," he said, "to have those students visit schools, pry into their methods, and quiz the superintendent about how to conduct his business? If so you are barking up the wrong tree. All that the superintendent wants the public to know can be found in his reports. As for myself, I have never visited another superintendent except as a friendly caller, or perhaps to steal a

teacher. Snooping around just can't be done; it isn't ethical." Nonetheless, after prayerful thought and repeated conferences, he gave the
course and started us on the road so well paved by Dutton, Snedden,
Strayer, and their associates. (pp. 34–35)

The road to which Russell alluded was certainly well traveled by
Professor Strayer. The observational, fact-gathering, comparative (of one
situation against the norm of other school systems), and extrapolating
techniques he employed in his doctoral dissertation, *City School Expenditures* (1905), were basically the same tools he used throughout his
career. He saw his work, including his innumerable school surveys, in
Hollis Caswell's (1929) terms as, "determining human thought and
human conduct by facts objectively measured, rather than by assertion of
authority. What are the facts and what do you have to do sequentially to
move from the present to a desired goal?"

In a 1917 survey of building needs in Omaha, for example, Strayer
and his colleagues used locally expressed aspirations about school curricula, available census data, comparative norms of pupil per classroom
use for different school subjects, analysis of Omaha's actual and potential
tax base, and extrapolations from new housing permits and district
growth trends to base recommendations for new school construction.
Strayer, Engelhardt, and Hart (1917) introduced their Omaha report
thusly:

> The object of this survey is to determine the adequacy of the present
> school plant, the relationships that should exist between the building
> program and the educational opportunities to be offered to the chil-
> dren, the determination of the facilities which must be provided
> during the next fifteen years, the location of new buildings erected, the
> cost of such facilities, and the ability of Omaha to pay for them. (p. 2)

It is interesting to note that essentially the same techniques were
used by members of The Institute for Field Studies, which Strayer
founded at TC, in recommending plant expansions during the baby-
boom period, and plant abandonment in response to more recent population statistics. There is at least some pertinence in recalling, also, how
frequently contemporary scholars have pleaded—for example, Nathaniel
Gage for close observation of what teachers actually do, Joseph Schwab

for theoretical constructs emerging from analysis of curricular practice, or Alan Tom for conceptualizations of teaching, not borrowed from the behavioral sciences, but arising directly from instructional experience—for the study of practice as one important source of professional knowledge.

I have no quarrel with Callahan's primary estimate of George Strayer's impact upon the field of administration. Certainly his methods, and possibly his predilections, were far more applicable to studies of technical efficiency, of school business questions, and often of the more trivial aspects of administrative responsibility than to broader problems of the field. There is little doubt, too, Strayer encouraged his students to concentrate, particularly in their dissertations, on matters which matched his own statistical sophistication and his own, admittedly narrow, definition of what was worth knowing or able to be discovered. Callahan observed that few discerning persons, not including the unfortunate students for whom such reports were required reading, voluntarily plowed through the voluminous school survey literature. I must personally admit that while, out of deference to Professor Callahan, I attempted a modest sampling, I found little worth resurrecting for contemporary use. One is obliged to lament with Callahan that Strayer oversold the "science" on which his own research was based, and thus provided a protective respectability to directions he inaugurated. Finally, one must conclude, however reluctantly, that Strayer earned enshrinement in the cult of efficiency.

Looking at his career through an internal, more sympathetic, perspective, however, reveals George Strayer to have been a person of deep commitment and outstanding ability, extraordinarily productive, and totally dedicated to the task of building a new profession. One can readily empathize with his basic premise—that the study of practice is a viable, potentially highly rewarding source of professional knowledge. I am impressed by the reports of former students, particularly those who held appointments in The Institute of Field Studies, of how exhilarated they felt in being active inquirers into actual school situations rather than passive recipients of already discovered information. One must admire, too, the vigor and intelligence with which he initiated and defended his professional positions. I, for one, can more readily comprehend his membership among the cultists of efficiency by attempting to understand, and thus appreciate, his qualities as a person.

An Embarrassment of Riches

The 1897 agreement with Columbia University, renewed and amended periodically, established Teachers College as an integral part of the university while retaining its fiscal separation. The Columbia trustees had no gambling urge to subsidize what must have seemed an exceedingly poor risk. But the early years of the college coincided with an enormous expansion of the nation's schools and a concurrent drive for the professionalization of school personnel. Hence students appeared in ever-increasing numbers, tuition in hand, to seek their educational fortunes. TC, like colleges of education in general, proved exceedingly profitable.

What the separation did, as Lawrence Cremin explained, was to permit the college to spend its total income on its own mission, with no control or restraint by the university. At a time when other schools of education were forced by central university administrations to subsidize everything from Sanskrit to medicine, Teachers College subsidized nothing but itself. The result was an unprecedented opportunity: located in the nation's first city and associated with one of the nation's first universities, the college was free to develop as it saw best, to the limit of its resources.

It was this opportunity which James Earl Russell seized so decisively during his 30 years as dean. He recruited an outstanding faculty, made certain that individual professors had challenging, and not simply agreeing colleagues, and encouraged all to write and to speak to audiences far larger than what could be assembled in their own classrooms. Students from every state in the Union and from every area of the world responded in an uninterrupted flow.

But there were dangers in this abundance. Greatly expanded enrollments in the Department of Administration necessitated new staff if only to serve as advisors and to sponsor doctoral dissertations. The difficult question was what should be the teaching and research specialties of newly appointed professors. The perceived success of Strayer's emphasis upon the details of practice suggested an ever more precise targeting of administrative tasks. Hence specialists in every level of administration— early childhood education, elementary education, secondary education, normal schools, adult education, and even higher education were eventually appointed. Similarly, using a different method for subdividing administrative responsibility, such areas as educational law, educational finance, facilities planning, plant management, personnel, and educational accounting all eventually found their special representation in the department.

In important ways, of course, the degree of specialization thus achieved had positive results. The new professorial appointees, given Russell's sensitivity to potential talent, were, for the most part, able and energetic people. In a few short years, they and their students accumulated an imposing array of information about their respective specialties. Sam Evendon, for example, was the country's ranking expert on teachers' colleges; his recommendations of particular persons for normal school presidencies were always attended to and most often accepted. Henry Linn, unquestionably, knew more about school plant maintenance (his courses were affectionately, if sometimes derisively, known as Mops and Brooms I and Mops and Brooms II) than anyone before or since. Policy recommendations by representatives of educational finance greatly influenced state foundation programs, and contributed significantly to public awareness of gross inequalities in school funding practices. Without question, too, this enlarged department, through its foreign students, many of whom later became college presidents and ministers of education in their native lands, spread the American ideal of universal education throughout the world.

While George Strayer is in the foreground, other men and events are clearly visible in Callahan's portrayal of TC's contributions to the cult of efficiency. Callahan does not focus specifically, however, on the departmental expansion that paralleled and usually exceeded the college's general growth. Had he chosen to examine this ever-enlarging Department of Educational Administration with the same lens he used in *The Cult* as a whole, he would have quickly identified inherent dangers.

"In the first place," he might have stated, "it is impossible to increase course offerings at a rate faster than knowledge worth teaching is produced. The inevitable result is gross duplication in course content and intolerable padding of individual courses with trivial detail." Surely he would have asserted that such a massive concentration of presumed experts results in a false sense of departmental self-sufficiency and further discourages exploring relevant ideas and theories developed in the university's other units—for example, political science, sociology, philosophy, public administration, and, forgive me Professor Callahan, business administration—and in the college's own Division of Educational Foundations. "Where," he might also have asked, "are the unifying themes in a field so severely fragmented by declared specializations?" He would certainly have noted that training for specific jobs at a particular educational level is singularly unsuitable in a field where careers take unpredictable turns. In his section on "The Great Diffusion," Callahan (1962) documents the frequency with which graduates in school administration actually became college professors and college presidents, foundation directors, and officials in state departments of education and in the United States Office of Education. Even when they held jobs as practicing school administrators, rarely were they in positions for which they had specifically prepared.

One can almost hear Callahan concluding in his reminiscently populist style, "Enjoying an income greatly in excess of expenses does not guarantee wise investments. To the degree that new appointees in the Department of School Administration were more specialized versions of the original George Strayer model, the college contributed even more decisively than I previously judged to institutionalizing a business-manager conception of educational leadership. While I can rejoice in TC's fiscal good fortune and in Russell's taste in the recruitment of an able and diverse faculty, I can only grieve that in the field of school administration it was an embarrassment of riches."

Departmentalization in a Professional School

There may be a modicum of rationality, although many would deny it, in establishing autonomous departments in graduate schools of arts and sciences. To the degree that an academic discipline utilizes distinct methods of inquiry, particular conceptual schemes, and unique modes of analysis, it seems relatively sensible that its practitioners control their own and their students' destinies. If the singularity of a discipline be granted, it follows that only those already initiated in its mysteries are qualified to determine curriculum and to guide neophytes.

In professional schools, autonomous departments, except perhaps to bear responsibility for the final phases of training, are clearly absurd. No one would deliberately delegate control of preparatory programs for physicians to a cadre of surgeons. Similarly, it is difficult to imagine scholars in comparative theology making the crucial curricular decisions about the education of ministers, or specialists in corporate tax law determining unilaterally what insights into justice should be transmitted to prospective lawyers. It seems equally ludicrous that specialists in various aspects of administrative practice should exclusively define the nature of educational leadership and the proper course of study for its attainment.

I have long been personally convinced, and have given voice to that conviction on countless occasions, that educational issues could not be resolved by educationists acting in isolation. In a 1959–60 report to the Dean of the Graduate School of Arts and Sciences at Washington University, for example, I stated:

> The staff of the Graduate Institute of Education is constituted on the assumption that education is not in itself a distinct and single scholarly discipline, but is rather a complex phenomenon which requires vigorous analysis from many approaches and with the analytical tools of a number of disciplines. The faculty is composed, therefore, of professional educators who have had successful experience, and have reflected seriously and systematically on that experience, in teaching, guidance, or administration, and of scholars trained in particular fields who are committed to applying their disciplines to the analysis of educational problems. It is assumed that the greatest contributions to the understanding of education can be made when 'clinical' professors work in close association with representatives of the basic disciplines underlying the study of education—history and philosophy, psychology, political science, sociology, and social-psychology. This association of experienced educators and persons highly trained in specific fields makes possible, it is felt, a more fruitful interaction of theory and practice and a questioning rather than a dogmatic approach to educational issues. (Schaefer, 1960, p. 3)

Callahan (1962) does not discuss problems of departmentalization in a school of education, but his views on "educational science" are clear. Using John Dewey as collaborator, he concludes:

> [Dewey] pointed out that there was no such thing as an independent "science of education" but that material drawn from other sciences furnished the content of an educational science when it was focused upon the problems in education. Recognition of this fact, he said, *would compel educators to attempt a mastery of what these sciences had to offer.* Failure to understand this fact, he said, led to a "segregation of research which tends to render it futile" and accounted for the tendency of educators "to go at educational affairs without a sufficient

grounding in the non-educational disciplines which must be drawn
upon, and hence to exaggerate minor points in an absurdly one-sided
way." (pp. 247–248)

James Earl Russell had to have been aware of Dewey's views, and he
certainly never abandoned his personal commitment to professional
training based upon broad liberal education, advanced study in a substantive field, systematic pedagogical and technical study and practice,
and serious examination of the psychological and social foundations of
education. Apparently assuming that the subspecialties of education
could become equivalent to academic disciplines in their authority, he
did not foresee any dangers in the departmental system he inaugurated at
TC. Indeed, he specifically declared that once a professional program
had begun its directions, emphases should be determined by "professionally minded" rather than "academically minded" professors.

As long as Russell's departments consisted of one, two, or three
persons, it was physically impossible, even if professors had been willing
to accept teaching loads comparable to those they advocated for instruc-
tors in the lower schools, to offer the full 90 semester hours required for
the doctorate in education. Association and negotiation with colleagues
in the college as a whole, and, when congenial, in the university as well,
was inescapable if only to staff a full curriculum.

But by the 1920s, given the continuing availability of surplus funds
to be invested in new faculty, departments expanded enormously and the
tradition of departmental autonomy became firmly entrenched. In psychology, despite Edward L. Thorndike's example to the contrary—his
impact on educational practice was at least as significant as his influence
upon psychology itself—many professors felt secure forgetting that their
appointments in a professional school carried a concomitant responsibility to contribute to the illumination of educational issues. They preferred
to behave instead as if their primary mission were to produce psychological offspring. In the Division of Instruction, comprised of departments
charged with preparing teachers, supervisors, and teacher-educators in
the school subjects, new appointments were made in the substantive
fields themselves, thus making it unnecessary to depend exclusively upon
cognate departments of the university. Had such disciplinary representatives been attracted to the college in order to work closely with learning
theorists, child development specialists, and pedagogical scholars, their
presence might have proven excitingly fruitful. Since departments effec-

tively controlled work assignments, continuing appointment, promotion, and tenure, new appointees quickly adapted to departmental norms. They were thus effectively deprived of any real opportunity to experience the intellectual rewards inherent in attempting to discover how youngsters develop a sense of history or an appreciation of poetry. Gradually, perhaps inevitably, the Division of Instruction became indistinguishable from a typical liberal arts college, its professors, from their vantage point as "pure" scholars, looking somewhat disdainfully upon educationist colleagues in other parts of the college.

With professorial reinforcements regularly provided, and students appearing in numbers far exceeding the general growth of the college, the Department of Administration could easily dismiss external critics as amateurs, and ignore, with impunity, internal skeptics who might disagree with departmental policies. Secure in its choices and insulated from outside criticism, the department became increasingly self-contained and self-satisfied. Even if a Callahan had been available to offer a few suggestions, it is doubtful that his advice would have been heeded.

Jesse Newlon and His Heirs

If James Earl Russell is primarily remembered in *The Cult* as the impressario who supported the villain George Strayer on the stage at TC, there is only dramatic justice in recalling that he also presented the hero, Jesse H. Newlon. Newlon's 1925 presidential speech to the National Education Association—in which he vigorously denounced the cultists of efficiency and presaged his own conception of democratic administration—was delivered two years before Russell's retirement as dean. While Newlon did not begin his professorship until the fall of 1927, his appointment was offered and accepted while Russell was still active. The dean's vision of a diverse, challenging, and often opposing faculty still prevailed.

Whatever Russell's introductory role, however, it seems more appropriate that Callahan (1964) himself describe Newlon.

> The leader in the movement to establish a new conception of the superintendency was Jesse H. Newlon—and he was perfect for the job. He was not only a man of great ability and courage but he was a rare combination of scholar and successful practitioner. He could and did hold his own in a company of outstanding scholars that included John

Dewey, George Counts, John Childs and Charles Beard and was probably the most able and stimulating group of professional educators ever assembled. More important from the point of view of having his ideas listened to with respect, and perhaps accepted, by a field of practical men was his background and experience. He came from a small town in the midwest and had risen to the top. He was successively a teacher of history, a high school principal, a superintendent of schools at Lincoln, Nebraska and then at Denver, and finally a professor of education at the most important school in professional education—Teachers College, Columbia University. He had received national recognition for his work as superintendent at Denver and in 1925 as elected president of the NEA. As one prominent professor of educational administration put it, "No man can justly say that Dr. Newlon's thinking had not been tested both in the crucible of theory and under the withering fire of practice. He can neither be characterized as an 'educational upstart' nor a 'visionary college professor.'" (pp. 16–17)

In his 1925 address to the NEA, Newlon worried that "The greatest danger that besets superintendents at the present time is that they will become merely business managers." Many, he said, were "more concerned about the purchase of pencils and paper, about the employment of janitors and clerks, about mere business routine than they are about the educative process that goes on in the classroom." Such individuals, he added, "would make good bookkeepers." He wanted superintendents to be students of the social sciences and to draw constantly on knowledge of these fields when confronting educational policies and problems. A particular theme was educational leadership within a democratic framework. He wanted to make it possible for teachers to participate "in the study of educational problems and in the development of methods of procedure." "I like to think of the teaching staff," he remarked, not as a labor force, but "as a company of scholars engaged in the education of youth." (NEA, 1925, pp. 658–660)

During his career at the College, Newlon developed and focused his picture of the socially aware, educationally purposeful, and democratically oriented administrator. In his teaching, his vigorous participation in faculty debates, his writing, and, climactically, his highly successful book, *Educational Administration as Social Policy* (1934), Newlon dedicated himself to changing prevailing images of appropriate administrative behavior. He was not alone in his crusade, but his voice was the most persistent, and, as Callahan believed, probably the most influential.

But Newlon's appointment at TC was not as a member of the Department of Administration, but in the Department of Social and Philosophical Foundations. His distant colleagues in administration were not obliged to listen to his heresies, nor to recommend his classes to their students. Persons who had been appointed as representatives of the functional specialties of administration, or of particular educational levels, were not likely to change their orientations in response to the most well-reasoned rhetoric.

For almost a decade, Newlon's presence made few discernible differences in programs for preparing administrators. An examination of student transcripts for the period revealed a continuing pattern: ordinarily, there was only minimal use of courses outside the department, almost no advanced studies beyond introductory level courses in the foundations, and dissertation topics of embarrassing narrowness. Now and then, one found a transcript of an enterprising student who was wise enough to recognize the intellectual richness of the institution and courageous enough to demand his right to partake of it. Departmental rigidity never prevented breadth of training in any field; it only obscured the possibility for most students.

By the mid-1930s, however, social circumstances forced even the most recalcitrant to heed Newlon's admonitions. The Great Depression had seriously weakened public faith in the omniscience of business aphorisms. Radical democratic notions were in the air and the beginnings of teacher militancy could be dimly perceived. Kurt Lewin's classic experiments in authoritarian, *laissez-faire,* and democratic leadership were everywhere discussed, and schools of business were beginning to favor more open styles of corporate management. Even George Strayer allowed in 1938 that teachers should participate in the formulation of school programs and in the development of educational policy. Some members of the department, as well as Strayer himself, began to stress the desirability of breadth of training in the social sciences and the need for the administrator to have a social and educational philosophy as a basis for providing educational leadership.

To conclude that Newlon's crusade ended in complete victory, however, would be to underestimate the hostility of the antagonists. Even in the individual, there is a latent conflict between the urge to complete a task efficiently and the need to decide which tasks are worth tackling. Similarly, in a school of education, there is a just below the surface tension between those who wish to improve practice immediately and those who prefer to raise complicated questions of educational purpose, or to inquire, patiently, into possibilities not yet comprehended. Creating conditions which assure optimum communication and respect between persons of such differing motivation and temperament is the primary institutional goal. As might be readily anticipated, such an associational balance is not easily maintained and repetitions of the Newlon-Strayer conflict were bound to occur.

In the 1950s, Kellogg Foundation funds gave promise of a new synthesis of Newlon' social concerns and Strayer's identification with the needs of practice. As one of eight members of the Cooperative Program in Educational Administration, Teachers College received significant support in research funds, student fellowships, and new appointees with developed skills in the behavioral sciences. Kellogg's intent was to improve the quality of America's schools by encouraging broader, more sophisticated, and more research-oriented training for superintendents. The hope was that an infusion of new staff, new research opportunities, and cadres of full-time students would create such excitement as to effect permanently the manner in which school administrators were prepared.

At TC, however, rather than being integrated into the department as a whole, the Kellogg Project was established as a semi-autonomous unit, comprised of a few assigned departmental members and personnel expressly recruited for the work. Instead of forcing fresh conceptualizations of training or new patterns of collaboration, old suspicions and enmities were left intact. By the time the funds were exhausted, most of the project staff had accepted positions outside the College. If anything, department members who had watched the Kellogg Project come and go were reinforced in their conviction that the old ways were clearly best.

In 1968, a new Program for Educational Leadership was initially funded by the United States Office of Education and later by the Ford Foundation. The dominant theme in the grant request was the need to prepare administrators who comprehend broad and basic policy issues. It was alleged that former programs had been characterized by an overreliance on management skills and a lack of real concern with the great issues of the politics of popular education. Quoting from Lawrence Cremin's *Genius of American Education* (1965), the proposal stated:

Few educational leaders in the United States are genuinely preoccupied with educational issues because they have no clear ideas about education. And if we look at the way these leaders have been recruited and trained, there is little that would lead us to expect otherwise. They have too often been managers, facilitators, politicians in the narrowest sense. They have been concerned with building buildings, balancing budgets, and pacifying parents, but they have not been prepared to spark a great public dialogue about the ends and means of education. And in the absence of such a dialogue, large segments of the public have had, at best, a limited understanding of the whys and wherefores of popular schooling.

I think we need to train up a new kind of educational leader in this country if the great questions of educational purpose are to receive intelligent discussion by teachers and the lay public. This new kind of leader will obviously need fundamental preparation in the humanities of education, those studies of history, philosophy, and literature that will enable him to develop a clear and compelling vision of education and of its relation to American life. (pp. 117–118)

As a corollary to this emphasis upon questions of educational purpose, the proposal asserted that preparation for educational leadership was broader than training for administrative careers. The program was envisaged as the collaborative responsibility of the college's Division of History, Philosophy, and Social Science of Education (formerly Social and Philosophical Foundations) and the Department of Educational Administration. It was hoped that establishing the project as a genuinely joint concern would enable TC representatives of the humanities and the behavioral sciences to focus their disciplinary studies upon important professional issues, and, at the same time, allow professors of educational administration to broaden and illuminate their work through immersion in collaborative research and teaching. Indeed, it was anticipated that dedication to a common task might serve a larger institutional purpose than the program itself, that it might provide a significant exception to the long-established tradition of departmental autonomy in the training of students.

The Program for Educational Leadership thus began with an enthusiastic emphasis upon policy analysis and joint research on a particular school system and its social setting. Professors Cremin and Ianni (Francis A.) collaborated in a policy seminar, and young scholars in both

departments attempted to carry out their research and teaching coopera-
tively.

Within a few years, however, it became apparent that the dream of
building permanent programs upon the collaborative efforts of two college departments was not to be fully realized. Professor Cremin and
Ianni, both carrying unusually heavy all-college assignments, were unable to continue their joint seminar. The external funds supporting
situational analysis and research were exhausted. Younger, nontenured
professors, perhaps lacking the support and encouragement such high risk
ventures required, found the press for within-department focus too persuasive to be resisted and most turned away from interdepartmental
commitments. In retrospect, it seemed that the ghosts of Newlon and
Strayer had spooked the effort.

Footnotes on Footnotes

A footnote, by definition, is a modest addendum, intended to elucidate an author's point, but not sufficiently important to necessitate its
inclusion in the text itself. These "Footnotes on Callahan's Teachers
College" certainly meet the definition, but they were not appended by
Professor Callahan himself. I am assuming this departure from accepted
footnoting procedure grants me license to conclude with a few footnotes
of my own.

Without disputing Callahan's contention that early training programs in administration amounted to capitulation to business ideology, I
have no doubt that those involved at TC fervently believed they were
building a profession. The positive testimony of students who partici-
pated in surveying schools is too clear, and Russell and Strayer's writing
too full of pride and a sense of adventure to judge otherwise. I find myself
sympathizing, also, with their decision to build course content by directly
examining practice. Surely, this was intellectually preferable to depending upon old campaigners from the field to recount their personal
experiences. Their observations, comparisons, and computations in actual school settings at least attended to "facts" rather than to declared
authority.

The essential disaster of their approach, I believe, was its perceived
success. Given the blessing of the dean, and reinforced in their self-
esteem by the avalanche of students who sought their wisdom, Strayer

and his associates were able to establish and entrench their concern for the details of practice as the preparatory norm of the field. Hence, school administration was developed independently from the study of administrative behavior in other settings. Therefore, school administration was almost from its outset divorced from disciplinary perspectives which may have challenged its insularity and broadened its goals. It might even have been possible, given the patience and the collaborative will, to work out the conceptual schemes and the theory to organize and interpret the massive factual data so avidly collected. Hence, finally, the kind of problem it was best suited to attack—the technical, managerial, and often trivial matters *The Cult* so decries—characterized the field for so long.

But my joining Professor Callahan in regretting the kind of training departments of school administration customarily provided should not obscure my admiration for many of the individual professors involved. Strayer was not simply hardworking and fortunate in his timing; he earned his reputation as a leading educator of the period. Thomas Briggs, John Norton, and later Paul Mort—to recall only a few who achieved national recognition—well demonstrated the capacity of gifted persons to transcend the conceptual inadequacies of their craft. Whatever the constraints of autonomous departments in a professional school, there are always, fortunately, persons able to break the organizational fetters which bind their less venturesome colleagues.

I feel a similar obligation to attempt to elucidate my several footnotes on collaboration among persons of diverse preparation and perspective. In a medical school there is a natural tension between the M.D.'s and the Ph.D.'s. While M.D.'s enjoy the greater power and prestige, the most perceptive fully recognize the contributions of the Ph.D.'s to the resolution of medical dilemmas. The Ph.D.'s, on the other hand, may sometimes feel they are the "purer", more research-oriented scholars, but the most sophisticated understand that attending to medical questions can at the same time enhance their disciplinary development. There is inevitably internal squabbling for status and power, but the well-organized and well-run medical schools understand that collaboration and congenial working relations are essential.

In a school of education it is easy to empathize with a professor of administration's impatience with the irrelevance to his concerns of much of what an academic seems to feel is important. It is similarly possible to understand a sociologist or a social psychologist's bewilderment with the educationist's insistence upon attending to the practical situation in all its complexities. Our basic problem in schools of education, it seems to me, is to achieve at least the degree of cooperative action ordinarily characteristic of good medical schools. In the field of education our commitment to research is as yet so tenuous, our grappling seriously with the reciprocal relations of theory and practice as yet so tentative, our faith in the authority of the processes of inquiry as yet so fragile, and our resistance to ephemeral issues as yet so incomplete, that we do not always grasp the need to develop a community, rather than a mere collection, of scholars.

4 Raymond Callahan and *The Cult of Efficiency:*
About the Writing of History of Education

H. WARREN BUTTON

This chapter is an outcome of a coincidence: that coincidence makes it possible to describe the research for and writing of an important book, and with that description illuminate some aspects of historical research and writing. It is hoped that it also demonstrates part of what was to be learned from working with Raymond E. Callahan.

Of course there are rules for historical research and writing, even beyond the rules for such mundane matters as citations and indentations. Philosophers clarify—or at least intend to clarify—modes of explanation. Any one of half a dozen handbooks painstakingly describes theses, organizing ideas, standards of evidence, explanations, and modes of exposition and narrative. There is even an informative and amusing compilation of historians' errors in logic (Fischer, 1970). Some historians have not yet been amused, however. I might not be if I had been cited for having committed one error or another. There are even delightful satires on historians. Some advice to and criticism of historians can be informative, much of it is harmless, and a little of it amusing. In honesty, much of it can serve only as an antidote for insomnia. But good historical research and writing often produces a good book. Therefore, an account of the genesis of a good history book can be informative.

One such book is Raymond E. Callahan's *Education and the Cult of Efficiency* (1962), a book of importance, lasting importance. *The Cult* was one of the first history of education "revisionist" books, a revisionist book before that term was often used. It was an account of the impact upon school administration and schooling of business management methods; of cost accounting, of the growth of school systems' central bureaucracy intended to emulate those of private enterprise, of research growing from industrial efficiency studies, and of educational research intended to foster business management and efficiency in the schools.

It dealt critically, for the first time, with the "rationalization" of schooling, and the accompanying centralization of authority in school systems. It described the historical origin of the great eruption of bureau-cratization of schools, if not the origin of bureaucratization. The develop-ment of aggrandizement of the profession of school administration was justified in the name of "efficiency." *Education and the Cult of Effi-ciency* described the development of quantification in educational ad-ministration, or at least for educational administration. It described the immediate sources of efficiency studies in machine shops and in factories, and the importance of measurement for the sake of administration. As to measurement, Robert L. Thorndike had said often enough that "if it exists, it exists in some quantity, and is therefore measurable." Some administrators' faith went beyond that. They believed that if "it," what-ever "it" was, was measurable, it existed. The idea was not stated so baldly in *The Cult*, but the thought was there.

The book "casts a light upon the present," and it has all too much relevance for education at the end of the 1980s. When Callahan was writing what would be entitled *Education and the Cult of Efficiency*, "efficiency" and business management methods in schools seemed ata-vistic, crude, and disagreeable survivals, at most nascent and potential hazards. Callahan cited school efficiency articles in the 1950s. No matter how repugnant, expressions of those views were then rather unusual. Thirty-odd years later, school efficiency and business management are manifest, dominating. Their cost, I would add, is catastrophic.

What is to be learned from *Education and the Cult of Efficiency* is of substantive importance. *The Cult* is in print 26 years after its publica-tion, 25 years after other books on education published that year have been forgotten. What is to be learned from an account of how *Education and the Cult of Efficiency* was written is a lesson in methods of historical research, of how a book that is still poignant was written. Rules and rubrics aside, good historical research is research that produces good history. From that point of view, this is a case study, a case history of history.

A part of the coincidence is that I was present at the birth of—or at the conception of the research for, and writing of—*Education and the Cult of Efficiency*. The GI Bill saw me through undergraduate majors in English and history, and a master's degree in history at Washington

University. Callahan was a graduate student in history there too, although I cannot recall meeting him then. We were the advisees of Dietrich Gerhard. Callahan went from Washington University to Teachers College, Columbia University. I met him again, briefly, after he had returned to Washington University and I was teaching in a St. Louis high school.

We were only casual acquaintances until I again became a part-time student and lecturer at Washington University. I had taken a few, very few, courses in education when, as I recall it, Callahan wanted the summer off for research and I taught the Introduction to History of American Education. I relied on Callahan's help and reading lists to teach a course that I had not taken. Of course, we were not equals: Callahan was a professor and I was not. But he was my advisor, and we shared interests and I suppose we shared values. The topic of my dissertation augmented, in a minor way, Callahan's research. We were engaged in the same grand enterprise. During a later summer, I shared his office. The net results for me were a longlasting friendship and the best of opportunities to learn.

Education and the Cult of Efficiency is Callahan's personal, individual triumph. (Valuable historical writing invariably rests upon the author's interests, concerns, and talent.) But it would not have been the same book, and might not have appeared at all, without the influence of those with whom he had studied, especially Dietrich Gerhard and George S. Counts. Surely its writing was supported, and in some ways shaped, by his colleagues in the Graduate Institute of Education and by the concerns of the university generally. The Graduate Institute of Education, more than a department yet less confining than a school, was nurturing.

Callahan's conviction, when I returned to Washington University, was categorical and driving, almost compulsive. He was fully convinced that there were terrible flaws in American society, and that they could be and should be remedied or ameliorated by schooling. He was emphatic and eloquent about flaws and shortcomings of society. Subtopics in his *An Introduction to Education in American Society* (1956) enumerated some: imperialism, nationalism, militarism. Even in the 1960s, there were other themes. There were things terribly wrong about schools. What happened there was far more often than not trivial, ineffective, damaging, stereotyped, and phony.

About these things curriculum makers, administrators, and other educationists who determined schooling's content, form, and conventionality were far too milk-and-toast bland and accepting. School "policy" and administration depended far too much on fad and hocus-pocus, often hocus-pocus with numbers. Callahan's (1961) piece on Leonard Ayres' (1909) *Laggards in Our Schools* had demonstrated that a business-oriented author could mislead the public with numbers. America had terrible flaws. Schools had not helped remedy them. Therefore, the schools and education must be rejuvenated and reformed. Callahan had indignation about these matters—towering, dark indignation. Callahan's convictions on society and schooling were unremitting matters of principle: reforms in schooling were imperative and urgent. They were not only to be expressed in lectures, but also convictions to be demonstrated and developed in his scholarship. *Historians' convictions direct much of the best of historical research, although historical research affects convictions.*

Education and the Cult of Efficiency was, and still is, an unusual book that falls outside the conventions of the histories of education written in its time. It forwent the deterministic optimism of Ellwood Cubberley, which was still the accepted view. It was not, except in an odd sense, intellectual history, history of the thoughts and philosophies of the great proponents—and critics—of education. Its unconventionality, which cost delays in publication and a few torpid reviews, is an essential part of *The Cult's* importance. In one way, it was a high-risk book. *Nothing risked, little gained.*

Education and the Cult of Efficiency was the result not only of principle and conviction, but of years of strenuous, unremitting work. Callahan started with a conviction, not with a clearly formed thesis. With not much more than his gut feeling to guide him, there was no sharp focus for research. To proceed, he must find his way into a forgotten part of the past, searching wherever inklings and obscure citations led. He spent years, literally, in his search for relevant and informative sources. Finding them and digesting them was time-consuming and energy-consuming, something that demanded more than an occasional visit to the library, more than reading an occasional source. If "efficiency" was to be tracked to its source, a search of sources in education would not be enough by themselves. It was necessary to go beyond them: to information on efficiency in industry; to the work of Frederick Taylor, his colleagues, and his successors; and to hearings before the Interstate Commerce Commission. Callahan's sources were articles and books, textbooks, contemporary journal articles, an occasional book-length exposition and dissertation, the National Education Association's (NEA)

Proceedings, and a scattering of NEA and other speeches that were printed. Without photocopying, except for prohibitively expensive photostat, the alternatives were longhand notes or possession of the source. Callahan's office bookshelves were laden with library books. The cost was most of Callahan's time and energy for several school years and summers. He worked and wrote in the daytime and at night. School vacations were opportunities to get more work done. *Education and the Cult of Efficiency* was the product of unrelenting search, reading, and reflection.

I remember, with a little ruefulness, commencement day of 1961. I was working on a United States Office of Education project then. I think Callahan was making final revisions of *The Cult* manuscript. For degree candidates, attendance at commencement was mandatory. For that reason and others, I attended. To celebrate the end of two decades of often interrupted studenthood, I invited my family—children, wife, parents— and a few friends to lunch. It was mid-afternoon before I got back to the office I shared with Callahan. He was there, in his usual cloud of blue cigar smoke. He greeted me with a grumble. I had surely squandered that working day, he said. *Barring pure genius, historical research demands time and demands energy.*

Along with conviction and energy, Callahan had the important ability to avoid distractions and historical byways. His definition of relevance to what would become *Cult of Efficiency* was broad, but it did have limits. Beyond them, nothing much of historical importance existed. It was not history generally in which he was absorbed, but his topic, his subject. Of course there were byways, but he carefully avoided them— no matter how interesting these detours and digressions might be. Callahan avoided the temptations of detours and the futility of tracing ideas and events to their "real" beginnings. *Historical research should be broad, but must have limits.* Historians must avoid the analogue of the "retroactive existence" of Stephen Leacock's (1946) Mr. Juggins, whose study of French led to the study of Old French, which demanded the study of Latin, which in turn necessitated Sanskrit, which was based on a lost root-language, so that the enterprise came to naught. There have been real and unfortunate instances of this sort.

Callahan's spending commencement day revising was, in another way, revealing. My recollection is that the manuscript that would be *Education and the Cult of Efficiency* went through at least four drafts, each more or less reorganized, often rephrased. The final, printed draft is simple and forceful. If there were circumlocutions, they were edited out, and complicated phraseology was simplified. Part of *The Cult*'s effectiveness comes from its forthright prose, its simplicity and power. *Any first draft needs revision, and revision again.*

Callahan's convictions, his indignation, his energy, patience, and determination, his broad research and, not quite contradictorily, his ability to avoid bypaths, led to his clear expression of the findings. Perhaps some of his ability and drive came from the professors who most influenced him. In *The Cult*, and in *An Introduction to Education*, he acknowledges others but says that his greatest debts were to Dietrich Gerhard and George S. Counts: the foreword to *An Introduction to Education in American Society* was by Counts, and *Education and the Cult of Efficiency* was dedicated to him. What one can or does learn from even an outstanding professor seems to some degree obscure and equivocal, but many outstanding scholars have studied with outstanding professors (Ziman, 1976).

Although it may not have been true, I thought I knew Dietrich Gerhard as well as any of his students did. He was born in Prussia a few years before the turn of the century. His mother, tiny, and by then frail when she visited him in St. Louis after the Second World War, had been an important German novelist and feminist. Gerhard had served on the German General Staff in World War I, although we heard of that only in the context of a self-depreciating comic story or two. He had studied at the University of Berlin and taught there. On the night of the burning of the Reichstag in 1933, he and his wife had decided to flee Germany. These early refugees from Nazism escaped with books on history and a Bechstein pianoforte: The historian had foretold the future. Gerhard arrived at Washington University via England and Harvard University.

There was a Teutonic thoroughness about Gerhard's scholarship, a willingness to search with the greatest care. Beyond that, he was intent on going beyond the narrative, on conceptualization and reconceptualization. He was willing to consider several fields of history—after the war he taught American history some semesters at Goettingen—but he devoted his life to research in history. Gerhard valued historical research on the basis of content and contribution: the counting of publications probably seemed to him to be immature.

Counts was probably as well known by Callahan as by any man. Callahan's (1971) commentary on Counts' autobiographical sketch is praise-filled. Callahan had been enormously impressed with Counts at Teachers College. After he had completed his degree, he had visited

Counts in New York City, and he spoke of driving the 130 miles from St. Louis to Carbondale, Illinois, to visit Counts again at Southern Illinois University. Callahan's perspective, his critical view, in some ways echoed Counts. Counts' original interest had been sociological rather than historical, although as one of the founding polymaths of "social foundations" he pursued a variety of topics by a variety of means. Above all, Counts was a reformer, a man anxious to support and help produce change in schooling and in society. Callahan's zeal for reform, a real and abiding feeling, must have been strengthened by Counts.

Although historical and other commendable scholarly work has been done by scholars working in isolation, that is the exception. Although it did not break new ground, Callahan's *Introduction to Education* (1956) had been capably done under less than stimulating circumstances. But at the end of the 1950s, and into the early 1960s, Washington University's Graduate Institute of Education (GIE) was an active research community. Faculty members there were engrossed in educational research, research that was being reinvigorated by concepts and techniques from behavioral sciences. Richard DeCharms was extending Henry A. Murray's theory of motivation. Louis Smith was starting his transit of the social sciences, which has since carried him from psychology to participant observation, to history, and, from reports, currently to biography. W. W. Charters, Jr., would be writing on the social origins and background of teachers for a piece that is still cited (Charters, 1963). Ryland Crary, a sometime writer if not a researcher, a social reconstructionist in the spirit of those at Teachers College, offered support. Each of them listened, and as researchers, shared goals. Robert J. Schaefer, who had become Director of the GIE, had a clear vision of the ways in which research and scholarship could contribute to the improvement of schooling. Laurence Iannaccone, who arrived at the end of the 1950s, had useful suggestions: it was Iannaccone who, as I remember and as the preface to *The Cult* acknowledges, suggested that school administrators' "vulnerability" explained their quick wholesale conversion to management and efficiency. There were other faculty members, some of them our friends, admirable individuals, but with other nonresearch interests.

Students, at least some of us, were as much involved: Bryce Hudgins who has stayed on at Washington University, and Joseph Gore, whose dissertation on the economy of time (1962) was, in a way, a forerunner of *The Cult*, were well along toward their doctorates when I returned to full-time study. It is hard to understate our contributions to *The Cult*. At most they were only tactical. I seem to remember that I turned up the Spaulding autobiographies (1952, 1955), innocent yet damning, but Callahan probably would have found them anyway. I may have suggested a description of the careers of some of those who wrote dissertations about one or another aspect of school efficiency and management. Callahan's wife, Helen, was also a critical member of the team. Putting up with the irregular life of a dedicated scholar would have been enough, but she also managed to assist with proofreading chores and, most important, provide encouragement.

The GIE was an exemplary example of *Gemeinschaft*, of professors and students, of masters and apprentices, bound by common interests, engaged in a common task. Historians of education ideally choose a supportive atmosphere, although real choices more often than not fall short of the ideal. *Prospective researchers in history of education, if they have the opportunity, will benefit from study in productive departments and schools.* Granted, the recommendation is more readily made than followed.

The Graduate Institute of Education was housed in what had been a 1907 World's Fair exhibition. It did not offer impressive physical facilities. Offices were shared, crowded, and worn. While they were not too cold in winter, they were almost unbearably hot in the St. Louis summers, when classes met starting at 7:15 A.M. to avoid the worst heat of the day. But that was not important. It was important that Washington University's library was large and well seasoned, and its staff helpful. The sources for *The Cult* came from this library, augmented by an occasional interlibrary loan.

The prepublication history of *The Cult* was mundane. Producing the final draft of what would be *Education and the Cult of Efficiency* was laborious, far more laborious than it would be now with the use of word processing and photocopying. It was typed, revised, and typed again. To Callahan's great anger, it was categorically rejected by Alfred A. Knopf, Inc., which had published Callahan's first book. The University of Chicago Press acceptance came only a day before acceptance from another university press, causing embarrassment. The manuscript, titled *An American Tragedy in Education*, evoking Theodore Dreiser, was retitled by the publisher, using, I think, a phrase that had been coined by sociologist Daniel Bell. The original title survived as the heading of *The Cult*'s concluding chapter. There were few reviews, and one of the more important of them, in a history journal, was disparaging, to Callahan's dismay. It must be consolation that it is still cited, and sometimes paraphrased at length (Wise, 1979).

Perhaps the success of *Education and the Cult of Efficiency* rests upon the questions Callahan asked and upon his final development of a thesis. The questions had several virtues. Each of them was at least partially answerable. Each of them suggested another question, more specific or somewhat differently directed. For the first question Callahan cites Gerhard, who viewing American education as a European, asked, What were "the origins of the business influence on American education?" (p. vii). The question, as it stood, was too broad to direct specific inquiry, but it did point in a general direction.

A subsequent question was much narrower, more specific: What was the origin of the Carnegie unit, that coin of the realm of American high schools? I recall Callahan and Gerhard discussing that. The answer was somewhat less than satisfying, because it did not fully reveal the impetus.

"Leonard Ayres and the Educational Balance Sheet" (Callahan, 1961) shows Callahan's indignation and anger. Ayres' use of numbers and statistics was misleading, misinformative, and inappropriate. As purest conjecture, I think Counts would have shared Callahan's feelings. Gerhard might have been less pleased with the article's organization and logic. Ayres' was a business approach to a phenomenon outside the realm of business accounting methods. (Ayres' study did lead to calling pupil attendance records "child accounting.") His *Laggards in Our Schools* (Ayres, 1909) was often cited as the beginning of the application of statistical research in education, but did not in itself reveal its origin and did not account for its general and overwhelming acceptance.

Education and the Cult of Efficiency, in its final form, had become a capably organized description and argument. From the conviction that schools were all too much like factories, and that school administrators far too often acted and thought like businessmen, the description and argument followed.

School efficiency, logically, could not win wide and general acceptance until "efficiency" was seen as a remedy, a panacea. Although the word "efficiency" had long been used as a general term of approbation, concrete meanings and applications were required. They came from the work of Frederick W. Taylor, the engineer from Philadelphia who had extended his study of the efficiency of machines to the study of the efficiency of people. Callahan described them in the first substantive chapter of *The Cult*. Taylor's own example of "Schmidt," a worker whose efficiency in loading iron pigs into freight cars was increased from 12½ to 84 tons a day, demonstrated the method.

At Interstate Commerce Commission hearings in 1910, Louis Brandeis, later best known as a liberal Supreme Court Justice, called efficiency experts as witnesses to show that "scientific management" would make railroad rate increases unnecessary. "Efficiency" and "scientific management" caught the attention of admiring journalists. Commending articles appeared in many journals and magazines: efficiency and scientific management were popular, widely known, and polarized as principles. The application to schools of efficiency and scientific management soon followed.

These would take two forms, sometimes fused. In part they were copied, however imperfectly, from Taylor and the other industrial efficiency experts: Bobbitt's (1913) formulation, which appeared as a yearbook of the National Society for the Study of Education (a publication of highest prestige), exemplified that. The school was a factory, the child was material and product, and the teacher was worker. The step-by-step orders given to teachers were to be identical in kind to those on moving pig iron given "Schmidt" the laborer.

There were other similarities. "Schmidt's" productivity was easily measured, in minutes and hours, pounds and tons. For school efficiency there must be something like equivalent measures, achievement tests, and teacher rating forms. These appeared quickly and were widely applied. The school surveyor resembled the efficiency expert of industry. As an outside expert, he examined the school system in the most minute detail, and produced book-length, sometimes multivolume, reports. Callahan (1962) detailed this in a chapter on the Gary schools and the "platoon school," designed for maximum use of school "plant" (the term seemingly borrowed from industry).

In these ways scientific management in the schools aped factory and shop efficiency studies. Another approach was the use of techniques copied from business cost accounting methods. Frank Spaulding had begun that process in seeming innocence when he had calculated the per pupil cost of heating schools, and then had extended the same logic to costs of instruction, per pupil per lesson. It followed that lessons in Greek were less desirable than lessons in French, solely because per pupil per lesson costs were more (Callahan, 1962). Cost accounting could be extended to purchasing of school supplies, and was, *ad absurdum*. There would be published "research" on economies in buying chalk, towels, even toilet paper.

All this described the introduction and proliferation of efficiency and scientific management in the schools. It did not explain its wide and enthusiastic acceptance by school administrators and did not provide a motive. Iannaccone, as Callahan acknowledges, suggested that school administrators, especially city superintendents, were "vulnerable," at risk of losing their positions, if they could not allay or satisfy the criticisms of school board members and businesspeople. The doubts and dissatisfactions of board members, businesspeople, and the community at large, had been aroused by the "muckraking journalists" of the era. The "vulnerability" of school superintendents and other school administrators was a central, unifying theme of *Education and the Cult of Efficiency.*

There was a succinct summing up of the cost of efficiency and scientific management. Business considerations preceded educational considerations. Educational administrators were not educators. The unscientific was labeled scientific. Antiintellectualism was strengthened.

The best of history argues a point. It is in some ways like a lawyer's brief, or the presentation of a case in court. The historian may amass data, and he may narrate. But data without a purpose is useless, and narration without a thesis or theme, an organizing idea, is meaningless.

There have been addenda to the account in *The Cult* in the last quarter-century. As David Tyack (1974) has said since, the orderly reorganization of schooling, its rationalization, had begun before 1910. David John Hogan (1985) has documented the appearance of the thrust of efficiency in Chicago well before 1910. We have noted that the chain of thought that led to scientific management reaches at least as far back as Joseph Lancaster's monitorial schools at the beginning of the nineteenth century (Button & Provenzo, 1983). But these reflect other historians' somewhat different agendas. Tyack's account is broader, while Hogan is pursuing history in one city, with a different purpose. Our interest was in the ancestry of an idea. But these do not detract from *Education and the Cult of Efficiency.* Cuban (1974) raises questions as to the nature of "vulnerability," but vulnerability may arise from sources other than a job at hazard. The worst fate for a historical work is for it to be stillborn, to be ignored. If nothing else, *The Cult* demonstrates that this has been averted.

To reiterate briefly, on the research and writing of history: The topic must be interesting—for the researcher, even consuming. Convictions count, but must not be immutable. A "safe" topic is probably an insignificant one. Even those with talent face drudgery, time-consuming work. Too broad an approach means an unending search. An approach too narrow leads to parochialism. A first draft is for revision, not for submission or publication. Historical study and historical research are enhanced, or impeded, by the milieu of the historian. And, finally, good history considers hypotheses and labors to convince its readers.

These precepts, learned by Callahan through instruction and trial, are worthy guidelines for historians who, like Callahan, would succeed.

5 One Road to Historical Inquiry:
Extending One's Repertory of Qualitative Methods

LOUIS M. SMITH

This essay attempts to make a simple point or two—how one researcher, trained in contemporary social science methods, came to do history, and then tried to think about the implications of that decision. As such, it is a tale of personal experience, a story of assumptions, of beliefs, of intellectual problems, and of learning a craft called inquiry.

The basic format of the essay will be a stringing together of a series of partially related beliefs, supported mostly with anecdotes of personal experience. Then I will try to deepen the discussion with reference to a large research project that my colleagues John Prunty, David Dwyer, and Paul Kleine and I are just now finishing and a reference to one I'm just beginning, a project on the history and sociology of naturalistic research. Next I will widen the issues with extended references to several methodological accounts from history and life history and the intersection of the two. And, finally, I would hope to reach a simple conclusion or two.

A Series of Beliefs and Assumptions

A series of beliefs strung together, like clothes on a line, is one step before a pattern or structure of beliefs that have coherency in the form of chronology, parts of a drama or narrative of human action. A series is also less than a pattern of part to whole, that is superordinate and subordinate relationships. Finally, I would add, a series is less than a pattern of coherency in the form of antecedent and consequence relations, if not hard cause and effect connections. Just suggesting these alternatives raises the possibilities of where the essay might turn in future extensions.

Problem, Method, and Personal Style

One of the clichés in research training is that there must be a congruency between the research methods one uses and the problem one is seeking to attack. Experiments can do certain things regarding causality that other methods cannot do. Social surveys have other advantages and limitations. In turn, historical inquiry brings other strengths and weaknesses. And so on. But the point I really want to make is that the individual researcher, as a person, brings a cluster of personal characteristics and dispositions to the research method and the problem which facilitates or hinders his or her ability to make the method work creatively on the problem. I think these characteristics are beyond the usual content of research methods training courses, those typically offered in Ph.D. programs—beyond a little more statistics here, or a little more work with observational schedules there, or another course in historiography. For instance, Karl Rasmussen (1931/1967), one of the early researchers into Eskimo culture, grew up in Norway and thus had, at the least, tacit knowledge of cold climate and adapting to it. He knew the Eskimo language from his childhood, and his family history intertwined with that of the Eskimos. It is not that you or I could not study Eskimos from an anthropological perspective, or that we might not bring other strengths and weaknesses to the study, but rather that these other characteristics become part and parcel of how we inquire. At this point, my question becomes: What is the unique set of personal dispositions that contributes to doing creative work in educational history?

Triple Threat Inquirers?

A corollary of the first point regarding personal dispositions, intimately associated with the problem by method interaction, argues that the dispositions may be considerably more important than the fitting of problem to method. Even a cursory reading of the literature suggests that the number of social scientists who can do classic research in more than one methodological mode is a very small set. For instance, there seem to be a few Leon Festingers who do classic experiments, classic field surveys (as in the MIT housing study), and then do a classic piece of qualitative observational research, as in *When Prophecy Fails* (Festinger, Riecken, & Schachter, 1956/1964). In my view his creativity in multiple modalities is a remarkable intellectual achievement, one seldom duplicated in social science or education.

In a sense the argument is this: It is very difficult to do important research in any one modality. To do publishable research in several is practically unheard of. The moral I seem to be reaching for is: Try one's hand at several modalities (preferably in one's training program, but if not, later) until finding one that permits the best exercise of one's creativity.

On Knowing One Method Well

Once one has found a research niche, a method that fits one's underlying dispositions and intuitive understandings, a related belief arises. I think that one should come to know that method from the inside out, from the bottom side to the top, from the left side to the right, and from one diagonal to the other. You need to get all around it, to "really" see what it can do. In practical terms, that means that you should try it out in project after project, each partly the same and each a little different so that all the little "wrinkles" become clearer and clearer. "Pushing the outside of the envelope" was Tom Wolfe's (1979) metaphor in his account of the astronauts (p. 12).

At this point a craft, if not an artistic, metaphor comes to mind. The worker in textiles who spins, dyes, and weaves with different wools, textures, colors, patterns, and with different looms seems to run into a neverending series of combinations and permutations of design elements. I think that doing research is like this. Being facile in all this does not come in a one-shot Ph.D. program or after one or two pieces of work. I suggest that inquiry is something like what Henry Murray (1951) called a serial, an ongoing personality process that can last a lifetime.

Many of us get diverted for all kinds of reasons, most of which are sensible, into other activities—committees, administration, consulting, and so on, most of which are also important—before the farther reaches of that serial or that craft can be run out. I believe this to be a loss to the profession as well as to the individual. Preventing that loss has a lot to do with the social structure and dynamics of one's work setting. But that is another story for another time.

Genres of Research Modalities

I do not have a list of all the possible educational and social science research methods, much less a factorial structure of those that hang together as genres of research modalities. But the point I wish to make in this section is that ethnography, biography, and history have some basic and important similarities. In some one-upmanship games and byplay with my historically oriented colleagues, Raymond Callahan, Arthur Wirth, and William Connor, I once tried to capture the point by the comment that "history is *nothing but* participant observation with data fragments," a kind of less adequate ethnography. Beyond the joy in trying for epigrams and the friendly tug of war on doing different kinds of inquiry, I think I perceived then that there were fundamental similarities in the methods and also some very real differences in the kind and quality of the data that one had at hand, or might develop. For one who views himself as a participant observer, an ethnographer, or a field worker, the conception of there being a larger genre of qualitative methods suggests that this is a direction that one might flow into. And so we did. We are now trying to make it work creatively.

Excursions in History and Biography

In keeping with the general theme of this essay, that making research methods work creatively is a peculiar mix of problem, method, and personality disposition of the inquirer, I raise several comments on our learning to use historical and biographical methods. To do this I would make reference to two projects, one completed and one in the initial stages of exploration, discussion, negotiation, and implementation. The first is our return to the Kensington Elementary School and the Milford School District for what we initially called, *Kensington Revisited: A Fifteen Year Follow-Up of an Innovative School and Its Faculty* (1983), later published by Falmer Press as a trilogy of books titled "Anatomy of Educational Innovation: A Mid to Long Term Restudy and Reconstrual."

This first project consumed my colleagues John Prunty, David Dwyer, Paul Kleine, and myself for almost a decade. Our return to the Kensington School as a 15 year follow-up of our ethnography of the first year in the life of the Kensington School (Smith & Keith, 1971) grew from our initial conception. Eventually we had three books, a trilogy. The first of these we called *Educational Innovators: Then and Now* (1986). It amounts to a cluster of life histories of the original faculty and administration who conceived and started the school and who have now gone on to a variety of other career and professional activities. Our data came mostly from long (up to seven hour) taped interviews. Because there were no older male teachers or female administrators, we clustered the faculty into four groups—male teachers, male administrators, younger females, and older females—and looked for patterns. A variety of these arose: careers; what we called "educational reform as secular religion" (p. 144); and "you *do* go home again" (p. 202), a return to geographical and attitudinal origins. We were into biography and life history with a vengeance.

The second book we called, *The Fate of an Innovative School: The History and Present Status of the Kensington School* (1987). We did an ethnography of the school during the 1979–1980 school year, and we combined this with the data from the ethnography of the first year and with data from the intervening years. In effect, we had an historical account of the 15 years of the school's existence anchored on both ends with intensive ethnographic field studies. That, we argued, is a powerful way of doing history. Substantively, we had a multiple perspective view of the school: from the central administration in the design and building of the school and its program; from each of the four principals who served the school and who both influenced and were influenced by the changing school; and finally, a community perspective on the 15 years. More abstractly, we raised themes of "school identity: from the culture of intellectual excitement to the culture of poverty" (p. 168); of "teachers and teaching and innovation and change" (p. 197); and of "demography, cultures, neighborhoods and the longitudinal nested systems model" (p. 234). The relationship of educational innovation to social change became a major issue in its own right.

The third book in the trilogy, *Innovation and Change in Schooling: History, Politics, and Agency* (1988), carries the exploration into the heart of the relationship between innovation and change. This was done through the exploration of the history of the Milford School District, the immediate context of the Kensington School. The basic documents were the 65 years of minutes of Milford School Board meetings. These were supplemented by interviews and more informal interactions with a number of individuals connected with the district from the 1920s through to the present. The chronicle was captured in three broad headings: "genesis and early evolution of a school district" (p. 43), "the longer rhythms of stability and change" (p. 97), and "radicalism and conservatism: the high drama of innovation" (p. 173). The more abstract conceptions were organized as: "a systematic and diachronic perspective on innovation" (p. 258), "innovation and educational administration" (p. 284), and "the many faces of democracy in innovation and schooling" (p. 311). The experience in this work has shifted our view of educational inquiry toward triangulation of multiple qualitative strands and toward perspectives of multiple actors—school board, central administration, teachers, and patrons.

The second project is a complex of substudies in the history and sociology of science. The initial project involved what I called "The Voyage of the *Beagle*: Field Work Lessons from Charles Darwin" (Smith, 1987). The essential data came from reading and analyzing Darwin's letters written during the five years, 1831–1836, he was on the *Beagle*, doing the field work for what would become *The Origin of Species* and a number of other monographs and books. A second piece of this same strand of work is a biography to be entitled, "Nora Barlow and the Darwin Legacy." Briefly, Nora Barlow is Charles Darwin's last surviving grandchild. She is the author of four books on Darwin manuscripts. One of these she did just before she turned 50, one in her 60s, one in her 70s, and one in her 80s. That seems an enviable productive scholarly career, especially, one might add, for a woman at the turn of the century with only a secondary education. In addition, she did early research in genetics with William Bateson, the Cambridge biologist who coined the term *genetics*, and she was the principal force in establishing the *Darwinism* collection at the Cambridge University Library, a remarkable piece of "intellectual social activism." My intent is to explore her life in the form of an intellectual biography.

But the point to be made here is how a sometime ethnographer has gotten involved in studies that are "really" history and biography. The initial prompting was relatively simple: Research problems arose, and their solutions necessitated forays beyond the traditional bounds of ethnography; I have written accounts of that elsewhere (Smith, 1979, 1982). Second, the methods of history and biography seemed to me to be qualitative and thus similar to those of ethnography. We made some initial narrative and analytical excursions into some of this expanded territory (Smith et al., 1986, 1987, 1988). In the present essay I want to continue this discussion by reference to three "models," intellectual statements that were so vivid, so relevant, and so phrased that I could put myself into them and "dialogue" with the author regarding what I was hoping to do. The three authors are Jack Hexter, Lawrence Stone, and Catherine Drinker Bowen. In keeping with the central theme, I believe I had interesting and important research problems, I found models that were highly stimulating, and these seeds of thought fell upon reasonably fertile soil in terms of my prior background with similar methods.

Classic Statements as Models

Some years ago, in a context now long forgotten, we hit upon the gambit, "Who did the classic piece of research on X?" or "Who wrote the classic essay on Y?" as a way of grounding the discussion of one's problem or ideas in the best of literature. "Classic" was used in the sense of the individual who defined the field or the way of looking at the field. This "classic" gambit helped define the perspective that one had to challenge, criticize, or modify if one were to have anything new to say about the area or the issue. In addition, it was a sure lead into the literature that one needed to read to fill out the ordinary science of the area. At this point I would like to modify the gambit one step further, as a methodological resource. The thesis is simple: Can classical statements be used as models to guide, in the sense of helping, as one stumbles and fumbles along in one's methodological and procedural forays? In our work with history and biography, we were fortunate to hit upon three such pieces. Early on, the late Lawrence Stenhouse suggested Hexter's *The History Primer* (1971). Arthur Wirth pointed out a review of Stone's *The Past and the Present* (1981) which led us to the book itself. I think I found Bowen's *Adventures of a Biographer* (1959) and *Biography: The Craft and the Calling* (1969) by myself, having read several of her biographies over the years.

Hexter's Processive History

One of the best analyses and guides to writing the history of educational innovation and the life histories of the Kensington educational reformers arose in reading Hexter's (1971) account of processive explanation in history. In his view, one selects and organizes one's presentation to make the essential point that one feels the data convey:

> It is this outcome that warrants the substance, the structure, and the tone of the introductory section. . . . In other words, the outcome defines the appropriate historical macrorhetoric, and the macrorhetoric in turn dictates the selection of "facts" or more accurately data to

be drawn from the record. Or to put it more bluntly, amid a mass of true facts about the past too ample to set down, historians choose not merely on logical grounds but on the basis of appropriate rhetorical strategies. (p. 190)

This seems congruent with our attempts to maintain the integrity of individuals qua individuals on the Kensington Elementary School faculty as we tended to tell each story in conjunction with a major thematic point. Also, it relates to our attempts to maintain the integrity of the collectivity of the individuals as a group, for the larger point, *Educational Innovators: Then and Now* (Book I) and the meaning for the entire project, Innovation and Change in American Education, an initial title we gave the trilogy of books resulting from the project.

When one gets this kind of help in the practical tasks one is trying to do, a potent kind of validation of the methodological theory occurs. This seems to be an instrumental or pragmatic criterion for the adequacy of Hexter's theory of methodology. On the surface it seems to carry more weight than the criterion of internal consistency of the point of view.

To be a bit reflexive and more homespun, perhaps, Hexter (1971) speaks of the same phenomenon as "moving the work along":

In their piecemeal work they unconsciously accept the notion that an adequate explanation "why" is one that provides them with all the information and understanding they need in order to be moving along with their inquiry. The very moving along is a sort of "o.k." in action responsive to the query "o.k.?" that they tacitly posed before they moved along. (p. 32)

But Hexter also gives help on the larger metatheoretical and paradigmatic aspects of our work. He speaks to the classical assumptions underlying social science when he contrasts his approach with the two standard views from the philosophy of history:

Hitherto we have encountered two philosophical views of what constitutes satisfactory historical explanation yielding true knowledge of the past. One, associated with the analytical philosophers Hempel and Popper, is usually described as covering-law explanation. The other, most fully propounded by White, attempts to adjust the Popper-Hempel argument derived from their conception of scientific explanation to the "story" form of much history writing; it propounds a logical schema of explanation by narration. We have also seen that these views of philosophers coincide roughly with two looser conceptions, current among historians, on the one hand that they explain the past analytically, on the other hand that they do it narratively. (p. 188)

As he continues his discussion, he seems to imply these different modes of explanations reflect differences in types of personalities among researchers in history.

Narrative historians regularly confront the complex rhetorical problems of storytelling. Consequently, they are likely to be keenly aware of what those problems are. But because they are not by temperament analytically inclined, they have not paid systematic attention to the relation between their concern with historical rhetoric and their concern with historical truth. On the other side, most analytical historians, if pressed, would probably admit that history cannot wholly dispense with narrative, with its concern about the conjunctions of specific persons at specific moments in specific localities. They would, however, regard analysis, which obliterates or at least obscures such conjunctions, as the place to go for high octane historical truth. Analytical historians tend to orient themselves toward what they imagine the sciences to be, and to conceive of rhetoric as an unseemly concern with mere tricks of language rather than as it is—the commitment to any coherent discourse that aims at persuasion. To them the notion that the truth-attainment of history is linked at all with the rhetoric of history is repugnant; for them, as for the analytical philosophers, truth resides only in the "facts" and their logical adumbration. Two common assumptions seem to provide the common ties, such as they are, among the four groups—two of them philosophers of history, two of them practitioners of history—that we have identified. One assumption is that historical explanation has only two forms—a governing-law form and a narrative form—there is no *tertium quid*; the other is that explanation in history deals solely with why things happened. (p. 188)

But, and so it seems, not all philosophers of science agree with one another. Stephen Toulmin (1972) seems to be suggesting the breadth of a possible synthesis:

This thesis can be summed up in a single, deeply held conviction: that, in science and philosophy alike, an exclusive preoccupation with

logical systematicity has been destructive of both historical understanding and rational criticism. Men demonstrate their rationality,
not by ordering their concepts and beliefs in tidy formal structures,
but by their preparedness to respond to novel situations with open
minds—acknowledging the shortcomings of their former procedures
and moving beyond them. Here again, the key notions are "adaptation" and "demand," rather than "form" and "validity." Plato's pro-
gramme for philosophy took it for granted that the functional adequacy of geometrical forms was self-guaranteeing—so that there must,
in the last resort, be only one Idea of the Good, and that a mathematical one. The philosophical agenda proposed here sets aside all such
assumptions in favour of patterns of analysis which are at once more
historical, more empirical and more pragmatic. (pp. vii–viii)

For us, this raises both short- and long-term time perspectives. Does
the idea, the strategy, the tactic help in solving the problems of the
immediate projects: life histories of educational innovators and the biography of one individual in the history of science? Second, what does the
idea have to say to the longer term research serial of which the projects
are one small piece? Does it integrate, conflict, expand, or perhaps
illuminate the broader stream of activity?

Stone's Revival of Prosopography

The day we found that we had been doing "prosopography" rather
than interviewing a group of teachers rivaled the elevation in status we
experienced some years ago when we found that we were doing the
"microethnography of the classroom" rather than collecting anecdotal
records of a teacher and his classroom (Smith & Geoffrey, 1968). Our
concern with historical methods led us into the work of Lawrence Stone
and his book, *The Past and the Present* (1981). There, among other
insights, we found an important linkage between the work of classical
historians and what we had been calling life history methods.

The introductory paragraph to his second essay, "Prosopography,"
overwhelmed us with its relevance to our work and its explication of how
historians think about programs similar to ours:

In the last forty years collective biography (as the modern historians
call it), multiple career-line analysis (as the social scientists call it), or
prosopography (as the ancient historians call it) has developed into

one of the most valuable and most familiar techniques of the research historian. *Prosopography is the investigation of the common background characteristics of a group of actors in history by means of a collective study of their lives.* [italics added] The method employed is to establish a universe to be studied, and then to ask a set of uniform questions—about birth and death, marriage and family, social origins and inherited economic position, place of residence, education, amount and source of personal wealth, occupation, religion, experience of office, and so on. The various types of information about the individuals in the universe are then juxtaposed and combined, and are examined for significant variables. They are tested both for internal correlations and for correlations with other forms of behavior or action. (p. 45)

Rather than take each of the ideas in his essay and spin off insights of historical thinking contributing to life history and biographical thinking, I opt for a brief summary of his position and a brief commentary on its implication for what we have done in our *Kensington Revisited* project. In part I do it this way because we came to Stone late. We struggled and came out where he starts. The quest becomes more one of legitimation of our efforts than hard debate.

Stone's essay breaks into eight sections, from "Origins" to "Conclusion." His initial generalization accents why we felt tacitly that our life histories were important:

Prosopography is used as a tool with which to attack two of the most basic problems in history. The first concerns the roots of political action: the uncovering of the deeper interests that are thought to lie beneath the rhetoric of politics; the analysis of the social and economic affiliations of political groupings, the exposure of the workings of a political machine and the identification of those who pull the levers. The second concerns social structure and social mobility: one set of problems involves analysis of the role in society, and especially the changes in that role over time, of specific (usually elite) status groups, holders of titles, members of professional associations, officeholders, occupational groups, or economic classes; another set is concerned with the determination of the degree of social mobility at certain levels by a study of the family origins, social and geographical, of recruits to a certain political status or occupational position, the significance of that position in a career, and the effect of holding that position upon the fortunes of the family; a third set struggles with the

correlation of intellectual or religious movements with social, geographical, occupation, or other factors. Thus, in the eyes of its expo-
nents, the purpose of prosopography is to make sense of political
action, to help explain ideological or cultural change, to identify
social reality, and to describe and analyze with precision the structure
of society and the degree and the nature of the movements within it.
Invented as a tool of political history, it is now being increasingly
employed by the social historians. (p. 45)

If we were rewriting our Kensington research proposal, we could not have
focused it better. Now as I contemplate the proposed biography "Nora
Barlow and the Darwin Legacy," I seem involved in part, in the sociology
and politics of scientific inquiry.

Stone's discussions of the intellectual roots of prosopography raises
the crisis in history after World War I:

This crisis stemmed from the near-exhaustion of the great tradition of
Western historical scholarship established in the nineteenth century.
Based on a very close study of the archives of the state, its glories had
been institutional, administrative, constitutional, and diplomatic history. . . .

In their search for new and more fruitful ways to understand the
working of the institutions, some young historians just before and after
the First World War began to turn from the close textual study of
political theories and constitutional documents or the elucidation of
bureaucratic machinery to an examination of the individuals concerned and the experiences to which they had been subjected. . . .

The unstated premise is that an understanding of who the actors
were will go far toward explaining the workings of the institution to
which they belonged, will reveal the true objectives behind the flow of
political rhetoric, and will enable us better to understand their
achievement, and more correctly to interpret the documents they
produced. (pp. 51–52)

A first reaction I had was that he sounds like an ethnographer of
contemporary society. Not being trained in history, I found approaching
the history of the Milford School District from this "great traditions of
history" perspective a major peak experience for me. In our work, the
close study of the school board minutes became the prototype of Stone's

position on this great tradition. Our life histories, in part, began then with the accounts of the five superintendents of Milford and the four principals of the Kensington School. Now the perspective we are elaborating comes from the even more intensive study of the original administrative and teaching staffs. In an interesting way, we blended Stone's elitist and popular perspectives, though from a case study perspective.

Stone raises the "limitations and dangers" in the nature of the data and the evidence in prosopography: the approach is possible only "for fairly well documented groups" (p. 57); however, "At all times and in all places, the lower one goes in the social system the poorer becomes the documentation" (p. 58). The evidence "is abundant for some aspects of human life and almost not existent for others." With our "before and after" year-long ethnographies, adaptations of ethnographic interviews and oral history, and the more aggressive hunt for all Kensington teachers and administrators, we developed data sets that supplied very well— better than most historians are able to do—information on the lives of our people. In part, we are replaying an earlier point: "Historical method is just, nothing more than, participant observation with data fragments."

Further, Stone speaks to "errors in the classification of data":

> Meaningful classification is essential to the success of any study, but unfortunately for the historian, every individual plays many roles, some of which are in conflict with others. He belongs to a civilization, a national culture, and a host of subcultures—ethnic, professional, religious, peer-group, political, social, occupational, economic, sexual, and so on. As a result, no one classification is quite rare. . . .
>
> The second danger which threatens every prosopographer is that he may fail to identify important subdivisions, and may thus be lumping together individuals who differ significantly from one another. Good research depends on a constant interplay between the hypothesis and the evidence, the former undergoing repeated modification in the light of the latter. (p. 60)

If we have a quarrel with this, it's not so much the substance per se, but the way the comment is cast. In our view, and from our experience putting meaning into our topic, "educational innovators: then and now," one of the key problems, if not *the* key problem, was the construal of classifications of people, of characteristics, of ideas about them. The idiosyncracies, if not recalcitrance, of individuals to fit or be construed into meaningful categories and patterns is, from our perspective, what social science is all about.

Stone's next point, "errors in the interpretation of data," has to do with samples and populations and the relationships between the two. Our 20 individuals are the entire population of Milford-Kensington educational innovators. Whether they are a sample of any larger populations anywhere, any time, is unknown. It is our hunch that they belong to some larger group of true believers, utopians, reformers, and innovators in education in American, and probably Western, society and probably at several time periods over the last several hundred years. But obviously, we don't know. However, we don't believe this is a fatal flaw. Some people argue that the flaw might be in the nature of the reasoning (Diesing, 1971; Geertz, 1973; Hamilton, 1981).

Stone's succeeding cluster of concerns are "limits of historical understanding" in the work of historians. He reaches for three generalizations: historians' concentration on elite and ruling classes; the relative unwillingness to build into their perspective, sentiment, ideas, and ideals; and a neglect of the stuff of politics, the play of individuals in concrete institutional setups. In summary, Stone comments,

> Many elitist prosopographers instinctively opt for a simplistic view of human motivation, according to which the springs of actions are either one thing or another. . . .
>
> In real life, human nature does not seem to function this way. The individual is moved by a convergence of constantly shifting forces, a cluster of influences such as kinship, friendship, economic interest, class prejudice, political principle, religious conviction, and so on, which all play their varying parts and which can usefully be disentangled only for analytical purposes. (pp. 64–65)

Our overall theme in the *Kensington Revisited* project—the natural history of true belief—and such subthemes as origins of educational ideology, educational reform as secularized religion, you *do* go home again, old innovators never die (and some don't even fade away) all suggest we are attempting to push through these limitations.

Stone's brief comments under "achievements" seem a call to the possibilities of prosopography; we find the emotional appeal attractive:

If past errors can be avoided, and if the limitations of the method were recognized, the potentialities are very great. Indeed, provided that it is accepted—as it surely must be—that values and behavior patterns are strongly influenced by past experience and upbringing, the power of the method can hardly be denied. All that is needed is more willingness to recognize the baffling complexity of human nature, the power of ideas, and the persistent influence of institutional structures. Prosopography does not have all the answers, but it is ideally fitted to reveal the web of sociopsychological ties that bind a group together. (p. 65)

If I were to generalize this point, it would be to entertain a strong argument for the importance of social and cultural anthropology, and its central cluster of methods, with ethnography as the broader perspective.

The last paragraph of Stone's "Conclusion" section raises a more general integrative social science perspective with which I am in substantial agreement:

Prosopography nevertheless contains within it the potentiality to help in the re-creation of a unified field out of the loose confederation of jealously independent topics and techniques which at present constitutes the historian's empire. It could be a means to bind together constitutional and institutional history on the one hand and personal biography on the other, which are the two oldest and best developed of the historian's crafts, but which have hitherto run along more or less parallel lines. It could combine the humane skill in historical reconstruction through meticulous concentration on the significant detail and the particular example, with the statistical and theoretical preoccupations of the social scientists; it could form the missing connection between political history and social history, which at present are too often treated in largely watertight compartments, either in different monographs or in different chapters of a single volume. It could help reconcile history to sociology and psychology. And it could form one string among many to tie the exciting developments in intellectual and cultural history down to the social, economic, and political bedrock. Whether or not prosopography will seize all or any of these opportunities will depend on the expertise, sophistication, modesty, and common sense of the next generation of historians. (p. 73)

My only additional concern lies in the disciplinary place of education in social science. And that can only be "solved" if we have a conception of social science and its more fundamental assumptions. If social science is in a paradigm crisis, as some believe (Fay, 1975; Bernstein, 1978; Bredo & Feinberg, 1982), then our solution only prefaces a larger problem.

This discussion of prosopography seems to link life history to one important strand of history. If we had seen it sooner, it would have been a heuristic model of importance to us. Getting there on our own, though, has had its rewards, one of which is that Stone's discussion serves as a major methodological legitimation of our efforts.

Research projects, in spite of most Ph.D. programs, are not individual incidents. They are parts of serials, long-term and loosely related strands that run on for years, sometimes decades, sometimes entire careers. As we were finishing our *Kensington Revisited* project, we were reading Oscar Lewis for clarification of the "culture of poverty" concept. In his *The Children of Sanchez* (1961), one finds another variant of prosopography: "In this volume I offer the reader a deeper look into the lives of one of these families by the use of a new technique whereby each member of the family tells his own life story in his own words" (p. xi). In retrospect, we seemed to be doing this with our teachers and administrators from the Kensington School and the Milford School District. The school was the organizing unit. In contrast to Lewis, who tends to be a more narrative-oriented rather than an analytical anthropologist, at least in this work, we wanted a more analytical account, and we broke the interviews apart according to themes and subthemes in the analysis.

In regard to the Barlow biography, it is not which choice one finally makes, but rather remaining aware of Stone's work and Lewis' similar work which opened hitherto unseen options. As soon as the options are made explicit, the pros and cons spring forth and weave into the fabric of one's overall thinking about what one wants to do. That seems a real gain and seems to illustrate well the point I wanted to make in the first place about models, as well as legitimating rationales. It illustrates the overall thesis of this essay on learning new genres of inquiry.

Bowen on Biography

Craft Insights.   One of the problems in reading Catherine Drinker Bowen is that one can hardly read a page without turning up some major or minor item that is helpful in thinking about what one wants to do. Just now I was rereading her comment in the opening chapter of *Adventures of a Biographer* (1959) that her description of Moscow in a biography of Tchaikovsky had moved some readers to tears. The fact is she had never been to Moscow. Much of her data had come from old nineteenth-century guidebooks, full of such detailed instructions to travelers as to avoid sleeping in rooms at the front of a house because of the noisy nighttime taps of the watchman's stick on the wooden sidewalks of the city. Maybe it is common knowledge to historians that guidebooks would give one an image of time and place, but as a neophyte it was news to me.

Bowen has the ability to convey the adventure and excitement of the varied activities involved in researching a biography. On an actual trip to Moscow later, she wrote of convincing border guards in Poland (in 1937) to let her pass through to Russia without a Polish visa, which her travel agent had neglected to obtain. To be on that train, to be a part of that experience, to be on the way into a new book, this time on Tchaikovsky's teachers, the Rubinsteins, has an emotionally exciting quality. If all that be biography, it is something I could not help wanting to sample.

And then there is her mix of courage and creativity in the face of problems and frustrations. She had not been picked to do the "definitive" biography of Justice Oliver Wendell Holmes, Jr. Access to all his letters and private papers had gone to someone else. The emotional blow started a train of thought that led her to find all the people who had been present at occasions of importance—his 80th birthday, his last illness, and death—and to talk to them as "living witnesses." It also led her into analyses of "definitive," of "evidence," of "hearsay," and of how other notable biographers and historians—such as Collingwood and Goethe— had handled similar problems. Eventually she interviewed 11 of the 12 lawyers who had served as clerks to Holmes and she also interviewed other employees, friends, and relatives. Some of them were present at key times and some of them had letters written at the time about those events.

Into these stories she drops other significant points, phrased in a compelling way, "But the subject of a biography cannot remain at one age—at fifty, at twenty-five, at forty. He must grow old and the reader must see and feel the process. It is not easy to describe a person, even a living man or woman whom one has seen an hour ago" (1959, p. 65). And that poses the further problems of how to do such descriptions. The social and intellectual chase around hurdles and blocked pathways brought out the best of her creativity.

And Bowen speaks of scene and small detail. She inquired of individuals, "important and unimportant," judges and court messengers, people who had seen Holmes in all kinds of "mundane" daily activities and "significant" occasions. The quotation marks are mine, only to highlight the commonsense meanings of the terms and the fact that for Bowen, all were critical for capturing the detail of scenes in which Holmes' actions would reveal him to the reader.

Manuals on interviewing techniques abound, but the subtleties often escape the technician qua technician. Bowen comments on her experience:

> And they had taught me, not only by what they remembered of Judge Holmes, but by what they were themselves. Sometimes I had been impatient, I had thought the personalities of those bright talkers got in the way of the past and of the picture I was seeking. I had wanted to turn the conversation away from themselves and back to Holmes. But I had been wrong. A man's memory is part of himself, it cannot be taken out of context. (pp. 76–77)

As I think about my initial interviews with the family and friends of Nora Barlow, I come away with images of individuals important in their own right, whose knowledge of her is idiosyncratic and particular to the special relationship they had with her, and they, too, become a part of the image of her. Capturing that is difficult in itself, talking about it is doubly difficult.

In a final summary paragraph to the Holmes study, Bowen creates another image as guideline for the neophyte biographer:

> Yet Holmes, the young man and the old, had begun to take shape, emerge, protest his quality. Interviews, letters, scenes from printed volumes, the remembered sound of voices, the rooms where one heard testimony and took down evidence—there was a fusing, a sense of continuity. I could not recreate a man. But with the material I had gathered I should be able to suggest him, perhaps evoke him, with his living quality. (p. 77)

The account goes on and on, but for the moment the importance of Bowen as model and teacher is clear. Adapting that to the time and circumstances of one's own subject becomes a next step. Some of those steps seem easy translations, and others suggest the need for one's own line of thought and reasoning. All part of learning to be historian and biographer!

   A More Fundamental Perspective.   But another side—or two—exists in the reading of Catherine Drinker Bowen. For me, she strikes hammer blows on the anvil of my experience in a way that few social scientists have. She makes observations that I find penetrating, guidelines and models for more than just the writing of history or biography. In her comments after an interview with Judge Brandeis, while doing the Holmes book, she raises a number of issues about aging. She cites Chief Justice Stone: "Holmes grew, after eighty, grew in legal stature." And Chief Justice Hughes concurs, but also comments, "but make no mistake. Holmes was mature when he came" (p. 75). And then, later after the Hughes interview, "Eighteen years have passed, since that day, but as I look at the notebook the spell is still upon me. 'Great men confess old age,' I had scrawled in the margin, sideways. 'They accept old age, and thereby deepen the narrowing channel that remains open to them'" (p. 73). I find that a fascinating insight on how some people live out their later years.

   The farther reaches of those remarks, describing Holmes as coming to the Supreme Court at 61 "mature" but still growing, with his celebrated dissents to occur between the ages of 60 and 90 years, left a deep impression. The continuity with Nora Barlow, a continent away and a generation later, writing her books on Darwin, the first as she approached 50, one in her 60s, another in her 70s, and the last in her 80s, is fascinating. That the later years, for some subjects, need clarification if not a reconstrual, seems a worthwhile agenda. Fertile soil for one in his own mid- to late 50s.

   Finally, I would comment on Bowen's accounts of one of Holmes' most basic life perspectives, that of action. She tells of his advice at 83 to a young man: "If I were dying my last words would be, 'Have faith and pursue the unknown end'" (p. 76). And on an earlier and more tragic occasion, the death of his wife, one of his colleagues commented, "I saw philosophy tested in a hard hour. Holmes had always believed that life was action, the use of one's powers. His wife died, and Holmes' routine never broke. He just kept on and did his work. He was living out his philosophy" (p. 71). In that instance he returned to write one of his most famous dissents on the principle of free thought, in the Rosika

Schwimmer case. Here the blend of the individual under study and the biographer interplay in a powerful way for understanding the nature of biography.

Bowen as Human Being.   In a brief story of "John Adams' Bowl," she reveals another segment of herself, as sensitive outsider snubbed at an auction of the Adamses' household effects. She was so full of sentiment, so full of information leading to further questions, so eager to share with strangers at the auction, yet unrecognized, being outside the social class of the potential buyers, and thus frustrated and angry. "What business had a biographer, then, to be so vulnerable, so eternally thin-skinned where her subject was concerned—was I never to outgrow it?" (p. 116).

Bowen possesses the ability to communicate with the subjects of her biography. As she meditates about the nature of "possessions" and the ambivalences surrounding the Lowestoft bowl of John Adams, she comments:

> How quiet it all seemed and how beautiful. It was good to sit here alone, with the people gone. What was it John Adams used to write in his diary, back in the 1760's before the fighting began, when Britain and America were, as he said, staring at each other? 'I will stand collected within myself and think upon what I read and what I see.' I got up, put my things carefully on the chair and made ready to go. (p. 122)

She had an uncanny ability to talk with her subjects and have them respond empathetically to her in her own words. She knows them so well that conversation seems to flow naturally, as with old friends.

In the early stages of the Nora Barlow biography, I find myself reaching for the young girl, described by her cousin Gwen Raverat (1952), as "Quiet Nora, who always reminded me of a little, obstinate grey Quaker donkey, so clever and sober and pretty" (p. 112). And the older Nora visited in her 70s by her granddaughter, then six or seven, and the granddaughter's friend. They walked in "Granny's garden," where the friend picked a leaf from one of the bushes and the grandchild knew that Granny would know that one leaf was gone from the garden from that particular bush. Then there is the Nora in her late 80s, being described by her Ph. D. granddaughter as "a formidable competitor in a Scrabble game." How does one get to know a person so well that one can converse with them as Bowen does with the subjects of her biographies? It seems an incredible skill. Seeing the possibilities seems a long step on the way to actualizing it.

Catherine Drinker Bowen makes me laugh and cry. In the "Biographer's Holiday" of her *Adventures of a Biographer* (1959), she tells an anecdote about a Henry Stevens mentioned in an essay she was reading:

> There was a young man in the speech named Henry Stevens, who in mid-nineteenth century had begun to help Mr. Brown to collect his books and who styled himself "Henry Stevens of Vermont." This Henry Stevens of Vermont, with whom I fell in love at first mention, went to England to buy books, then became a book trader and settled down in London. Not to be out done by the gentry, he commenced adding capital letters after his name, "Henry Stevens, G. M. B., B. B. A. C." *Green Mountain Boy*, the letters signified; and in memory of an incident from which he carried scars, *"Black Balled Athenaeum Club."* (p. 129)

I chuckled. "Lou Smith, A. L. A. C. L. A.," Lou Smith, Ate Lunch Athenaeum Club Ladies Annex. The images of a delightful meeting with Nora Barlow's daughter and her eldest son, a challenging and penetrating series of methodological and ethical questions on doing the biography, and a world of delightful stories of Nora and the Barlow family remain fresh in my mind. Yes, my wife Marilyn and I had eaten at the Athenaeum Club, in the ladies annex through the front door, to the left and down the stairs. On that late September day we were in our fourth meeting with members of the family and in the series of discussions which I hoped would lead to support to do the biography. And now, who is this Henry Stevens and why was he blackballed from the Club a century ago? Once again, if this is the biographer's life, I believe I have found a niche.

Reading on, I cried as Bowen recounts her visit with Dr. Randolph Adams, whose *Political Ideas of the American Revolution* (1958) "said things never before hinted at, descriptive of John Adams's genius, his prophetic view" (Bowen, 1959, p. 130), which, in turn, had provoked her interest in doing the Adams biography. He took her through the Clements Library and showed her rare manuscripts of early explorations of America, *terra incognita*. "I took out a handkerchief and blew my nose. Randolph leaned down to look at me. 'Well!' he said. He sounded gratified. 'Let's say the emotion does you credit'" (p. 133). I was back in the rare manuscript room in the Cambridge University Library, opening a folio of letters written in the 1830s by Charles Darwin's three sisters, Catherine, Susan, and Caroline. "My dear Charlie," one of them had begun. After months spent with Charles on the *Beagle* and his letters to them, collated and published by Nora Barlow, I was now able to fill in "the other half of the conversation." I couldn't believe it. The emotion overwhelmed me at the time. Now I read Catherine Drinker Bowen and tears well up. I'm reminded once again of a song I used to sing, when I first started doing educational ethnography, "It may not be science, but it sure is fun. I seem to be learning a lot." Biography seemed to be doing the same thing for me.

Bowen as Ethnographer. In reading Bowen's (1959) scathing but delightful accounts of her contact with the academic historical establishment, a number of issues and images arose. The overriding label, "Bowen as ethnographer," captures, at least in part, much of what she was saying to me, as I read the account. With Malinowski, she pursued her quarry into its most intimate lairs. After a morning of pursuing John Adams in his homes near Boston, Bowen had gone to lunch with an academic historian, also working on Adams.

> 'What luck,' I told the professor, 'what extraordinary, unequaled luck for us biographers, that those Adams houses still stand!' Had the professor seen John Adams' beaver hat and the red wool cloak he wore, riding circuit? Fire-engine red, it was, and must have covered him to the boots. And the attic room that John slept in as a boy, with the hired man's room behind it—that was a sight for biographers! Sitting on John's bed I could touch the ceiling with my hand. From the front door downstairs to the stone wall by the road was only fifteen steps; I had paced it off. 'Professor,' I said, 'do you think the old Plymouth Road ran that close to the house in, say, 1745, when John Adams was ten years old?'
>   The professor shook his head. 'Haven't seen those houses,' he said. 'Don't intend to. I never go to Boston, I hate the place.'
>   . . . Was this professor an exception, or was the academic mind deliberately trained to distrust the evidence of the senses? Your artist, when it comes to the pinch, trusts little else. Surely, it takes all five senses to apprehend mankind, past or present? History was not made by ghosts and should not be told as if ghosts made it. (pp. 88–89)

She riles at the arrogance of the pedagogue who disdains in actions and words "writing a popular book"; the historian who loses the sense of drama in the lives of people who are making history; the denial of the writer's point of view as important; and the patronizing pigeonholing of her position rather than the legitimate debate on the issue being raised.

In one of the best one-liners in the book, Bowen concludes her observations on the American Historical Association convention she had been attending: "There are ways to come at history, I thought, pursuing my way down the hotel corridor. Let us say the professors come at it from the northeast and I from the southwest. Either way will serve, provided the wind blows clean and the fog lifts" (p. 102). Ah, to make the wind blow clean and the fog to lift, that is a bit of a challenge. But there are ethnographers, and then there are ethnographers. Bowen's words move one's thinking along. And that is a part of what this essay is all about.

Conclusions and Implications

The Craft of Educational Inquiry

One of the not-so-minor misconceptions held by many students in education is that the only practical activity in education is "teaching a self-contained third grade class" or "teaching Algebra I" to a group of adolescents. In my view, "doing research" is very much a practical activity, or in C. Wright Mills' (1959) words, the practice of an intellectual craft.

> To the individual social scientist who feels himself a part of the classic tradition, social science is the practice of a craft. A man at work on problems of substance, he is among those who are quickly made impatient and weary by elaborate discussions of method-and-theory-in-general; so much of it interrupts his proper studies. It is much better, he believes, to have one account by a working student of how he is going about his work than a dozen "codifications of procedure" by specialists who as often as not have never done much work of consequence. Only by conversations in which experienced thinkers exchange information about their actual ways of working can a useful sense of method and theory be imparted to the beginning student. I feel it useful, therefore, to report in some detail how I go about my

craft. This is necessarily a personal statement, but it is written with the hope that others, especially those beginning independent work, will make it less personal by the facts of their own experience. (p. 195)

I have raised a number of "practical issues" in doing historical and biographical research. The substance of these and the processes by which we worked can be captured briefly in another half-dozen observations, which seem to qualify as limited generalizations if not conclusions in a theory of research methodology.

First, the issues are practice oriented, to use Atkin's (1973) term, that is, they arose as we carried out our *Kensington Revisited* research project. They are grounded in the lived experience of the work activities and the worker as a craftsman.

Second, the issues are also reflexive in the sense that we thought about what we were trying to do, made decisions, carried out alternatives, reflected on what we were doing, and tried to make continuing sense of what we were up to. And then we iterated the process. Obviously, the actual process was much more ragged, emotional, and lumpy than this orderly sentence implies.

Third, we perceived the issues to be an extension of our earlier use of qualitative field methods over a number of years (Smith, 1979). Lurking in the background here was one of the most important admonitions we had ever been taught. In an offhand comment about more quantitatively oriented research, Fred Strodtbeck (1964) had mentioned that in any new research project one should be using instruments that had been used before for two-thirds or three-fourths of the variables. As new instruments were included, one found out what they could do, beyond the reported reliability or validity coefficients. In keeping with the idea, we believe we have gradually integrated history and biography into our earlier modes of ethnographic qualitative inquiry.

Finally, and most important, as we discovered along the way, our *Kensington Revisited* project evolved as C. Wright Mills (1959) seemed to be advocating: "No social study that does not come back to the problems of biography, of history and of their intersections within a society has completed its intellectual journey" (p. 6). This essay attempts to redress that part of our quest. In the course of all this, trying to finish a large and evolving project and looking for similarities and differences within and among problem statements, multiple methods, and varied theoretical perspectives, we have been trying to approach in education, what Mills called the sociological imagination, a quality of mind which "enables us to group history and biography and the relations between the two with society. That is its task and its promise" (p. 6).

Knowledge: Public and Personal

The Sociology of Educational Inquiry.   Although Kuhn (1970) is more recognized and Campbell (1979) more recent, it was Ziman's little book, *Public Knowledge, An Essay Concerning the Social Dimension of Science* (1968) which raised my consciousness about the sociology of science, the social relations among scientists as a key element in the nature of science. In his view, science is public knowledge. Its objective "is not just to acquire information or to utter all non-contradictory notions; its goal is a *consensus* of rational opinion over the widest possible field" (p. 9). In its training program, science is clearly social:

> To understand the nature of Science, we must look at the way in which scientists behave toward one another, how they are organized and how information passes between them. The young scientist does not study formal logic, but he learns by imitation and experience a number of conventions that embody strong social relationships. In the language of Sociology, he learns to play his *role* in a system by which knowledge is acquired, shifted and eventually made public property. (p. 10)

Such ideas raise an agenda large in scope:

> The "Science of Science" is a vast topic, with many aspects. The very core of so many difficulties is suggested by my present argu-ment—that Science stands in the region where the intellectual, the psychological and the sociological coordinate axes intersect. It is knowledge, therefore intellectual, conceptual and abstract. It is inevi-tably created by individual men and women, and therefore has a strong psychological aspect. It is public, and therefore moulded and determined by the social relations between individuals. To keep all these aspects in view simultaneously, and to appreciate their hidden connections, is not at all easy. (p. 11)

But my purpose here is not to raise all that in some grand form, but rather to tell a story or two, particular incidents with a point that bear upon Ziman's bigger issues.

Invisible Colleges and Problems from Kensington Revisited.
Sometimes it is difficult to tease apart what seem to be chance events
from those events which one unconsciously is precipitating or selecting or
creatively construing and causing. The Archival Case Records Conference at York, England, in September 1980 is an important case in point. I
have had a decade-and-a-half relationship with several individuals at the
Center for Applied Reasearch in Norwich, England. Among the variety
of contacts and joint activities, the possibility of presenting a "Case
Record" of some of this work was raised in December 1979. The chance
to return to England on a relevant and important issue made the choice
impossible to refuse.

I include a paragraph from a brief two-page statement "Archival
Case Records: Issues and Illustrations," that I prepared for the conference.
It shows clearly the kind of thinking that the conference encouraged.
Further, one can see elements of both the substantive and the method-
ological issues that were enhanced by the opportunity to participate:

> The very preparation for the conference on Case Records requires a
> series of decisions which highlight many of the issues that the confer-
> ence will be treating as problematic. The first of these issues might be
> "Which case study project, among the several with which we've been
> involved, should we pick?" For a number of reasons I chose our
> current project *Kensington Revisited*. We might want to explore the
> reasons at the conference. A second question, "Which records to
> include in the package of material?", is even more important and
> problematic. I finally decided to try and capture the entire process of
> the case study from the beginnings of the idea to preliminary drafts of
> the final report. I don't know whether that was a wise decision, but it
> seems that that, too, is something we need to talk about. A third
> decision has to do with "sampling" the totality of possible materials.
> So far in the Kensington Project we have several file drawers of data.
> We couldn't bring all of that so we sampled. A fourth issue involved
> "tidying up" the materials. We deliberately left some items just the
> way they are—handwritten, partially reworked, and so forth. Some of
> it may be unreadable, illegible, isolated and unconnected. And that's
> an interesting and important archival problem. Fifth, and perhaps our
> most difficult problem, we've tried to anonymize all the documents
> we've included. That's taken considerable time. It involves issues in
> the rights of human subjects, informed consent, and potential harm to
> the people in our settings. That issue, above all others, needs discus-

sion. Finally, these materials were collected originally "for research purposes," which is a "funny" set of underlying intentions, guiding the selection, storage and now reproduction of the items. (1980, p. 1)

In a sense we were playing out a further episode with our friend and colleague, the late Lawrence Stenhouse. He had put us on to Hexter's *The History Primer* (1971). Now we were countering with items illustrating Hexter's important distinction of "the first record" and "the second record." By so doing, we were implicitly asking Lawrence how his archival project would come to grips with that distinction, an idea we had not considered before.

While a number of stimulating events occurred at the York Conference, the event most relevant to this part of our continuing methodological reflections concerns the informal subgroup on History and Life History which arose out of a conversation with Ivor Goodson. This activity and decision then led to a series of other important events: (1) direct involvement in thinking about a historical approach to case study; (2) a chance to rethink part of *Kensington Revisited*; (3) meeting of several individuals intimately involved in history and life history methods; (4) rephrasing of our interviews with former teachers of Kensington as a mix of biographical accounts based heavily on autobiographical statements; (5) reference to R. G. Collingwood's *Autobiography* (1939) and Carl Becker's (1935) critique of Henry James' *Autobiography*.

But most significant, socially it led to participation in the 1982 and 1983 St. Hilda's Conferences. There are boondoggles and boondoggles. Sometimes we feel guilty that running about to national and international meetings is nothing more than simple pleasure in travel or an ego trip for all the rewards of fame and fortune. Then, occasions such as the St. Hilda's Oxford meetings on History and Ethnography of School Subjects occur.

These meetings provided a forum for a number of ideas on the relationships among history, life history, and ethnography. The formal give and take of papers, presentations, critiques, and informal discussions proved very helpful in those most critical, and difficult to do alone, dimensions of one's work—problem redefinitions, alternative metaphors, and reference from domains far from one's immediate experience.

In addition, it led to quite specific discussions with a number of individuals. Perhaps most specific and immediate were those with Goodson, who was pursuing issues from his experience with the innovative

Countesthorpe School. For example, as we compared and contrasted post-Kensington and post-Countesthorpe faculty careers, the historical context in which each school ended arose as a major variable in the later careers of the staff. The Kensington teachers "returned to the world" in 1965 and 1966. In American education, the force of President Johnson's Great Society conceptions and the resources of the Elementary and Secondary Education Act (ESEA) were to spread over the land. Shortly thereafter, the Vietnam War and schools desegregation were to inter-twine in the lives of a number of our people. In contrast, the teachers of Countesthorpe moved in the early 1970s into a world of recession, unemployment, declining enrollments, and the conservative tide of government.

This idea seemed to anchor, contextualize, and help focus the free-floating cases of Kensington and our data from the lives of our 20 educational innovators and reformers. And that was very important for us.

This brief section might also have been written as a letter "Dear Ivor, Stephen, et al." It reflects the good fortune when one is doing a report or an essay to have a specific audience in mind. As we were finishing the final analysis and writing of *Educational Innovators*, we were also writing various pieces of a methodological appendix, trying to get straight on what we had done and how it both contributed to and constrained the substantive report itself.

The work all seemed to be moving along very well; that is, slowly, painfully, joyously, unendingly, and so forth. Along the way, a separate but partly related string of events was developing. In the autumn of 1982, Ivor Goodson and Stephen Ball were implementing plans for a conference at St. Hilda's College, Oxford University, a year hence. The topic was to be "Teachers' Life Histories and Careers." The substantive and methodological fit seemed close to perfect. I had been a part of the previous conference on "History and Ethnography of School Subjects" and now was looking forward to the coming one.

The important point here is that the methodological essay, while hopefully of some interest to a larger audience, could be brought now into the St. Hilda's Conference. A number of individuals whose interest in the issues had been evolving for almost a decade and who were part of the conference would act as a specific target audience. "How will it play at St. Hilda's" became the summary way of speaking about the impact of such a focus. In our view, having an image of such an audience is a very powerful factor in shaping and finishing a piece of inquiry. If "science" is redefined as having a social dimension, then such items as this become an aspect of the conception per se.

There are several further implications, for the work itself, of this phrasing that makes it more than a simple truism. First, who are the people at St. Hilda's? Which ones have published within the career or life history area either methodologically or substantively? Have any worked with issues of innovation and change? Or with innovative schools as organizations? Or with the relationships between teachers and administrators? Where are they on the metatheoretical issues of positivistic or interpretive or critical stances toward education? Are they people mostly out of sociology, anthropology, psychology, or professional education? Within that mix, do they have an explicit or only an implicit theory of personality, a set of ideas so important for our data and analysis?

That's when we began to get tired. The perspective on audience seemed to give us not just a knoll or small hill from which to see. Rather, it is its own kind of range of mountains, each climbable, but each requiring huge resources in time and energy for that ascension. Perhaps we could do a later revision; the first draft needed to be done next month for the final report. Or better, that's part of what the conference should be about.

But our major point accents the power—motivationally and intellectually—of one small group of educationists to help shape and focus our efforts. In a quite simple, mundane, concrete instance, for us, this is what all the fuss raised by Kuhn, Campbell, and others is all about.

Even more important, when one begins to think of educational inquiry from this perspective, all the issues of the human condition become part and parcel of the inquiry process. We believe part of the malaise in educational science (e.g., Cronbach, 1975; Jackson, 1981) reflects the dissolution of the Thorndikian paradigm and the search for a new perspective. Our history and life history problems, methodology, data, and interpretations and the group of people who have coalesced at the St. Hilda's Conferences are part of our quest at that level. It seems significant to us now.

Getting the Methodology Straight

In our work, we have found that there is a much more complex interplay between methodology and results presented in reports than the usual description in the methodology books. In each of our projects, while there has been commonality, usually also there have been large areas of "first time through." These first time through areas have provoked a need "to get the methodology straight."

In this instance we find that our methodological reflections are always being tried out in classes and seminars with graduate students learning to do field work. Part of the advice to students is to do short methodology and procedural papers. This often begins with an initial paragraph at the beginning of the semester that accompanies the first problem statement before going to the field. At this point, students think they know what it is they are to be about. Later, after the problem has evolved and they have collected data and are beginning to think seriously about the analysis and form the report, it is often propitious for them to write the methodology section. That assignment is usually for a relatively straightforward, almost behavioral document of the decisions made, of what it is they have done, where they have been observing, whom they have talked to, what the kinds and quantities of data, and the strong and the weak spots are. In effect, one tries to get an overview of what one's got and how it bears on the initial and evolving questions. This is what we mean by "getting the methodology straight."

The biggest trap to be avoided occurs with individuals, and they are more than a small minority, who find the observational exercise such a potent personal learning experience that they want to make the term paper, thesis, or dissertation a revelation of personal impact, a phenomenology of the research experience. They forget that there once was a substantive problem which they were exploring and that the qualitative methodology is just a potentially potent way to explore such a substantive problem. The issues become most complicated when the students are educationists and you, as instructor, have been urging them to develop—in the sense of extend, deepen, and articulate—a "personal theory of teaching or education" which will be of use in their own teaching, supervising, administering, or other roles they play in the educational process.

But the point that I am reaching for here, in spite of my meandering about more generally, is that our volume on the 20-odd innovators and my speculations on the biography of Nora Darwin Barlow posed some very special problems that were different from those I had encountered before. Each section of this essay involved a different aspect of the general issue, "getting the methodology straight." Once I got into the projects, things wiggled more than a bit. This essay hopes to have straightened some of that out. In that process, I may have fallen into the very trap about which I caution students. I have written an overly long, involved essay on the phenomenology of historical and biographical research with an overall label "one road to historical inquiry: extending one's repertory of qualitative methods."

6 Reforming Education American Style

FRANK W. LUTZ

There are two meanings of "reforming" as it will be used in this analysis. First, as used here, "reforming" tends to be something seen by one person as necessary for another person. Churchgoers reform sinners, legislators reform state agencies, managers reform the labor-production line, and so forth. Reform or change most often is initiated from some external, superordinate locus (Griffiths, 1964). In this sense, an educational reform is what occurs at the end of an extended period of public criticism. The reform statement is a public mandate. The reform as a process is the partial evasion of and partial compliance to the new mandate.

But reform also has a second aspect. In American political culture, reform is a steady shift from a society characterized by personal values, familial structures, and informal processes to one with impersonal norms, bureaucratic structures, and formalized procedures. In classical sociology, this transformation is termed as moving from *Gemeinschaft* to *Gesellschaft*.

While reform may be necessary, it is always Machiavellian in that it justifies its means in terms of its ends. In such a way the reforming process, its description and evaluation, is value laden. Most evaluations of reform use a logical positivist set of assumptions which coincide with the value biases of the reform. These parallel processes, the reform and its evaluation, "justify" each other, rationalize failure, and tend to prohibit "real" reform.

The Political Process of Reforming Education

The trend of reform in America has been from *Gemeinschaft* to *Gesellschaft*, particularly in the last century. It has significantly diminished rural populations and even more significantly reduced economic opportunity in rural areas. Since 1900, supported by the writing of

110

Wilson (1887) and commensurate with the idealization of American business written about by Callahan, government reforms have persistently reflected the shift from sacred to secular values, from machine to reform governance, moving government further from the people and placing it deeper in the bureaucracy of professional government experts. This has been the process of "Reform American Style" for at least 100 years, and public education has not been left unaffected by that process.

The Cult of Efficiency: Model of Reform

Early in his *Cult of Efficiency*, Callahan (1962) introduces "scientific management," the principal catalyst in his description of educational reform. Describing the pervasiveness of that system of organization and management, Callahan notes that it found "its way into China and the Soviet Union, where it was endorsed by that old friend of capitalism, Lenin" (p. 19). This humorous note about Lenin, I believe, becomes more significant than Callahan intended. We will see later the Critical Theorists of today and yesterday point to "scientific management," Russia's adoption of it, and the bureaucratic industrial domination of the proletariat by the Politburo as the most significant failure of the Marxist movement in Russia. Strange if "scientific management" should also prove as significant and as negative an element in the public education system of the largest, most powerful capitalist nation in the world as the Critical Theorists believe it did in Communist Russia.

The second factor of reform, as established in *The Cult*, was the "fourth estate," the print media in the United States. Callahan shows how the media adopted scientific management as the panacea for public education and used it, over time, with skill and intensity to criticize the public schools and their administration, thus whipping up national dissatisfaction with public education.

The third factor was the domination of American culture by an American business myth and ideology. This, in Callahan's analysis, plays the most mischievous role not only in the development of the administrative and governance structures of public education, but in the curriculum of the public schools as well.

Fourth was the surrender, or worse yet, the alliance without objection, of the majority of the influential education professors of the time and the total capitulation of the programs in educational administration in the nation to the precepts of scientific management, thus establishing a cadre of *trained* (as different from *educated*) educational managers who focused on business practice in their role as educational experts.

The final factor, and central focus of Callahan's analysis of the 1900 public education reform, was the vulnerability of the superintendent. He quotes the following conversation between three superintendents attending the 1916 meeting of the Department of Superintendence of the National Education Association (now the American Association of School Administrators).

Said one, "Are you going to remain in _____ next year?"

"No, I'm not," replied the one addressed. "The floral tributes are now being prepared."

"My case exactly," said the first, "in fact, I am expecting to find a job while I'm at this meeting. When I go back home I am supposed to resign. I haven't anything yet. Probably I shall be forced to discover the necessity of taking advanced educational work at Columbia."

The third man volunteered the information that at the last election of his board of education, the balance of power which had for the past several years enabled him to retain an eyelid hold on his position, has been disturbed. The odd man was now against him. The petitions for his retention were being circulated but the obituaries were even then underway. He considered himself lucky that the board did not require him to prepare his official death notice, all of their other official communications having been prepared by him for several years.

The fourth man drew from an inside pocket a small morocco-bound note book. "Gentlemen," he said, "your conversation is full of information. I have in this little book the reasons, compiled at some expense of trouble and correspondence, for the enforced resignation of school superintendents in my state for the past ten years. While sympathizing with your several misfortunes, I have the strong interest of a professional collector in your experiences. With your permission I shall record the details of your official executions in my directory of the professionally defunct."

Nothing ever assailed me with such violent tenacity as my curiosity to see the contents of that morocco-bound book. The thought immediately entered my mind that here was an object of educational interest compared to which the *roof-garden exhibit of door knobs, burlap, and plumbing would be insignificant.* I knew this man possessed information of consuming interest to the thronging thousands in attendance at the convention. (pp. 206–207) [Callahan is quoting from a piece that appeared in the May, 1916 issue of the *American School Board Journal.* The author chose to remain anonymous.]

The fact of superintendent vulnerability is well established and the above conversation is repeated frequently today at meetings of school administrators. Seventy years after the original conversation, we think we have established the causes (without having found the morocco-bound notebook) of that vulnerability. Its explanation is called the Dissatisfaction Theory.

The course and political fate of the school board member and the superintendent have long been tied together, but this went largely unrecognized for many years. As a matter of fact, the political nature of the school district and its superintendency follows closely the general nature of politics, particularly city politics.

Corrupt machine politics, which dominated large cities in the late nineteenth and early twentieth centuries, were all too prevalent in the big city school districts as well. The call for political reform by Woodrow Wilson in the early 1900s inspired changes in school district governance and big city governance alike. At the center of Wilson's reform government model is the separation of the management of government from the politics of government: the establishment of the "expert manager" as separate from the elected political council. In cities, we have the city council and the city manager; in school districts, the school board and the school superintendent.

The establishment of a separateness between education and politics dominated the idealistic myth of the school board/superintendent relationship for 50 years and, according to Ziegler (1985), still dominates the manner in which many school superintendents manage conflict and maintain control. Callahan (1962) notes that by 1920 the role of "expert" was enshrined and likely to prove the safest haven for the vulnerable superintendent. Although not the "only port in the storm," the role of "efficient business expert" was highly visible and acceptable to a business-oriented school board (pp. 210–220).

To summarize, in *Education and the Cult of Efficiency,* Callahan presents a very practical model of the forces behind school reform in the early twentieth century. It includes (1) a new national technology: scientific management; (2) a highly visible and media-centered public criticism of the schools; (3) the business-oriented value system dominating

American culture and controlling public education; (4) a response by professors and major programs which brought the "efficiency expert" ideal to the school superintendency; and (5) the vulnerability of the individual superintendent. The acceptance of the business manager model (as opposed to the scholar model of Horace Mann) was the best protection against that vulnerability.

The Dissatisfaction Model of American Democracy

It is probably not simply a coincidence that Larry Iannaccone and I were at the Graduate Institute of Education when Callahan was writing *The Cult of Efficiency*, and that the Dissatisfaction Theory, for which we are essentially responsible, documents and accounts for superintendent turnover. Although taking very different approaches, both *The Cult* and the Dissatisfaction Theory hold as their major interest reforming education policy. Both focus on the departure of the superintendent and the function the local school board plays in that departure. Until this writing I have never consciously realized how much *The Cult of Efficiency* must have influenced our thinking in the development of that theory.

Essentially, the Dissatisfaction Theory says that local school districts are structured in such a way as to be the grassroots model for American democracy. In that manner, through the election of local school boards, the people have access to the policy decision mechanisms in public education. Thus, when the people are dissatisfied enough with current education policy outputs, they can and do act to defeat school board incumbents. That event is often followed within three years by superintendent turnover, outside succession, and policy changes. Further, it is noted that this process is episodic, occurring generally once every ten years and that among the visible precursors of the incumbent defeat is a vigorous display of public rhetoric and criticism. It is clear, then, that in many ways the process by which local school districts are reformed every decade or so closely parallels the model set forth by Callahan 25 years ago when Iannaccone and I began this line of research.

Local, State, and Federal Reform

Education in the United States is a state function usually carried out through local agencies or school boards. Callahan describes this process in the education reform of the nineteenth century. In his description, the

locus of governmental reform initiative is ambiguous. There was a national mania about scientific management and the concept was adopted
by the press, national professional associations, and the recognized educational administration programs and professors. Callahan says little
about government or politics. State agencies were, with few exceptions,
unobtrusive. Real educational reform, however, can only take place at the
local school district level with its board and its superintendent. Regardless of the original locus of the reform, it is at the local school district
where any national reform must be operationalized, but all levels, federal,
state, and local, will be involved in some fashion.

From Cult to Cult with What Result?

As noted, reforming education is akin to politics and runs a close
second to politics as, to quote Skeffington in O'Connor's *The Last
Hurrah* (1956), the nation's greatest spectator sport. Periodically, the
public press, supported by the politicians, seizes upon education as the
scapegoat for some national difficulty and demands reform of the public
schools. The issue varies from substance abuse, to student protest, from a
lack of qualified workers for American business, to school dropouts and
truancy. Whatever is the matter with the United States, the public
schools may be blamed.

Reform in the Early 1900s

It may be that the only significant reform in American education
occurred between 1900 and 1930 as described by Callahan in *The Cult
of Efficiency*. Perhaps, even at that time, the reform was merely a
reemphasis of values that had always pervaded public education but had,
due to Theodore Roosevelt's attack on corporate business in 1900, mo-
mentarily failed to dominate the scene. In any case, Callahan makes the
case for the scholar superintendent, such as Horace Mann, prior to 1900.
Then came Frederick Taylor and his scientific management.

A good summary of the 1900 reform is provided by Callahan in his
preface to *The Cult*.

[This reform] had started about 1900 and had reached the point, by
1930, that, among other things, school administrators perceived them-

selves as business managers, or as they would say, "school executives" rather than scholars and educational philosophers. . . . By 1905, as James Bryce pointed out, business was king in American society, and certainly between 1910 and 1929 (if not down to the present time) the business and industrial group had had top status and power in America. . . .

What was unexpected [by Callahan] was the extent, not only of the power of the business-industrial groups, but of the strength of the business ideology in the American culture, on the one hand and the extreme weakness and vulnerability of schoolmen, especially school administrators, on the other. . . . I was surprised and then dismayed to learn how many decisions they made, or were forced to make, not on educational grounds, but as a means of appeasing their critics in order to maintain their positions in the school.

I am now convinced that very much of what has happened in American education since 1900 can be explained on the basis of the extreme vulnerability of our schoolmen to public criticism and pressure. (pp. vii–viii; emphasis in the original)

Callahan goes on to document the changes in the organization and administration of public education. Specific changes at local district level include

1. Standardized tests as measures of teaching efficiency
2. Score cards for school buildings
3. Cost analysis of instruction
4. Questioning of small class size as useful to instruction
5. Use of terms such as school plant, effective products, investment per pupil, cost per pupil recitation, platoon school, and education balance sheet.

These and other concepts and techniques were adopted in wholesale fashion in an effort to demonstrate that the public schools were as efficient as private business and that superintendents were not excelled by corporate executives in their "scientific management."

Of major significance was the change in programs in educational administration so as to be dominated by the scientific management and the business perspective. Those programs trained thousands of school administrators, steeping them in that ideology. More importantly, those programs produced hundreds of professors by the 1930s who, in turn, trained tens of thousands more practitioners and professors from 1940 to 1960. In such a way, the business management perspective still dominates the practitioners of today and is still preeminent in the majority of university programs in educational administration. University programs are still largely influenced by the practical point of view taught by ex-practitioners and include such how-to-do-it courses as school business management, school law, school facilities, school/community relations, the principalship, and the superintendency. To the extent that the reform of 1900 was a radical departure from the thrust of public education pre-1900, it was only a radical reform but, more is the pity, it has been a pervasive reform.

The Sputnik Reform, 1958

The isolationist views following the First World War came to an abrupt end with World War II. Since that time, a new dimension has been added to the business ideology which, as Callahan pointed out, dominates the American culture. If school administrators were no match for the power of American business, they are certainly no match for the power of the military/industrial complex.

Beginning with the original Land Grant Act of 1862, military interests always played a role in American public education. But, its direct influence was not strongly felt in K–12 general public education until the National Defense Education Act of 1958. The NDEA bill referred to the national security or national defense three times in its first three paragraphs. Stimulated by the technological/space achievements of Russia, the nation was alarmed about its safety. It was felt that national security was threatened, and the blame was placed upon the public schools for not preparing mathematicians and scientists. The public was told that the Russians were ahead of us in space exploration, because they were ahead of us in education. Our nation was threatened, and something had to be done. What should be done? Reform the schools!

And what was recommended? Schools should be made more efficient by increasing high school size to a minimum of 1,000 pupils (Conant, 1959). Teachers who could teach science and mathematics should be recruited from other professions. Such teachers, we were told, would be better and brighter than teachers obtained from education colleges.

What then were the ingredients of the Sputnik reform? They were (1) a new space technology; (2) a highly visible, media-centered, public criticism of the failures of public education; (3) a military/industrial ideology dominating the nation and public education; (4) introduction of new technology in school administration programs; and (5) vulnerability on the part of the school administrators which caused them to join immediately the criticism and adopt the panacea of the proposed reforms. In 1900, we took Greek out of the high school curriculum. In 1958, Russian was added!

The weakest item from the list of 1900 reform ingredients that appeared again with the Sputnik hysteria was a far-reaching reform in educational administration programs. There had been reforms, but perhaps not quite so pervasive. The business orientation was already well established in these programs. Sputnik introduced certain innovations into those programs such as Program-Planning-Budgeting Systems, imported from the Defense Department via American industry.

Inadvertently given a boost by the Sputnik reform was the Theory Movement in educational administration. The Theory Movement produced a major shift in research in educational administration, but left the practice of educational administration largely untouched. Borrowing from the social sciences and using logical positivistic epistemology, the movement radically changed, and, I think, improved research in educational administration. The impact on the practitioner was minimal, however, due to the traditional chasm between research and practice and the fact that most programs in educational administration are offered at institutions that are not research oriented and which do not have a research based curriculum.

The Nation at Risk, 1983

Fifteen years ago, I warned that our schools were headed for a neo-Cult of Efficiency (Lutz, 1971). I noted a sense of déjà vu when observing the educational scene, and what I saw were "striking similarities between the press [for reform] in the early 1900s that resulted in 'The Cult of Efficiency' and today's press [for reform] and the educator's response" (p. 25). The antecedents of reform are observable. In 1983, education reform was almost a consuming force in state legislatures from coast to coast. The 1986 National Governor's Conference report, *Time for Results*, dealt solely with reforming education.

President Reagan had appointed the National Commission on Excellence in Education (1983). Their report, *A Nation at Risk*, stimulated the education reform of the 1980s. Often seen as a set of separate state reforms, that reform has been clearly a national phenomenon. Declaring that "if an unfriendly foreign power had attempted to impose on America the mediocre educational performance that exists today, we might well have viewed it as an act of war" (p. 5), the commission fired the opening shot in this reform. Emphasizing the "nation at risk" aspect of the problem, Mr. Reagan's commission stimulated a public media criticism couched in national defense terms and deeply embedded in the business orientation of high-tech international markets and profit.

Already a public issue when Mr. Reagan was elected in 1980, favorable public opinion about education continued to decline, reaching a low just after the release of A *Nation at Risk*. That release was followed by publicly stated presidential concern about the terrible condition of American education. Media coverage came to a peak with the three hour TV series on the public schools in the fall of 1983. As one might predict, the 1984 Gallup Poll indicated the lowest confidence rating for public schools in a decade. The President declared this a national problem that could not be solved by throwing federal money at it. Rather, he said, states and local governments would have to come up with the solutions, which, more often than not, required hundreds of millions more dollars per state. Most states responded by legislating reform through state law and providing large amounts of money to accomplish those reforms. By 1985, Mr. Reagan's administration took credit for reforming public education, and the Gallup Poll gave public schools the best opinion rating in the decade.

"The Great Communicator" had worked his magic once again. He had, in 1983, declared what public opinion polls showed the public already believed—that the public schools of the nation were in miserable shape. That declaration stimulated a media event unprecedented since Watergate and was couched in the military/industrial ideology of a free-market democracy. The new national technology was the "computer-microchip-electronic" phenomenon. Mathematics, science, and computer literacy, along with some sort of "back-to-basics" theme of reading, writing, and arithmetic, were to be the means of implementing it in the schools. (It is not quite clear how those things fit together.) The goal of the reform was to create the ability to excel in the technological revolution, guaranteeing United States' supremacy in space weapons and defense (Star Wars) and domination of world business markets.

Clearly, then, this has been a national reform. It is national in its political process, in its political rhetoric, and in its economic style. The

1983 reform is the very essence of President Reagan's political style. It articulated an already believed sentiment about a deeply held national value. It described the problem in national defense and free-market profit terms. It stimulated a national concern, if not hysteria, and placed the blame somewhere other than on the national administration. Finally, it shifted the tax burden from the federal government to state and local government. With the Reagan Administration having taken credit for improving the situation, the cost of reform was left to the states and is rapidly being shifted to local school districts in many states.

In my 1971 warning about a neo-Cult of Efficiency, I concluded, I am "not optimistic about the future of accountability in education as a functional output or as a process to improve education" (Lutz, 1971, p. 29). I am no more optimistic today. Today's reform in education is not a set of separate state reforms, but a single national reform couched in the same business ideology as earlier reforms. Callahan (1962) quotes Coolidge as expressing the major concern of the federal government during the early 1900s in the following manner: "The business of America is business" (p. 2). Could we expect less from Mr. Reagan when he uses President Coolidge as his presidential model?

Returning to the five elements of national public education reform set forth by Callahan, we can determine the extent to which the 1980s reform parallels the 1900 reform:

1900 National Elements	*1980s National Equivalents*
1. Scientific-Management	1. Computers—micro-chip technology
2. Media criticism	2. A *Nation at Risk* and follow-up
3. Business orientation	3. Military/industrial orientation
4. University program response	4. State Departments of Education centralization
5. Vulnerability of superintendents	5. Vulnerability of superintendents and local districts to state departments

It is the task of the oral historian in primitive cultures to articulate new, indisputable needs and facts in terms of the past so that the past still lives. Thus, in such societies, history repeats itself rather than the society learning from history and avoiding past mistakes. What was done before, is done again—putting "new wine in old bottles." What is new is offered in traditional trappings so as to be tolerable—and nothing much changes except the veneer.

The present reform emphasizes efficiency in schools; challenges the conventional wisdom of educators that small class size is an aid to better teaching; adopts standardized testing as a means of cross-school and interdistrict assessment of effectiveness; mandates teacher rating systems; calls for recruitment of educators from outside education to improve the quality of the teacher corps; suggests 12-month school as an efficiency measure and standardized curriculum as a means to improve instruction; and calls on the public schools to prepare workers for American business so that American business can be competitive and make a profit in the world markets. So, in a world of déjà vu, we travel from Cult to Cult, with no result.

Some Common Elements of Reform, 1900 to the 1980s

In addition to the elements spelled out by Callahan in his *Cult of Efficiency*, reforming education American style has another factor of a national, political nature. This, along with the five *Cult* elements, appears to account for American style of reforming education.

Conservative Federal Politics

Reforming education American style is a product of national conservative politics. Each of the reforms analyzed in this chapter took place under conservative presidents. Admittedly, there have been other important national changes in education—notably, the 1954 Brown vs. Board of Education desegregation decision under Eisenhower, the 1965 Elementary and Secondary Act under Johnson, and the 1975 Special Education bill, 94–142, under Ford. None of these, however, I would call a major education reform. The desegregation decision was an act of the Supreme Court and is generally thought of as a civil rights act, not an education act. Johnson was hardly a conservative, and his education act was thought of and treated as a support of public education, not a reform of education; it did not survive. Public Law 94–142 reformed education for less than 3 percent of the population, and it is generally considered as a civil rights act, not a general education reform. These events, therefore, while changing education, perhaps even reforming it, do not fit the usual definition of reforming education, leaving the three reforms investigated in this chapter.

The Cult of Efficiency 1900-1930. The majority of this period encompassed five federal administrations: Taft, Wilson, Harding, Coolidge, and Hoover. Taft's alleged support of reactionary Republican bosses and support of big business lost him the support of Theodore Roosevelt and the reformed segment of the Republican Party, and led directly to Wilson's election in 1912. Wilson contributed his notion of the separation of the bureaucratized expert management of the public enterprise as separate from the politics of government.

As it is not the purpose here to do a historical review of these administrations, a single, simple, but authoritative source published by *Encyclopedia Britannica*, will be cited as a source concerning the presidents in office during the reforms considered. It is recognized that some historians may disagree with the perspectives suggested here, but those perspectives appear to be generally agreed upon.

According to the American Freedom Library (1971), Harding was elected because "the people were so tired of the governmental restrictions and hardship imposed by the war, that they wanted a complete change in administration that would bring back the old days" (p. 165). A more conservative statement about an administration could hardly be formulated. Coolidge was described by his successor, Hoover, in the following manner: "Mr. Coolidge was a real conservative, probably the equal of Benjamin Harrison" (American Freedom Library, 1971, p. 157). And, Hoover himself is depicted in the same volume as, "opposed to direct federal relief to the mass of unemployed" (p. 140), as vetoing the Bonus act giving almost a billion dollars to veterans, as well as vetoing the Reconstruction Finance Corporation to make loans to business and home owners during the Depression, and ordering the military to march against the Bonus Army. Hardly a more conservative group of presidents in succession could be found in the history of the presidency.

The Sputnik Reform—1958. Eisenhower was probably the single interruption of "New Deal" oriented presidents from Roosevelt in 1932 to Johnson ending in 1968. He classified himself as a "middle of the roader" and a "dynamic conservative" (American Freedom Library, 1971, p. 80), but surely a conservative.

The Present Reform. Little is required to convince a reader of the 1980s that President Reagan was a political conservative. At the risk of overkill, and for the sake of the reader in the year 2000 who may not remember, a brief review will be sketched. Mr. Reagan's followers were called the New Right. He backed constitutional amendments prohibiting abortion and permitting school prayer. His justice department officially and publicly decided not to push hard in certain affirmative action cases. If Calvin Coolidge was his model, his administration might be termed a masterpiece.

The terms "liberal" and "conservative" fell out of vogue as concepts for political analysis during the 1980s because they failed to describe precisely the nature of some specific political actions. But no other descriptors have emerged which provide better labels for long-term political trends, individually or collectively. Of the group of presidents discussed above, Dwight Eisenhower is the most liberal, but surely no one would place him in the same category as the liberals Franklin Roosevelt, John F. Kennedy, and Lyndon Johnson. Clearly, reforming education American style had as its handmaiden conservative federal administrations.

Gesellschaft, Secular, Bureaucratic Aspects

Earlier, it was stated that reforming education American style was always from *Gemeinschaft* toward *Gesellschaft*, from sacred toward secular, and always more bureaucratic in nature, removing education farther and farther from the people. Let us now see how that statement fits the three reforms discussed here.

The Cult Reform. Scientific management and the industrial revolution that spawned it are the very heart of what Tönnies (1957) had in mind when he discussed the nature of the movement of society from *Gemeinschaft* to *Gesellschaft*. Scientific management is, perhaps, the single most important concept of the classical ideas about organizations, surpassed only by the notion of bureaucracy as a means of organizing work. The secular society is defined, in part, by its reverence for the "outside expert" and its valuing of reform or change. A set of bureaucratic elements—scientific management, division of labor, universalist rules, and standardized procedures—describe the reform. The business interests that dominated education during the 1900s had already adopted the same reforms. Now these reforms increased bureaucracy in the schools.

The development of the role of the business manager "or," to quote Callahan, "as they would say, 'school executives,'" (1962, p. 196) is a move away from the generalist "scholar" superintendent. Such a move along a sacred-secular continuum is a move toward the secular which values change and the "outside expert." The development of the platoon school, the school survey, and standardized tests for personnel are all indicators of moves from a *Gemeinschaft*-like society, where people knew one another and decisions were made on the basis of personal information, to a *Gesellschaft*-like world of impersonal decisions based on information obtained in bureaucratic fashion. Finally, the period of 1900–1930 was one of intense pressure to consolidate rural schools (Carney, 1912), moving schools, for better or worse, away from control of the people whose children attended them.

The Sputnik Reform.   The Sputnik Reform is slightly harder to categorize. For one thing, a lot of bureaucratization had already occurred in American society. The industrial revolution had already transformed a rural America into an urban society. But in several ways the Sputnik reform gave schools another push in that direction. Surely the federal money provided by the National Defense Education Act and the programs it generated carried with it new required paperwork, applications, record keeping, and reports that were added to the existing bureaucracy.

In addition, the Conant Study (1959), which was a part of this reform, and its recommendation for high schools of 1,000 minimum size, effected more consolidations of high schools and made the schools more secular.

The Present Reform.   The present reform may be something like Kansas City in the musical *Oklahoma*. It may have "gone about as far as it can go"—in creating bureaucracy and moving the schools toward a *Gesellschaft* society of secular values. Some suggest the present mandates were intended to put many rural schools out of business. While that was probably not the actual intent, it is likely to be the real effect (Lutz & Lutz, 1985).

Because of the cost of implementing the reforms and the fact that more and more of that cost is being pushed on local districts, many small rural districts will be hard-pressed to comply. In states that supply all or most of the cost, the state is having a difficult time justifying the cost of small rural schools. It is likely that the present reform will stimulate a further wave of school consolidation.

The new reform has, in almost every instance, increased the power of the state education agency and the number of inspections and reports required for compliance. It has mandated standardized testing of teachers as well as pupils, and has used those data to give decision-making power to the states rather than the local districts. In addition, and more surprisingly, it has usurped many of the certification prerogatives formerly granted to the universities, thus dictating university curriculum as well as public school curriculum.

Summary

It appears that in addition to the five recurring elements of reforming education American style developed from Callahan's *Cult of Efficiency*, another condition can be added: a conservative national administration (or climate). Such reforms, then, move the society in a secular, *Gesellschaft*-like direction making the schools more bureaucratic and moving them one step further from control of the people they are established to serve (Lutz & Lutz, 1985).

New Wine in Old Bottles

We probably all recall the problems of putting new wine in old bottles: "else the new wine doth burst the bottles, and the wine be spilled, and the bottles be marred, but new wine must be put into new bottles" (Mark 2:22). But putting new wine in old bottles is exactly what we do when reforming education American style. As a result, the new is spilled and the old is marred.

Everyone familiar with public education knows that it could and should be improved. Problems in need of attention include school dropout rates, functional illiteracy, gifted children who are underachieving and even failing, disadvantaged minorities, teenage pregnancy, substance use and abuse, and, probably, a *small* group of incompetent professionals who receive an inordinate amount of public attention. Schools, like all human enterprises, fall short of perfection. Like other enterprises, schools are often defensive about their shortcomings and almost always resist change. Public education can certainly use some fermentation and the new wine that would result. But we may need a new bottle: a new reform model.

Common Models of Reform

As we have seen earlier, the present reform contains the same elements as prior reforms and is consistent with the model described by Callahan in *Education and the Cult of Efficiency.* New individual needs, social demands, knowledge, theories, and technologies are poured into the old organizational bottles, albeit with new labels. The old bureaucratic business model persists as the inflexible parameters for new ideas.

Without intending to denigrate any author or publisher, the following are quotes from three advertisements of mid-1980 tests being touted by their publishers for adoption in educational administration courses: *"Offers step by step procedures* for every phase. . . . Explains clearly how a simple mathematical formula can be used to determine *cost effectiveness"* (Castaldi, 1986); "Get Help With Day-to-Day and Long-Term Financial Planning and Management" (Burrup & Bremley, 1986); "The author also details CIPP, DPM, linear programming, zero-based budgeting, management information systems, cash flow optimization, and other contemporary management techniques" (Candoli et al., 1986). In this aspect the present reform is affecting educational administration programs and could not be more like what Callahan documents as happening in the early 1900s when the authors were Bobbitt, Spaulding, Cubberley, and Strayer.

Callahan (1962) notes that one popular suggestion, ultimately unsuccessful during the Cult reform, was the 12-month school. I was reminded of this just the other day as I perused a popular educational journal which ran a feature on a local school district that had just implemented the concept. Local officials beamed with pride as national experts reassured the parents as to the wonders of the school's year-around scheduling plan. That article could well have appeared in 1906. It seems clear that we put our new reform into old containers.

The Cost of Educational Reform

Another aspect of our 1980 reform, that is apparently like the 1900 reform, is the question of who gets the bill for reforming. Although always couched in cost effectiveness, school reform seldom results in reduced costs. There is apparently no evidence that the 1900 reform resulted in any reduction in the total cost of public education. Clearly, the Sputnik Reform cost hundreds of millions and the cost of the present reform has been hundreds of millions per state. The Sputnik Reform was funded largely with federal dollars, but, like the 1900 reform, the cost of the present reform is being borne either at state or local levels. Thus, while all three reforms considered in this chapter are fiscally similar, the 1900 and the present reform are most alike, and although touting cost efficiency, cost more money.

This matter of who pays for reforming the *Gemeinschaft*-like sacred society toward the more *Gesellschaft*-like secular society also has its historic roots. The nineteenth century, during the time of British imperial expansion, was the heyday of British social anthropology. The Queen's government often provided the resources to study native cultures and then used the reports to determine the most effective ways for the Empire to govern and to profit from that relationship.

Today's reform, driven largely by urban, secular values and a need to assure states of attracting high-tech industry and a cadre of well-trained high-tech workers, is changing the face of rural America and of rural education. Of course, this trend, from rural to urban, has been in process for a century, interrupted briefly in the 1960s. The present education reform has clearly accelerated it and given it new life.

In addition, the current emphasis on "power equalization" of state education funding formulas has shifted the funding advantages toward metropolitan areas to the disadvantage of rural schools. Almost universally, rural schools are not only being asked to reform curriculum, educational values, and district management, but they are being required to assume, relative to urban districts, a great portion of the cost of that reformed education. Thus, like the native cultures ruled by the British Empire, they are not only asked to accept the bureaucratic rule of the Empire (the state department of education), to adopt the customs of the foreign land (the urbanization of the curriculum), but they are also asked to assume a greater share in funding the Empire (a greater share in the cost of education).

Rhetoric vs. Reform

Peterson (1985) views reform in the public schools as driven by pluralistic political values and power. While he presents interesting evidence for that position, one which both he and I *theoretically* prefer, I believe this argument is faulty in some ways. For instance, the pluralistic model fails to account for the failure of the community control movement in New York City in the 1960s. At that time the traditional power-holders in the New York City school system united with the support of organized labor of the state to recentralize power within the traditional power elite, and strip community control advocates of all but a vestige of the power they sought. Of course, that coalition of the school board, administrators, and teachers (the three traditional combatants) with the support of the union establishment of the state (because teachers in New York City are union members) represents some type of pluralism. But the fact is that, in oligarchical and elite or pluralistic and participative terms, the perceived results of the reforms have been the same. Given our different interpretations of the data, our conclusions about the result of reform are the same. To quote Peterson (1985):

> Whatever their talk of efficiency, school reformers were *expansionists* . . . the schools generally spend more. . . . Reformers not only held expansionist views, they also wanted to upgrade its standards, enhance the quality of instruction given, and *organize* its administration structure to be more *efficient*. (pp. 203–204; emphasis added)

Using Peterson's pluralistic explanation as one of two possible explanations of the recent Texas reform, Plank (1986) asks the question whether there is "rhetoric or reality in school reform." Again, there are some differences with the interpretation of some of the data he presents. But the data, uninterpreted, stand by themselves, and we agree on the major conclusion that there was more rhetoric than reform.

Plank states that the reformers called for "radical changes to adapt to the state's new economic circumstances" (p. 13). In describing that rhetoric, Plank says the reformers attempted "to adapt the school system to the presumed necessities of economic transition," repair the "damage [to] the local business climate," avoid "handicapping . . . new industrial investment," and improve "competition with other prospective capitals of high-technology industry" (p. 13).

Put another way, the reform consisted of rhetoric and its result was to reinforce, recentralize, make more secular and bureaucratic the educational system and the business-oriented value system that had always existed. New wine was put into old bottles, and the reform was mere rhetoric. Further, the reform was not a single state phenomenon. According to Plank, "curricular reforms similar to those approved in Texas have been introduced in almost every state in the past two years" (p. 14). And, finally, "the reality of school reform . . . proved to be profoundly conservative" (p. 16).

Happily, Plank offers two analyses of this rhetoric as a model, rather than just suggesting pluralism (Peterson, 1985): (1) Organizational fields constrain organizational change (DiMaggio & Powell, 1982); and (2) institutionalized organizations have powerful rationalized myths that strictly constrain both their structure and activities (Meyer & Rowan, 1977).

The Texas reform legislation was anything but pluralistic politics, however. The reform bill (HB 72) was opposed by almost every one of the usual actors in the state politics of education in Texas. It was opposed by the state school board, by the state's local school board association, by the three state teachers' associations, the state school administrators' associations, by most state education "support groups," and was not (until massive pressure was brought to bear) reported out of committee by either the House or Senate Education Committees. If, with that opposition, the politics of the Texas reform can be called pluralistic, we need a new definition of pluralistic. The Texas reform was clearly a case of elite power politics overriding the usual pluralistic coalition of education interests.

Plank's second model, I believe, serves the reality much better than does the pluralistic model. Based on the second model, Plank (1986) states,

Reform rhetoric notwithstanding, the Legislature acted on the assumption that the problems of the public school system were not structural. . . . In the end, the reforms approved by the Legislature were *not intended to change* the structure of the public school system, but rather to make the *present* system work better. . . . Despite the reformers' apparent success in the legislature, the recent campaign for reform . . . will leave the state's public schools and educational problems very like those it had before. (pp. 15–16; emphasis added)

What it will have done, however, is reemphasize the business-value orientation, increase the secular/bureaucratic nature of public schools, make the state agency more powerful, local schools more monolithic, and, to add a Peterson comment on reform, more expensive. When it comes to school reform, there is more rhetoric than reform, and the 1980s reform appears similar to past reforms.

The Tyranny of Methodology

Inherent in the above arguments is not only a Weberian model of bureaucracy but also the precepts of Marxian sociology. The use of those notions, as explanations of reform, requires some understanding of logical positivism on the one hand and of critical theory on the other as they are used as models for Western thought and science, and to structure the public schools of the United States.

Logical Positivism

Writing on logical positivism and political science, Gunnell (1975) says,

> [Its] influence . . . has affected nearly every methodological premise of the discipline. . . . The doctrine of logical positivism and, more recently, those of logical empiricism have been especially influential . . . in primary theoretical formulations and in works dealing with the nature of political inquiry. (p. 9)

This statement is important for our study of "Reforming Education American Style," for this chapter is an inquiry into both primary political theoretical formulations and of the political nature of education reform. Gunnell continues,

> there has been a failure to appreciate the full extent to which behaviorism has structured its identity in terms of doctrines uncritically appropriated from logical positivism and empiricism. . . . [We must either] . . . defend a set of philosophical doctrines that have become highly controversial, or . . . must begin a critical examination of these doctrines. (pp. 10–12)

The tendency in the political literature has not been to inquire and critically examine, but to reinforce present assumptions, Gunnell says. Small wonder then that political reform in the United States, and all education reform is political reform, has tended to reinforce present structures rather than to critically examine and change them.

As most social scientists and researchers in education are indoctrinated in logical positivism, a full and formal explanation of that paradigm is not necessary here. Suffice to note its widening of the gap between the philosopher and the scientist and its increased emphasis on formal logical models (Gunnell, 1975) parallels the increase in the scientific manager as superintendent as opposed to the philosopher-superintendent, as well as the increase of courses in school business management in educational administration programs noted by Callahan.

The positivistic approach to organizations produces an instrumental approach to people as well as it creates operational definitions of organizational roles devoid of concerns for individuals and competing values. In such a way, it is similar to the logical positivist canons for conducting research. It seems, then, that epistemological assumptions, those of logical positivism, have provided the rules for both structuring education reform and for assessing its success. It is hardly surprising that such an arrangement has produced little change. Rather, it finds the reform a success because the reform reinforces the structure and the paradigm that created it.

Critical Theory

The concepts of critical theory have their roots in Marxist thought and sprang from the work of the Frankfurt Institute for Social Research, later known as the Frankfurt School. Founded in 1929 as a part of Frankfurt University, it is important to note that at no time did the Institute actively support or have organizational ties with any political party. Its role, and the critical theory of society which it formulated, had to do with ideas, and an analysis of epistemology, the nature of mankind, and the institutions of mankind's creation. Major among such creations is bureaucracy and the domination of the many by the few in hierarchical bureaucratic, oligarchical fashion.

Bureaucracy, according to critical theory, is the bride of logical positivism which, like bureaucracy, fragments its object and is more concerned with results of abstractions than the theoretical reconstruction of the whole (Slater, 1977). Thus, it is easy to see that a reform which relied on bureaucratic concepts such as efficiency, regulations, centralization of power, and the canons of logical positivism (not to mention the goal of profit and of producing workers useful to and well-trained for the entrepreneurial needs of big business) would be a much different education reform than one spawned by the precepts of critical theory.

Here we have the fundamental reason why education reform has been more rhetoric than reform; why it results in putting the new wine into old bottles; and why, when everything is supposed to change, nothing changes. The reforms have always been driven by logical positivism thought which reinforces the bureaucratic structures that already exist and strengthens the secular power at the top of the hierarchy.

Reform Guided by Critical Theory

Perhaps John Dewey's reforms in education were doomed at their inception. They followed the precepts of critical theory more than those of logical positivism. They required a theory *praxis nexus* link so a part of original critical theory which, although it was not carried through by the Frankfurt School according to Slater (1977), remains a central concept of critical theory. Central to Dewey's notion of education was the individual, not the bureaucracy. Although theory was critical to Dewey's notion of education, it always required practical experience as prerequisite to the learning process. It considered the learner as a whole person and refused to fragment the learning into segregated elements.

Whether by design or not, John Dewey's "progressive" reform in education was patterned in a critical theory fashion. It did not fit the logical positivistic patterns and the bureaucratic structures of the public schools. Although Dewey's reforms were adopted by a few for a relatively short period, they never had a chance of surviving in schools without completely restructuring the public schools' bureaucratic organizational nature. Those bureaucratic patterns have persisted and have been constantly reinforced by every "successful reform" in American public education.

The above is not and should not be interpreted as a Marxist analysis of the American schools favoring communism over capitalism. Such a distortion would misdirect the argument. Nothing could be more bureaucratic and more hierarchically controlled than the schools of the Soviet Union. On the other hand, as noted by Loomis (1960), the United

States has developed the most democratic and people-controlled education system in the world. The argument here is neither for Soviet Communism nor Russian schools.

As noted earlier, it is interesting that the critical theorists have pointed to the domination of the Proletariat by a Soviet bureaucracy with its scientific management, supplanting czarist domination of the people, as a major source of the failure of that socialist revolution (Slater, 1977). It was to that end, then, that "it was endorsed by that old friend of capitalism, Lenin" (Callahan, 1965, p. 19). This rush to increase bureaucracy and efficiency via scientific management has apparently failed to free the human spirit regardless of geography or political style.

As suggested by Loomis and by the Dissatisfaction Theory of American Democracy (Lutz & Iannaccone, 1978), every step away from the local school board, every move toward more centralized state control is a move away from the people and toward a more bureaucratized and secular education system. In every case analyzed by this chapter, education reform has been a move in that direction, reinforcing the bureaucratic structure and further centralizing control of education at the state level.

Reforming the Paradigm

It has been argued here that education reform in America has been a cult of epistemology or of ideology. Bates (1986) and Willower (1986) have debated that issue. Each seemed to suggest that the position of the other was ideology and that his own was science. Both may be correct, for, as critical theory asserts, science and epistemology are based on some belief system and are certainly not value free. This is, in fact, one of the major points of the critical theorists' criticism of the exclusive use of logical positivism in education and educational research. Logical positivism not only requires the set of values that have structured a particular type of educational system in America, but has asserted that it, logical positivism, is value free and the only "scientific" method. Thus its dominance of the social sciences and of education has, until recently, closed out even the discussion of other options.

Such a contention is probably too strong. It, at least, provides a different hypothesis, however, about why "Reforming Education American Style" appears to have produced more rhetoric than reform. Certainly a reform based on critical theory's precepts would produce a different reform than the reforms examined in this chapter. The efficiency and the economic demands of big business would play a much smaller role. The bureaucratic hierarchy would be turned upside down and real decision-making on the part of students, parents, and teachers would take center stage. Certainly the trend toward the centralization of power in state departments of education would be reversed.

It is not argued here that such a reform would be better. The question is whether such a reform would produce change rather than merely reinforcing the present structures with more money and more power. The answer to that question is surely, yes. Reform follows the rhetoric. Change the rhetoric and one changes the nature, the structure, if you will, of the reform. To date reforming education American style always uses the same rhetoric and results in reinforcing the same structure and organization of education.

Conclusion

This chapter has inquired about the nature of reform in American education, but certainly has not asserted a final truth about education reform in America. Inquiry, as Schaefer (1967) stated, is the proper role of schools. Inquiry was the purpose and process of Callahan's efforts resulting in his classic work, *Education and the Cult of Efficiency*. Inquiry was the premier goal of the Graduate Institute of Education of Washington University. To paraphrase Mr. Lerner,

> There are those to tell the story
> So 'twill not be forgot
> Of what it was to inquire
> In that place called Camelot.

If only, from such recollections, could we rekindle the spirit of inquiry that was the hallmark of the Graduate Institute of Education. But, perhaps, like Camelot, it cannot happen again. Perhaps it can only happen in the imagination of the few. But with those few, its "ideal" lives to inspire others, in other places, to create centers of inquiry. Perhaps such inquiry may even initiate a better kind of education in America—some day.

7   Callahan's Contribution in the Context of American Realignment Politics

LAURENCE IANNACCONE

Within the limitations of a relatively new and small field of scholarship, this chapter attempts to follow Callahan's (1962) dictum in the second paragraph of *Education and the Cult of Efficiency*, where he set the stage for the beginning of the twentieth century:

> The story of the next quarter century of American education—a story of opportunity lost and of the acceptance by educational administrators of an inappropriate philosophy—must be seen within the larger context of the forces and events which were shaping American society. (p. 1)

Briefly, it attempts to use a perspective provided by a little more than a quarter of a century of theory-guided research in the politics of education, an applied subfield of American political science. In following Callahan's guidance, the emphasis here is on using some of the empirically grounded theory from the politics of education to reflect on his work. These theories did not exist when Callahan wrote *The Cult*. Instead, his work helped the development of the politics of education as an area of scholarship.

Theory from the politics of education provides a frame of reference, a useful window from another discipline, through which to view again the Callahan contributions. Note, in passing, the subtitle to *The Cult* is, *A Study of the Social Forces That Have Shaped the Administration of the Public Schools*. The relationship between educational government and general American politics is the larger context provided by this chapter to reflect on the story told by Callahan in *The Cult*. For in the United

States, as well as elsewhere, politics is the process by which the society's changing values are translated in governmental policy. Hence, the chapter's basic assumption, more often implicit than explicit, is that American politics is the mediating process through which the social forces Callahan speaks of shape American public institutions, including the public schools and their administration.

Three related sets of concepts from American political theory, also used in the politics of education, form the bulk of the conceptual framework of this chapter. The first of these sets emphasizes the role of critical elections. The second set of concepts hinges on the conflict between business values and democratic values. The third set concerns the role of federalism. All of the sets interweave and interlock.

The focus of the first set of political theory concepts used to shape this chapter is the theory of critical election eras as adopted, and especially as influenced, by the body of research in the politics of education. Much of this results from studies of local school districts undergoing their own critical election years. Together, this first set of concepts focuses on the nature and processes of abrupt political conflicts and policy readjustments, as these characteristically appear in American polities.

The idea of the importance of the conflict between business values and democratic values is borrowed from E. E. Schattschneider's *The Semisovereign People* (1960). The book provides an American political theorist's perspective on Callahan's (1962) first goal, "to explore the origin and development of the adoption of business values and practices in educational administration" (p. vii). In fact, Schattschneider's views of his classic work are used with all three of these conceptual sets.

American federalism is like no other federalism in the world. It may well be the most fundamental feature of the American political system, sustaining one of the two oldest large-scale governments in the world. The viewpoint on federalism taken in this chapter is based upon that of Morton Grodzins (1966) and his followers. Specifically, the perspective on federalism used in this chapter pays special attention to periodic redefinitions in the American creed, the configuration of beliefs undergirding political ideology, which in turn shapes governmental policy and programs.

Organizational structures embody social power. . . . As centers of social power, organizational structures both reflect and reinforce in-

> equalities in the distribution of influence among various social groups.
> Organizations . . . are not static. They can be changed . . . to redistrib-
> ute power among participants. (Mitchell & Iannaccone, 1980, p. 11)

Redefinitions of federalism occur in the United States incrementally as a new domestic policy grows over many years and as its value-laden premises spawn their logical podginess. Such redefinitions tend to appear rather abruptly instead of incrementally during critical election eras.

Critical Election Theory

Recent discussions of political realignments and realignment elec- tions have made some conceptual elements of critical election era theo- ries familiar. The theory basically says that American polities, including the nation, states, municipalities, and local school districts, are recur- rently brought into a more nearly balanced relationship with the realities of their changing socioeconomic structures, as these have come to be understood and conceptualized by their citizens. Such political readjust- ment periods are abnormally useful for reexamining and redirecting policies (including educational policy) and their implementation for years afterward. The research base for the view here presented is largely derived from studies since 1960 on the politics of education in the United States. Much of the research specifically about abrupt and significant educational policy redirections and the heightened political stress sur- rounding these comes from studies of local school districts. The primary scaffold of theory used here relies mainly upon the research on incum- bent school board member defeat and resulting policy adjustments (Ian- naccone, 1967; Iannaccone & Lutz, 1970). This line of research was begun at Washington University as Callahan was completing *The Cult*. Sec- ondly, its theoretical line of thought was initially derived from European political theory. Later, writings of Schattschneider were used. The earliest research on American local school districts, resting on this theory of political change in education, followed the work of the Italian political theorist of the nineteenth century, Mosca, and his school. Only later in the 1970s was the connection made between this body of research on educational governance and the work of American political theorists (Burnham, 1970; Key, 1955; MacRae & Meldrum, 1960; Schattschneider,

1960; Waldo, 1963). Implications of what had been previously synthe-sized at typical local school district, large urban school district, and state levels were applied to the national level (Iannaccone, 1977).

The Myth of Majority Rule

Whether from the politics of education or from American political science, critical election era theorists share the belief that episodic shifts in the distribution of power within a polity and its resulting policy redirection are systematic, not random. These shifts reconcile for them the reality of the existence of democratic societies and another empirical reality: in modern democratic societies the majority does not rule, what-ever normative democratic theory says to the contrary. From this point of view, democratic states exist in spite of the fact that the majority of the citizens in those societies do not govern, do not retain awareness (let alone oversight) of most public affairs, and do not administer the govern-ment. The inconsistency between the definition of democracy as govern-ment by the people and the operational reality of democratic society exists, not because of imperfections in realities, but because of weaknesses in the theory, especially in its classic definition. Majority rule is a slogan, one which obscures more democratic processes than it illuminates. The reality is that in a democratic society the public can and does periodi-cally use the electoral process to replace its governing elites. The majority simultaneously redirects government policy by altering the value-laden assumptions that operate as the long-term, underpinning premises of governmental policy with its related public affairs and programs.

Consequently, the theory argues that only longitudinal studies can test the propositions: (1) that critical election eras are not random; (2) that they are led up to by a tendency, exacerbated over time, of those in office to hold on to traditional policy when it is no longer believed in by the voters; and (3) that such eras are ones of unusually intense political conflicts. These years of conflict, often a decade or less, usher in new longer periods, usually of about a quarter of a century, of relatively quiescent politics and incremental policy development. Within this decade or so of conflict are critical election periods that exhibit depth, intensity, and coalitional realignment (Key, 1955). Such periods open the political system and force substantial policy redirection. Generally, that policy redirection, with its underpinning value-laden assumptions, there-after guides governmental actions for about a generation. "Why Is a

Generation the Proper Period for the Study of Politics? Schattschneider asked. Because ideas govern the world," answered Adamany in his Introduction to the second edition (1975, p. xxvi). Since adoption of the constitution, there have been about eight such changes in the national policies of the United States. The consequences of each of these have been so powerful, we could not understand American history were we to ignore them.

The Crucial Decade of Conflict

While Callahan and Button (1964) entitled their 1900–1913 chapter section, "The Transition Period," and the earlier *Cult* treated the decade of 1900–1910 as the "Prelude," Callahan's later research identified 1890–1900 as the crucial decade of conflict in the turn of the century politics of education. The 1890–1900 election era is seen by critical election theorists as one of the mainsprings of American politics (Burnham, 1970).

Schattschneider, writing in the late 1950s, says, "To understand what has happened in American politics in the past generation it is necessary to go back to the election of [William McKinley in] 1896, one of the decisive elections in American history" (1960, p. 78). The 1896 realignment was remarkably stable, and its policy values shaped governmental action far more than 30 years, including educational policy. The new alignment was born in the conservative fears of Republicans at the radical farm and mine populism west of the Mississippi, fueled by the fears of Southern conservatives when the Populist movement captured state legislatures there and moved to integrate poor blacks and poor whites. In return for a free hand in the South, conservative Democrats surrendered their chances for presidential victories, leaving it to northeastern Republicans, isolating the western radical Republicans into political limbo, and welcoming the Progressive's Municipal Reform in place of the more threatening populist movement. For at least a generation, it delayed movement toward racial equality; through one-party dominance, it decreased representativeness in state elections; through municipal reform, it decreased representativeness in local government. Most of all, it restructured local school district governments, largely eliminating any meaningful variation in social class, ethnicity, or religion on school boards. As will appear, using the theory and research about generational policy epochs from critical election era scholarship to add another context to Callahan's *Cult* is appropriate because of several complementary relationships between that school of thought in politics and Callahan's contributions. One connection, however, above all others would provide justification enough. The period of Callahan's research falls precisely between the two presidential realignment elections most studied by critical election theorists. These are the elections of 1896 and 1932.

There is a periodicity in the life cycle of American electoral governments. An electoral epoch lasts for approximately one generation. As a national election epoch runs from one generation to the next, so too does a national policy epoch. These are two aspects of the same historical happening. In passing, the years Callahan's research illuminates are approximately a generation in length, c. 1890–1930. Critical election eras are shorter episodes within these generational epochs. Such eras display the primary political processes of tension management, which characterize American polities generally, and the nation in particular. Political dynamics of critical election eras are the chief means by which the government of an American polity is recurrently brought into a more balanced and harmonious relationship with its (1) electoral system, (2) political structures and processes, (3) policy-making subsystem, (4) ideological policy assumptions as premises, and (5) policies and programs. Less significantly, the polity as a whole is, at the same time, brought into a new and more balanced relationship with its social and economic systems. The critical election era within political epochs is the American government's means of self-renewal.

Cyclical Patterns

Critical election eras are a universal of United States governments. They are a recurring stage in the customary life cycle of each of the American family of governments. This conclusion has been drawn partly from longitudinal research on the political dynamics of local school districts from coast to coast—large and small ones; surburban, rural, and middle-sized city districts (Lutz & Iannaccone, 1978; Criswell & Mitchell, 1980; Danis, 1981; Iannaccone & Lutz, 1970). Such eras have also been found by research on the largest American cities (Iannaccone & Cistone, 1974; Iannaccone & Wiles, 1971; Lowi, 1964; Peterson, 1976). Smaller municipalities with city managers also experience them (Kammerer et al., 1962, 1963; Danis, 1981). Similar political life cycles have been noted in states (Burnham, 1970; Iannaccone, 1966, 1967; MacRae & Meldrum, 1960). They are a significant feature of American national politics, especially in relation to changes in domestic policy eras, including education (Key, 1955; Iannaccone, 1981; Schattschneider, 1960; Sellers, 1965).

Within that universality, variations exist in the life cycle patterns due to a number of factors, for example: (1) demographic mobility; (2) technologically induced economic changes; (3) the impact of demands by supragovernments upon others, such as the state upon local governments, or made by one member in the family of American governments upon another, for example, federal on the local; and (4) the diversity of structural arrangements for representation. While noting such variations, the research still reveals a cyclical pattern in all the polities of the United States which have elected governments. The cyclical pattern's critical election era is its most important feature. Despite variations in specific election mechanisms or the mix of these with appointive offices, the dynamics of critical election eras are quite similar among the diverse governmental units of the United States. They have the common function of producing political realignment and policy redirection.

The life cycles of diverse American polities have many other common characteristics. Critical election eras fall between, in fact are, the overlapping transition phase between successive political epochs or episodes. They are a highly politicized stage in the intensity, visibility, and scope of their conflicts. The conflicts reflect the death throes of one epoch and the birth pangs of the next. Critical election eras are the briefer segment of a political epoch. There have been only a few national eras compared to the vastly larger number found in the local school districts, one polity in contrast to about 1,600 polities currently. However, the findings from school district research are consistent with the national government in this regard.

Features of Political Epochs

It may be useful to list more precisely a number of the characteristic features of political epochs, especially of their critical election eras and their periodicity. These are found in the corpus of critical election era research on the American family of general governments: local, state, and national, and in particular, local school districts.

1. American electoral polities display distinct epochs in their politics and policy premises.
2. The essential characteristic of each such epoch is the stability of its politics. This may be seen particularly in the stability of its constitu-

ency alignments for about a generation. A similar consistency may be noted in the epoch's public creed with its value-laden policy premises that shape policy and action.

3. Examination of these epochs reveal cyclical sequences in an alternating pattern of voter acquiescence and discontent.
4. The discontented portion of an epoch is its significantly shorter portion.
5. Such phases of discontent tend to unleash driving forces of citizen involvement in political processes, whereas quiescent phases tend to restrain these.
6. Critical election periods are preceded by a growing imbalance or mismatch between political and socioeconomic systems.
7. Critical election periods are also characterized by increased political conflicts around ideological issues.
8. Major and abrupt changes in the politics of American polities take place during their discontent phases. The most predominant of these abrupt changes is its realignment election.
9. These changes are lawful and cyclic adaptations of the polity's policies and service delivery. They reflect, more accurately than before, the changed social and economic conditions of the polity, and the particular governmental and service organization involved. In all these American polities, there is evidence that critical elections are cyclic—patterned over time.

As might be expected, given the enormous number of school districts, there appears to be more variation among these than in the nation as a whole. However, the length of a political epoch is remarkably similar in each of these otherwise quite diverse polity types. The findings from the school districts studied suggest that an epoch is about 32 to 40 years. The critical eras within these seem to run from about 4 to 12 years (Chase, 1981; Criswell & Mitchell, 1980; Danis, 1981; Peppel, 1986). Criswell and Mitchell (1980), reporting on a longitudinal study of local school district elections in four southern California counties, conclude that critical election eras in these were cyclical, not random. Using the indicator of frequency of school board incumbent defeats over two decades, they found that the outlying districts in their sample, the ones with the most and least defeats, fell within the normal bell-shaped curve, suggesting that critical election era phenomena are normal for most districts. They also found that the mean curve of high defeat districts at the beginning years of the study crossed over the mean curve of the lowest defeat districts after about eight years. The movement of the electoral results over the score of years studied suggests a recurring cycle of approximately 36 years. National realignment elections since the adoption of the constitution and Washington's first election suggest a similar length, about 36 years per national political epoch (i.e., 1828, 1860, 1896, 1932), avoiding for now the current debates about the meaning of the 1968 and 1980 elections.

The most important features of a critical election era are the simultaneous realignment of voter constituencies and the redirection of policy. These may be especially visible at the national level in the defeat of an incumbent president. The seductive visibility of such an event can misdirect attention. The loss of the White House by the party which had held it for most of an epoch, as in 1896, is not the most important feature of a critical election era. Nor is the more dramatic event, the defeat of a sitting president, as in 1932 and 1980. More important is the fact that, during a critical election era, intense disruptions of long-standing constituency commitments and traditional voting patterns of masses of voters take place. The more visible features—whether defeats of incumbent school board members after some years of uncontested elections or the defeat of a sitting president—reflect, are symptomatic of, a major restructuring of the polity's voting topography. The essential feature of a critical election era is the almost earthquake-like reconfiguration of the voting map. This involves the detachment of significant numbers of voters from their previous pattern, either by registering as independents or by switching parties. For others, it entails moving into the massive nonvoting portion of American citizens, while at the same time still others, customarily nonvoters, become active voters. The realignment realities of critical election eras influence both party affiliation and nonvoting statuses. The cyclic pattern of politics is matched by a parallel cyclic pattern in the character of the polity's policy making processes, because they are mutually dependent.

In critical election eras, the policy processes retrace some of their previous policy developments. The political conflicts of these eras tend first to challenge the most recent aspects of policy and later to address earlier policy precedents upon which recent policies relied for their legitimacy and guidance. As earlier policies are engulfed in the expanding political conflicts of these eras, their remote policy premises and the predominant political paradigm of the polity, sedimented a generation ago and then taken for granted, become politically salient. Eventually, as politicization of a general policy (or the governance of a public service, e.g., education) continues to expand, the newer conflicts force awareness of some of the government's ideological underpinnings, long and widely held governance philosophy and policy premises. These are now identified as issues once more requiring definition as part of a new public creed.

The Close of Critical Election Eras

Critical election eras characteristically draw to a close with the articulation of a new mandate and substantial voter support for it. After this, the new policy makers, their policies and programs, become increasingly more secure. Political conflict declines. A new era of voting quiescence emerges. Widely shared ideological assumptions about political, social, and economic organizations provide a needed base for policy making. Such ideological assumptions operate to take certain beliefs out of the battlegrounds of public criticism. They can then be introduced into policy making as settled fact and become the premises of future policy making. The characteristic policy making process of the longer eras of voter quiescence has been fitly described as incrementalism (Lindblom, 1968). Over time, incremental policy making produces, as it were, a chain of links consisting of the accretion of a body of previous policies. Each successive movement of policy becomes the immediate precedent for the next and draws the gunfire criticism of public debate to itself. Thereby, it automatically removes the political conflicts of the day one step further from the original ideological assumptions about philosophy of governance, authority, the criteria for distributions and value allocations, and the proper service functions of public authority. These policies have now become safely sedimented as governance myths in the unconscious "shoulds" and "oughts" of the society. For many years following, these myths indirectly and powerfully define the proper issues for political conflicts, determine the criteria for judging such conflicts, and separate the political from the apolitical.

The Competition of Business Values and
Democratic Values in the Context of Reform

Central to Callahan's 1962 work is the story of how, after 1900, business ideology was assimilated incrementally into the predominant public creed about governmental services, especially education. His focus is on part of the story of the municipal reform's ideology becoming the public creed of the United States. His specific concentration is on the processes by which the infusion of scientific management beliefs from industry become translated incrementally into the predominant doctrines of educational administration from its occupational training and professional ideology into its normative practice.

The Conquest of Business Ideology

Chapter One of *Education and the Cult of Efficiency* (Callahan, 1962) treated the 1900–1910 decade as the prelude to the story told by *The Cult*. That was appropriate. The story told by that book is one of the penetration of business ideology into the farthest reaches of educational administration. It is the story of how the ideological agenda of the winners of the crucial battles in national politics of the previous decade, 1890–1900, was first consolidated between 1900–1910, then restated in terms of a misunderstood scientific management, and finally progressively and pervasively misapplied throughout American education until the 1930s. The prelude would have been inappropriately applied to the 1900–1910 decade, however, had the research Callahan did subsequent to *The Cult* been included in it. It would have been a different chapter; it would have been a different book. From the perspective provided by the larger Callahan corpus of research, the prelude might be viewed as inappropriate for the first decade of this century. Instead, the previous one, the last decade of the nineteenth century, is the critical era. At least it is so in politics. Callahan's incomplete work, *The Superintendent of Schools: An Historical Analysis* (1967), clearly indicates the critical nature of the political conflicts in education during the decade of 1890–1900, prior to that 1900–1910 prelude, which then led to the injection of scientific management into the training of school administrators. As Callahan documents, there were many political conflicts faced by school administrators throughout the first decade of this century. These clearly preceded the infusion of the scientific-management panacea. But the political context of the United States saw its critical battles in the decade before 1900 and its decisive national politics battle in 1896, a presidential realignment election. As with the context, so it was in the area Callahan concentrates on. The conflicts in the politics of education between 1890 and 1900 were also decisive. They cleared the arena of combat and of combatants so that it could be converted into the stage on which the story of *The Cult* was played. It is 1895, the year before the 1896 realignment election, that, according to Callahan, saw the high point of attempts by school superintendents to reduce the vulnerability of that office by securing tenure for school superintendents. Callahan (1975) described that effort as, "the boldest attack ever made by school administrators as a group upon school boards" (p. 27).

Thus, Callahan's most significant period of study begins with the conflicts in the politics of education before the turn of the century. His period ends with the early 1930s. For one example, he uses a study of the misapplication of scientific management and misdefined efficiency in the doctoral training of 43 individuals who received their doctor's degrees in educational administration between 1910 and 1933 (Callahan, 1962). As he acknowledged the moderating impact of Newlon and Counts within the context of the 1930s depression, Callahan wrote, "But the damage had been done. Between 1915 and 1929 thousands of men had received professional training" (p. 249). The years he researched and reported upon run from about 1890 to 1933. In sum, in attempting the reexamination of Callahan's work with the lenses of American political science, it is essential to keep in mind the fact that his research period for *The Cult* falls between the two most studied American presidential realignment elections, 1896 and 1932. His later work, *The Superintendent of Schools* (1967), adds the critical election era of the 1890s. The whole episode he illuminated encompasses a critical election era c. 1890–1896 and its subsequent quiescent years, 1896–1928.

Social Conflicts

Different sorts of social conflicts exist. At the micro-level are daily conflicts within organizations. These are essentially private in nature and result in internal organizational adjustments. Public controversies over what are viewed as issues of public affairs are the central cleavage between the two major parties, each of which is a grand coalition of coalitions. These differences tend to remain rather stable over time during a policy epoch. So, too, the major coalitions, with their party affiliations, tend to display relative stability for about a generation. Critical election eras, instead, tend to produce yet another level of conflict. These election eras are about the mechanisms and processes for dealing with public political conflicts over public affairs. At the same time, they are concerned with defining the appropriate issues for political controversies and determining which social cleavages are appropriate for expansion through overt political conflicts. The outcomes of these sorts of conflicts have a shaping impact upon the political and policy cleavages for about a generation. Inevitably, in that process of defining the what and how of public politics for an epoch, they also separate these from the vastly larger realm of private affairs, with its many more social conflicts. Thus, what we call politics is the avowed conduct of public affairs. It refers to the management of conflicts about the allocation of value and the distribution of resources. In particular, it refers to the establishment and maintenance of rules and procedures by which such allocations are made. Implicit, therefore, is the suppression of some types of conflict. Often, these are relegated to the private sector and the world of apolitical institutions. The reverse of that coin is the exploitation of other kinds of conflicts in the public politics of the state. In Schatt-schneider's (1960) view, "The outcome of the game of politics depends on which of a multitude of possible conflicts gains the dominant position" (p. 62). The central political conflict in effect "overwhelms, subordinates, and blots out a multitude of lesser ones" (p. 68). Therefore, says Schattschneider of political strategy and tactics, "All politics deals with the displacement of conflicts or efforts to resist the displacement of conflicts" (p. 70).

Since only a few of a nation's social issues can command the society's central arenas for political conflicts at any one time, most social conflicts are left to the private sector or to apolitical organizations and groups. Here, the day in/day out organizational processes not only accomplish the work of the organization (for example, public transportation or police), but also simultaneously suppress in various ways, and sometimes temporarily resolve, the scope of social conflicts around the organization's decisions and actions. The term *apolitical* is generally used to refer to organizations and social events in which conflicts are, to a significant extent, privatized in this manner. Such apolitical organizations or events are set apart from the central political processes of the state.

All organizations were created through a series of value choices. In the case of special governmental institutions like schools, fire departments, police, and sanitation services, such choices reflect previous political conflicts in the central political arenas of the state. The factual memory of those conflicts may be buried in governmental archives and only recounted by the victors as tales of virtue triumphant over evil political scoundrels. The winning values of those conflicts, however, shaped the resulting apparatus of the state and built into them their peculiar value bias. These organizational biases, thereafter, provide the premises that guide policy making in public affairs. They also become the ideological bases for the internal apolitical organization's privatized politics. They become the premises of the doctrines of governance and administration, the institution's ideological underpinnings. In this century, the values and beliefs that justified education's separation from the central politics of the state simultaneously provided the *apologia* for its internal power relationships. The privatization of such conflicts confers special advantages on insiders as opposed to nonmembers and on organizational elites in comparison to rank and file members.

A New Public Creed

Callahan's focus in *The Cult* is largely on the internal politics of education during the years after the critical election era of that political epoch. Callahan gave particular attention to the processes in the politics of education by which the new age of educational administration began and gradually established itself around the new doctrines of educational administration centering on scientific management ideas. From the perspective of the larger political context, a similar development can be traced in the area of public administration and, of course, in business management. Dwight Waldo, in *The Study of Public Administration* (1963), points out how the naked empiricism of Frederick Taylor and the goal of the scientific management movement provided a necessary element in the administrative doctrine needed for a new philosophy of government in industrial America after the turn of the century. As described by Waldo, the goal of the movement was, "to discover the one best way to perform complex human operations . . . the dream of making social science really scientific" (p. 18). This was, for public administration, a solution for the quest for neutral competence in government officials. As Kaufman (1955) says,

> the core value of this search was ability to do the work of government expertly, and to do it according to explicit, objective standards rather than to personal or party or other obligations and loyalties. The slogan of the neutral competence school became, "take administration out of politics." (p. 1053)

The public school variant on this theme was: "keep politics out of education."

The general political context, its public creed, and its public administration doctrine went hand in hand with the doctrine of public school administration as it emerged from the politics of education. In the words of Heinz Eulau (1972):

> I think we have to think of politics, broadly conceived as including both government and social happenings, as the independent variable and of education as the dependent variable. (p. 3)

American public school policy has always been the caboose on the American domestic policy train. Thus, Callahan's early awareness of the adoption of business ideology in educational administration is supported not only by his own research but by the record of similar adoption in public administration at the same time.

Another common factor in both the larger political context and Callahan's report was the vulnerability of elected representatives, public administrators, and school superintendents prior to the municipal reform's political victories. Kaufman (1955) wrote, "legislators and administrators at every level of government proved themselves peculiarly vulnerable to the forces let loose by the burgeoning industrial system" (p. 1060).

The Municipal Reform and Administrative Doctrine

Since Jackson's day early in the nineteenth century, the dominant political ideology had advanced the claims of representative democracy through wide participation in elections and office holding, for example, advocating rotation in office and amateurism above tenure and professionalism. It had sought to balance the value claims of individual liberty and social equality with its widespread representative orientation and extended grassroots electoral system. By the end of the century, rampant individualism and political manipulation characterized the political order and education. The predominant political paradigm had lost its traditional credibility under the attack of intellectuals, especially those of the media, academics, and leading school administrators (Callahan, 1962; Tyack, 1974). Specifically, the belief in direct elections, grassroots decentralization, and amateurism were respectively challenged by the reform values of merit examinations, appointment, and tenure in civil service; centralized hierarchical bureaucratic structures; and professionalism.

The paradigm of ideological assumptions resting on beliefs about representativeness in government had become sedimented in public memory through the early and mid-1800s. The expanded conflicts toward the end of that century had increasingly challenged these assumptions. The desertion by the intellectuals of the older ideology, seen most clearly in the work of muckrakers, is characteristic not only of the eve before the great revolutions, but is also a characteristic early feature of critical election eras in the United States. The mounting threat of the new alliances of poor Southern farmers and Midwestern farmers, the embattled miners of the West, the growing populism, and the fear of the new ethnic political machines in the cities laid bare the failure of that previous political and policy paradigm. In effect, these forces indicated the bankruptcy of the old established ideology of the previous generation and that its myth of authority with its policy premises had not and could not solve the problems of the nation by further development of its techniques. Instead, the extension of representativeness through more direct elections and rotation in office had been followed by greater political corruption. The city machine was especially seen as the demon of the piece. Thus, the tools of Jacksonian democracy—amateurism in public service, direct election of officials, the long ballot, and rotation in office—were challenged by the reformers. This is characteristic of the political conflicts at the end of a policy epoch and the early themes of critical election eras.

The social forces fueling the political challenges to the established Jacksonian political paradigm also placed stress upon education (Callahan & Button, 1964). The conflicts between superintendents and boards were fueled by the 1893 report by Joseph M. Rice on education in the cities of the United States. Similar to the best work of the muckrakers in its research base, it also placed primary blame on the political system of the cities. It, too, espoused the doctrines of neutral competence, especially the separation of education from politics.

By 1910, the critical turn-of-the-century election victories were translated into a coherent package of governmental, political, and administrative reforms. Structurally, it was a highly centralized blueprint of policy making and control similar to Weber's rational bureaucratic model. It concentrated power in bureaucratic public service pyramids, walling off grassroots participation. Whether elected or appointed, the representational aspect of the model was a small local board, similar in size and function to the industrial corporation board. To eliminate the role of the political parties, its members were selected nonpartisan and at large rather than from specific neighborhoods. This system ensured the election of socially visible, upper-middle-class professional and managerial candidates, and the defeat of the poor and working-class candidates. This was precisely what was intended by its most influential advocates (Cochran, 1972; Hays, 1964, 1965). The reform was a successful political conflict to take power away from Irish urban machines, Mediterranean and Eastern European immigrants, Catholics, and small farmers, and to give it to the upper classes, the "better people." The reform model of government, shaped to reflect that of the private industrial organizations of the turn of the century, resulted in a similar manner as do stockholder elections in private corporations.

The reforms' stated aims were equality, efficiency, and strong, honest public service. The means for accomplishing these aims were seen as managerial control by professional administrators (city managers, civil servants, and school superintendents) trained in Taylor's "one best way" of scientific management. The brass instrument era of psychology and logical positivism, with its machine model of human motivation and behavior, was reflected in the ideology of a political paradigm. The essence of the political aspects of the ideology in the culture of professionalism is its faith in its definition of science as value-free and politically neutral. So, its judgments about social problems and its solutions for these ought not to be interfered with by political conflicts. It follows that such solutions are best undertaken by apolitical institutions and organizations, designed to scientifically deal with social services, and that these be administered by scientific professionals. This public creed has been the predominant myth of authority for most of this century.

Public service organizations and their governance are an expression of public authority. They are part of the apparatus of the state. Perhaps the most successful legerdemain of the municipal reform was its rhetorical victory in redefining public services as apolitical. The policy wars that make a difference are won and lost in the minds of citizens, often long before they vote. The delegation of some degree of autonomy to a public service (education or some other) does not make that tax-supported agency any less a part of the state apparatus. Its apolitical feature describes its status in the public creed as apart from the general public politics of the state and its political parties. Not only does its apolitical character not eliminate its basic nature as part of the state apparatus, it also does not free it from politics.

In their 1890 battles against elected neighborhood school boards, the school administrators had appealed to the Social Darwinism of Herbert Spencer (Callahan, 1967). The emergence on the political stage in 1910 of Taylor's scientific management—in fact a naive naked empiricism—provided the illusion of a solution to "the dream of making social science really scientific" (Waldo, 1963, p. 18). The elements of efficiency, tax savings, and scientific management supported the rationale claimed by school administrators of neutral competence, value-free, objective, and impersonal professional governance of the educational institution. This illusion allowed the definition of education as apolitical and its separation from the general public political conflicts.

The new apolitical doctrine of the twentieth century industrial state is power theory. It provides an *apologia* for a ruling class defined not so much by social birth and breeding (as did most previous theories of the ruling class), but by the newer culture of professionalism. The reform doctrine is a complete *apologia* for power in the strong bureaucratic state. At every level, the exercise of such power is buttressed by the illusion of scientific measurement as its essential characteristic. "In essence," said Waldo (1963), "this new theory of philosophy of government was a reinterpretation of the meaning of democracy. . . . It sought to attain the values of equality and freedom for citizens by making government strong and efficient" (1963, pp. 19–20). Its key elements were scientific management, training, and the hierarchical control structure of bureaucracy, guaranteed by faith in value-free measurement. Separated from party politics, it naturally becomes less vulnerable to party politics; however, by that same arrangement, it becomes more vulnerable to smaller, more narrow interest groups, at least until it develops its own internal politics with its own political defense systems. It tends to produce a low visibility politics of private agreements and informal consensus building among its insiders, its lay special interest groups, and its professional careerists.

> It is the politics of the sacred, rural rather than secular, urban community; a politics of the priesthood rather than the hustings. The two genres of politics are different in kind. The politics of the hustings are visible and thrive on conflict and its resolution. The colorful kaleidoscope and cacophonic calliope of the campaign is its milieu. They

subsist on the informal development of consensus prior to public
debate. (Iannaccone & Lutz, 1967, p. 161)

So, the scientific or professional character of the enterprise and especially
of its managers, does not and cannot operate scientifically, apolitically, or
with neutral competence. In the words of D. W. Brogan (1949):

> It is a dangerous and idle dream to think that the state can be ruled by
> philosophers turned kings or scientists turned commissars. For if
> philosophers become kings or scientists commissars, they become
> politicians and the powers given to the state are powers given to men
> who are rulers of states, men subject to all the limitations and tempta-
> tions of their dangerous craft. (p. xvi)

The use of the label apolitical is far from nonpolitical. It is a slogan
that identifies and reinforces in the public mind the political ideology of
the separation of an institution or interest group from the central political
conflicts of a democratic society. Its connotation is that such institutions
are above politics, somehow more sacred and purer than matters settled
by voters and their elected representatives. These characteristics do not
make the educational system any less a part of the state. On the contrary,
that ideology is a distinct feature of the public creed defining the modern
state. To wit: that public service is best rendered scientifically and
objectively in special structures of governance by a professionally trained
meritocracy of civil servants and public administrators.

Twentieth-Century Federalism

One of the central features of American federalism is the existence
of a family of governments within the United States. Included among
these are counties, municipalities, school districts, states, towns, water
districts, and the national government. From a constitutional law perspective, some of these exist only in virtue of the powers delegated to
them by the others; for example, the relationship of school districts and
towns to a state can be seen as a hierarchy of inferior and superior
governments. From that same perspective, others are neither hierarchically related nor dependent on some other government for their constitutional base of power, for example, the nation and the states. In fact,

operationally, these are even mutually dependent. Sovereignty is an even more slippery concept in the United States than elsewhere. Again, the operational relationship between school districts and a state is such that it would not have been politically feasible for the state to eliminate school districts, despite the constitutional competence to do so. These political and constitutional realities have been described as a condition of dual sovereignty existing between states and their local school districts (Iannaccone & Cistone, 1974). The existence of that dual sovereignty, despite a constitutional law view, accents a profound reality of our American system of governments. In the United States at least, the operating realities among its family governments are determined not only through Supreme Court decisions but also through the political processes. One implication of this is that significant features of the mutual dependence among the American family of governments may be materially changed by those same political processes that characterize the peculiar nature of American federalism. Conceivably, such change could be slow and incremental so as to be hardly noticed. In fact, Schattschneider's (1960) discussion of American twentieth-century political changes makes precisely that point. As in his preface to *The Semisovereign People,* he asked,

> What makes things happen? What is the process of change? What does change look like? These questions are worth asking because obviously tremendous things are going on in American public affairs, even in quiet times.
>
> While we were thinking about something else a new government was created in the United States, so easily and quietly that most of us were wholly unaware of what was going on. (p. vii)

He was referring to the incremental growth and changes in American government after the 1932 realignment election and its critical election years.

The political system's capacity to reorder the relationship among the members of its family of governments incrementally is matched by its potential to alter those relations abruptly. One outcome of a critical election era's political battles may be the modification of policy making processes to a point of no return, which continues incrementally, thereafter, to reorder profoundly the federal relationships. One of the most important consequences of the municipal reform's victory has been the coexistence of two conflicting philosophies of government for almost a century. One is the creed of federalism; the other, the doctrines of the reform. Portions of each were interwoven in the governmental ideology and structures as these were forged in the turn of the century conflicts. Federalism was lodged in the fundamental constitutional arrangements of the United States. It could be weakened, partly suppressed, altered, neglected, and redefined, but it could not be eliminated without the erasing of the United States. Its loose-coupled, relatively flat rather than pyramidal structure, and especially the semi-independent governments of federalism in the United States, easily appears to be an inefficient form of government. The rise of industrialism with its large, complex organizations led to new management concepts applied first in large-scale businesses and later reappearing as ideas for governmental reform.

Given the social composition of reform associations at the turn of the century, the transmission of industrial concepts into governmental services was inevitable. As Cochran (1972) points out:

> Characterizations of the twentieth century as one of managerial enterprise, labor bureaucracy, or dictatorship have one element in common: the emerging system had to operate through hierarchical administration. . . . Reform, in general, meant making the locally oriented politician more responsive to administrative control from above in the interests of efficient business and social policy. (p. 217)

Ironically, the loose-coupled structure of federalism both cushioned the shocks and provided a broken front opportunity for incremental but steady growth of the predominant reform orthodoxy. It moved incrementally toward increased centralism with more and more hierarchical policy making and control, without calling attention to the inherent contradictions in the system, at least until the latter half of the 1960s. The governance philosophy of the reform sought to redesign American government, at least its public service functions, according to the model of the large corporate pattern of the day. Its incremental spread and gradual growth across the country has often faced local or regional conflicts because of its basic inconsistency with American constitutional federalism and its political philosophy. The character of public services, domestic policy making processes, and domestic policy premises in the United States have been shaped by the tension resulting from the many contradictions produced by the coexistence of these twin conceptualizations and systems of governance. The reform view leads logically to big government; federalism rests upon the shared governance produced by independent governments. The reform concept of domestic policy making rests on the assumption that power should be integrated into pyramidal units, efficient monoliths hierarchically related so that the public good would result if the parts were kept in proper working order. Taylor's machine model of human motivation was central to the ideology and practices of scientific management. The ideology of the reform government was copied from the large industrial organizations of the day, designed for mass industrialism, and later assembly lines, with the same human motivational assumptions.

Hierarchical Control

A civics textbook picture of hierarchical control tends to reflect the reform philosophy. It assumes a cascade model of policy flow from Washington to state capitals to local governments. It assumes a relationship of superordination and subordination from one governmental level to the next. The cascade model assumes that all the intervening agencies and units of government are properly guided by goals from above. It is also assumed that neutral, competent professionals and civil servants in a merit system will interpret the goals appropriately for their level, influenced by their scientific training. Obviously, the essential elements needed for such a system are control of behavior by dispassionate professional norms, and scientific expertise working with scientifically produced data. The training assumptions are essentially the same as guided school administrator programs toward Taylor's "one best way." The assumptions of scientific management require centralization of authority and tight-linked hierarchical control of subordinate governments and employees by superordinate governments and supervisors working with scientifically determined decisions applied through explicit behavioral directives for measurable outcomes. The development of turn-of-the-century measurement in psychology and fiscal control systems provided the machinery for tighter internal controls. One ironic note in our day has been the label of accountability given such systems in response to grassroots demands for more control of individual and private destinies. Rapidly increased centralization and top/down domestic policy and control, proclaimed as a response to grassroots demand, led to the Reagan Revolution, whether these responses were supplied because of naivete or hypocrisy.

Characteristics of the Developing Paradigm

The principal characteristics of the developing paradigm consolidating the political victories of the reform after 1900 were centralization, professional bureaucratization, growth, and autonomy in public services. The nineteenth century political party and machine vulnerability of such services, including education, was increasingly offset as they were buffered by the ideology of separation from politics. In fact, it meant a separation from two party politics only, and a new vulnerability to special interests, many of which suited the new managers quite well in terms of their social class and ethnic and ideological character. The hierarchical assumptions of the reform, with the scientific emphasis of the day, fit the characteristics of the new managerial breed, as well they might since the progressive movement troops of the municipal reform were, to a significant extent, drawn from precisely the same new managerial and professional classes. Those who commanded the technical knowledge supported by the ideological victory and the new myth of authority eventually controlled the public service bureaucracies and agencies. And these expanded steadily. These same doctrines operated as an ideological buffer against pluralistic values, ethnic groups, and religious groups other than the predominant coalition, just as that buffer separated bureau politics from the political party conflicts. The public creed of the reform became, in fact, an ideology of centralization, justifying big government run by professional civil servants in evergrowing complex bureaucracies, hierarchically depicted in a cascade model of governance with the scientifically trained experts as the implicit ruling class of the society. In short, the municipal reform's public doctrines of policy making are pure ruling class theory, successfully functioning to weaken American federalism without being able to erase it. The shibboleth of the separation of public service from politics did no such thing. It did significantly weaken the two party system, as it does to our day. But just as it replaced twentieth century Jacksonian ruling class theory, it also replaced overt two party politics with politics of civil service bureaucracies and their related special interest groups. The American policy system continued to develop, with its basic contradictions of a hierarchical cascade model superimposed on the constitutional structures of federalism, by its nature fundamentally nonhierarchical.

The Roosevelt victory in 1932 resulted, in part, from the phoenix-like rise of the new coalition after the 1928 disaster of the Democratic party, as well as from the economic depression of the 1930s. The ideologi-cal shift of that realignment included an increased commitment to equality and compassion in government. It was reflected in new adminis-trative doctrines concerned with human relations and the human side of management. The 1932 realignment also significantly altered the rela-tionship between government and business. After all, the gods that failed in 1929 could hardly command the highest regard of the nation. The relationship between business and government, ushered in by the 1896 election of William McKinley and epitomized in Calvin Coolidge's election to the presidency in 1924, was rejected by the new Rooseveltian coalition of 1932. That winning coalition did not, however, repeal the cascade flow model of public policy. Neither were the centralizing ten-dencies nor the hierarchical government aspects of the twentieth century political ideology weakened. All to the contrary, 1932 and its later Rooseveltian years of political dominance embraced the essence of those two aspects of municipal reform doctrine. The growth tendencies of centralization in domestic policy making, an increasingly hierarchical restructuring of national government and its bureaucracies, continued during the same years as the national government spawned more and more bureaus at a more and more rapid rate until the late 1970s and the key election of 1980.

Redefining Federalism

The concern for equality translated into governmental policy and programs cannot become the increasingly dominant policy value except at the cost of some other values. No one element in a public creed can suppress effectively all others, however noble it may appear. Sooner or later, a predominant value of a public creed must be balanced against other important value elements in that same public creed. The increased concern for equality leading to the extension of the national government in domestic affairs, the proliferation of national bureaus and agencies, and the endless expansion of printed regulations had drastically rede-fined the meaning of federalism in America by the late 1970s. The impact on federalism of recent redefinitions of equality are profound. The redefinition of equality in national policy as equal results rather than equal opportunity is, at bottom, destructive of the essence of federal-ism. Aaron Wildavsky (1985) recently wrote:

> Uniformity is antithetical to federalism . . . were there to be a change in values toward equality of conditions, the political culture which undergirds federalism would fall apart. You can have a belief in equality of opportunity to be different, but you cannot have a belief in equality of results to be the same and still have a federal system. (p. 43)

The realignment of 1896, which ushered in a political epoch within which the story delineated by Callahan in *The Cult* is found, also shifted elements in the American public creed, especially at the expense of Jacksonian federalism. In effect, the municipal reform sought to produce Jeffersonian ends through Hamiltonian means. This meant, in part, the increased centralization of domestic affairs and faith in hierarchical government. The ideas of the reform had come from the private sector into politics by way of the rhetoric of the reformers and muckrakers. One of the clearest examples of this process was Taylor's scientific management in educational administration. This dominance of government by business models was dramatically arrested, but not reversed, by the 1932 realignment. In fact, key elements of the municipal reform, apart from the leadership of business, continued as part of the 1932 coalition's political ideology. Federalism continued to exist as a constitutional reality, but occupied a less and less prominent place in the American public creed.

The fundamental reality of the 1980 election was that for the first time since 1896, a deepening voter concern over centralization in domestic policy making, and the increased distancing of the making of policy from its points of application in the delivery of public services, broke through to replace a sitting president. That election reflected a lengthy but steady erosion in these same two municipal reform assumptions. It also fit some of the cases in the politics of education critical election era research (Iannaccone, 1981).

A rising tide of voter sentiment, beginning in 1964, has been directed toward the reduction of centralization in domestic affairs. Barring a catastrophe in international affairs or internal economics, such sentiment will continue. Voters unable to replace legislators, protected by legal advantages produced in the name of recent election reforms, continue to register their sentiments through the two avenues left to them: electing the executive and rejecting taxation as much as they can. This basic sentiment, more than party, explains the election and its after-shocks. The tenacious hold of incumbents on their offices was secured even more than before through the modifications of electoral laws in the 1960s and 1970s, although they were intended as reforms. Consequently, the Democrats have been able to ignore the need to reform fundamentally their party (Iannaccone, 1987). In effect, the leadership of the Democratic Party has chosen to become the party of the past and to hold onto their present offices, rather than restructure the party toward the future and risk the loss of present incumbencies. In the process, they have lost the presidency most of the time since World War II, even in spite of Watergate! As all established, long-term predominant coalitions tend to do, they have given the opposition the leadership toward change, holding onto what they have, while hoping for enough of a disaster to be returned to the presidency. It is, I believe, unlikely that even a major jolt to the nation, one putting the Democrats in the White House, could lead to their long-term return to political dominance without a major purging and restructuring of the party.

Conclusions

Public vs. Private: The Stressful Coexistence of American Governance

This chapter has given its attention to the political context, especially realignment politics, related to Callahan's historical contributions. Inevitably, it has concentrated on the figure of American politics, especially realignment politics, and resulting policy values, to the neglect of its contextual ground. But, as Gestalt schools are inclined to remind us, it is that ground which gives meaning to the perceived figure. American political conflicts tend to be about issues that divide established coalitions along the same lines for about a generation. These are the defined public affairs of a political epoch. What identifies some matters as res publica in contrast to others as res privata is not rooted forever in the world of nature. The definition of the public sector, whether explicit or implicit, is always a distinction from the private sector. In the United States, such definitions are created by the political conflicts of a critical election era. They are defined boundaries within which the subsequent political game of a policy epoch is played. They are also determined by the political battles shaping a political epoch. At the same time, an unbelievably large amount of social conflict is handled within the private sector, keeping it almost invisible. Thus, in the United States at least, the most profound consequence of a critical election era's processes is a redefinition of the ideological boundary separating public affairs from private matters. It influences which issues are political and which are apolitical; which conflicts are exploited by politics and which are suppressed; which citizens vote and which do not; and who the actors are and who the spectators are.

Business Values and Governmental Policy

Not the least important of the themes shared by Callahan and Schattschneider in their writings is the relationship between American governmental policy and American business. Schattschneider (1960) sees the relationship between American business and government as much more important than the view of business as a political interest group, or even as a coalition of interest groups. He views the pressure politics of interest groups, "as a stage in the socialization of conflict . . . an integral part of all politics, including party politics" (p. 39). In his formulation, pressure politics, while an important component of the political system and its processes, is a subsystem of and subordinated to the dominant political systems, the major American parties. And it is precisely the losers in the usually privatized business conflicts that seek to enlarge the scope of conflict in order to modify the private power relations of business, in hopes of recovering from or preventing their loss. In this process, such special business interest politics can be converted into party policy and enter the larger public conflicts of the political party system. Conversely, the winners in the privatized business power struggles seek to prevent this expansion of conflict. They try to keep business conflicts within the business privatized system and avoid the public arena (Schattschneider, 1960). This is the normal and normative pattern of American business power relationships.

Even more important within his theory, Schattschneider (1960) understands the American government and business relationship as a mature, unresolvable conflict. An unresolvable conflict is one in which "neither side can be overwhelmed, both sides are able and willing to continue and struggle indefinitely, and neither side can escape the necessity of continuing the struggle" (p. 114). Business is the principal nongovernmental focus of power in the modern world. The modern rivalry of business and government is like the church and imperial relations of the Middle Ages. The American contest between government and business is an irreconcilable conflict: Because almost everyone belongs to both groups, the clashes are seldom fully avowed as a struggle for power; the quarrel is pervasive in the political system; neither can disengage from their conflict; and it cannot become a war of extermination.

Ideologically the two systems are profoundly different. The business system is philosophically and operationally exclusive; in its competitions it tends toward secrecy; it is highly differentiated in its statutes and fosters concentrations of power. The economic system invites concentrations tending toward monopoly and fosters inequality. The political system rests upon numbers of votes, is broadly equalitarian, and avidly seeks publicity in its competitions. Schattschneider (1960) says, "The most significant difference between the private domain and the public domain is that in the private conflict the strong prevail whereas in the public domain the weak combine for defense" (p. 124). Thus, tension is inherent between the two systems, given their basic natures. At the same time, they are interdependent: Each needs the other.

Schattschneider (1960) argues that in America, "it was possible to democratize the political system without a bloody revolution because Americans invented a working model for splitting the two kinds of power. . . . If ever a contest was built into a regime, the conflict between government and business is it" (p. 120). This line of reasoning led Schattschneider to his conclusions: *"The function of democracy has been to provide the public with a second power system, which can be used to counter balance the economic power"* (p. 121). He adds that the public does not appear to want a final resolution of this basic conflict. It likes competitive power systems. He therefore concludes: "The public interest resides in no man's land between government and business" (p. 123). The rare, about once per generation, realignments of the political system result in a new political cleavage and new coalitions within the political system. At the same time, it changes the balance between business and government—the no man's land is inevitably redefined.

Louis Hartz (1955) offers a related view as the reason Americans have avoided bloody revolutions. He attributes American political ideology to the lack of feudalism against which to revolt and to the early American commitment to Lockian liberalism. Of the post-Civil War era, Hartz writes, "Unfurling the golden banner of Horatio Alger, American

Whiggery marched into the Promised Land after the Civil War and did not really leave it until the Crash of 1929" (p. 203). Nor did the New Deal reject the Lockian tradition. Hartz views Truman's second administration speeches as a "blend of fighting Roosevelt and the complacent capitalist oratory of Herbert Hoover. Surely such a synthesis would have been impossible if the New Deal had been defined in anticapitalist ideological terms" (p. 272). Thus, the business system with its values and the governmental system with its dissimilar ones are the Gemini twins of American society and its governance as a whole.

Innovation and Reform

Because politics is the avowed conduct of public affairs, its defined matters include only a very small fraction of the total conflict of any society. The bulk of conflict is inevitably left to the private sector. One consequence of this fact is that the private sector is a much better laboratory for social invention. Its fundamental structure is chaotic. At one end it tends toward monopoly, whether through mergers, takeovers, or governmental support. At the other end it creates new businesses at a rapid rate, whether through spinoffs, start-ups of subsidiary companies, or individual entrepreneurialism. In that chaos, however, a continuous formation, reforming, and new creating process goes on as large numbers of different businesses seek to cope successfully with changing social conditions. Only a few new ideas, inventions for coping with their changing social environments, work. Some significant trial and error learning takes place to the profit of some businesses, while usually many more fail. Some of these lead to useful changes in governmental action. Consequently, business produces an unintentional by-product of innovation for American government.

Government, in contrast, strains toward consistency. Its major output is law and regulation. It tends to shun risk and avoid insecurity. Its structures, agencies and bureaus reflect the opposite characteristics of the business system. Bureau pathology is endemic to the governmental system. Innovation is seldom found in governments. Indeed, the overwhelming evidence in the politics of education from research on school district critical election eras indicates that these eras are partly produced by the failure of school districts to change when their changing social environments require them to. The same characteristic is found at the late stages of a national political epoch, tenacious clinging to the policy of the past in the face of demands for change by the next generation.

The adoption and adaptation of business solutions and inventions by government during the late years of a critical election era are most probable. Since the private sector copes with social change on a broken front of trial and error, it almost inevitably leads the way during critical election eras. The 1896 realignment and its next decade did, as Callahan (1962) pointed out, display an extremely pervasive penetration of business ideology into the public sector, especially administration. Schattschneider provides us with a theoretical basis for understanding why and how the political process leads to the adoption of aspects of business ideology by the political system. As several researchers have noted, the rise of industrialism at the turn of this century had an overwhelming impact on American government (Cochran, 1972; Kaufman, 1955; Waldo, 1963).

In sum, paying attention to the general American political context provides another dimension from which to view the corpus of Callahan's research. The political theory and politics of education perspective used here help explain the Callahan findings. In particular, the dynamics of the tension between the American political and business systems help us understand the drift from business to government of new ideologies. One of these helped redefine the ideological meaning of federalism in the American public creed. The special significance of critical election era processes, combined with the historical period Callahan studied, 1890–1930, hopefully leads to a more complete, if not deeper, understanding of The Cult and the rest of the body of research and interpretation produced by Raymond E. Callahan.

8 The Violation of People at Work in Schools

ARTHUR G. WIRTH

I have been a teacher educator who has taken an eight-year detour into the world of American work. I think that there are parallel issues in work and in schools that we ought to be aware of.

A couple of quotations set themes I will be referring to. The first is by Hazel Henderson (1977), maverick economist: "For the first time in history morality has become pragmatic" (p. 235). That is the good news. It has become *practical* to act morally. The bad news is that we may not be insightful or courageous enough to act on it.

The second is by Mike Cooley (1981), President of the British Union of Engineers, who one sunny morning on the banks of the Thames, gave me this quote from a book he was writing:

> Either we will have a future in which human beings are reduced to a sort of bee-like behavior, reacting to the systems and equipment specified for them; or we will have a future in which masses of people, conscious of their skills in both a political and technical sense, decide that they are going to be the architects of a new form of technological development which will enhance human creativity and mean more freedom of choice and expression rather than less. The truth is we shall have to make the profound decision whether we intend to act as architects or bees. (p. 100)

The choice between architect or bee confronts us in both American schools and work. It is true that the bee-like way of treating teachers and students in schools came from American industry. Unfortunately, the chances of shifting toward the architect side may be better in American industry than in the schools.

The "violation of people" got into my title because institutions that treat us like bees violate who we are as human beings. Ernest Becker, in

The Structure of Evil (1968), helped me see that. Becker pointed out that since the rise of science and the Enlightenment in the seventeenth and eighteenth centuries, we have been confronted by two major images of humans: *l'homme machine* (the human as mechanism), and *homo poeta* (humans as meaning makers). The Newtonian image of the world as a physical mechanism moving according to mathematically regulated laws of force and motion gave powerful support to tendencies to see humans as manipulable objects within the grand mechanical design. That view was captured nicely by the eighteenth century philosopher Julien Offray de la Mettrie in his phrase *l'homme machine.* The problem with that concept, according to Becker, is that it is in violation of our deeper needs as *homo poeta.* We create structures of evil, Becker said, whenever we create institutions which deny persons the opportunity to stage the world so they can act in it creatively as meaning makers. In our time such institutions are not only immoral; they are also impractical. Our best chance of meeting successfully the problems of turbulent change of the momentous transition period we are now in depends on utilizing the full range of our creative strengths as *homo poeta.*

It has taken me a while to see things this way. In the late 1970s, I was aware of the growing concern about lowered productivity in both American industry and schools. I was aware, also, of the new press by educational policy makers to start treating children's learning as a measurable production function—with the assumption that the only learning that counts is learning that can be counted, and the parallel assumption that teachers will be made accountable in terms of test score results.

What disturbed me was my growing awareness that the teachers I thought of as the most committed and creative were becoming demoralized and thinking of quitting. Some of the rest were cheating to beat the test score pressures.

As parents, we had learned that the best bet for getting our own kids "hooked on learning" was to have them with teachers whose creative energies were engaged—teachers who worked from what the Greeks called their *entheos,* the personal God within which is the source of *enthusiasmos* or enthusiasm. If the new reductionist emphasis—"teaching is teaching for tests"—did damage to that, and in addition taught children that adults will cheat when fearful and resentful, then I assumed that something crazy and crazy-making was going on.

It was obvious that the new system's efficiency rationale was coming from the scientific management tradition in industry at a time of new fears about growing foreign competition. The question occurred to me, "If the scientific efficiency rationale is having crazy-making effects in schools, is anyone in management questioning its effects?"

About that time I was asked to join a new interdisciplinary Human Resource Management program at the university, which helped me to get in touch with the new thinking emerging in American industry. I found that while American management was split, and still is, advanced thinkers in industry and labor were beginning to hold that the scientific efficiency rationale was itself the *source* of productivity problems. These industry leaders, in effect, were saying to school people: "No, not that way! We're going the other way—thataway."

So I began my detour into American industry. It took me into fascinating places: from a pioneering auto mirror plant in Bolivar, Tennessee; to Work Research Institutes in Oslo, Stavenger, and Trondheim, Norway; to Sweden; to auto plants in Tarrytown, New York, and Flint and Detroit, Michigan; and to Anheuser Busch think tanks in St. Louis.

In *Productive Work in Industry and Schools* (1983), I described what I found. The alternative to scientific management was an emerging democratic sociotechnical theory of work that claimed that the dominant management tradition is guilty of the technical fix error; that is, the assumption that all system problems will yield to technical-type solutions. The new theorists were arguing that the reality of human work system is that it is "socio" as well as "technical." "Socio" refers to beings. The mainline efficiency model is out of touch with this dimension of reality, or worse yet violates it.

All of this gave me insight into what was crazy-making. To be out of touch with reality is crazy. Rational efficiency models are out of touch with the uniquely human "socio" dimension of human work—the *homo poeta* dimension.

A vice-president of General Motors in charge of new plant design helped me get the point when he said:

> GM used to boast that the production line had been broken down into segments so small that any task could be taught in fifteen minutes or less; any idiot could do it. If workmanship and morale were poor, the answer was to step up supervision and control. GM is now convinced, that a model based on increased control by supervisors, of a bored reluctant work force which produces shabby products is not viable for survival. (Duffy, 1980)

The Oxford dictionary gave me further insight. "Crazy" comes from the old Norwegian word *krasa* which means crushed or fragmented—not together. It showed up in fragmenting human work so that idiots could do it. It showed up in transforming school learning into information bits that would yield good test scores and ruin the enthusiasm and morale of teachers and students.

Where are we in industry and education by the end of the 1980s? Management and labor are still split, but as we all know industry has made moves toward participative work designs which assume that both the "socio" and the "technical" have to be taken with equal seriousness.

What about American schools? It is hazardous, of course, to make generalizations about the sprawling American school phenomenon, where happily many things different from what I am describing are also going on. But a safe guess is that for a large number of educational planners, the search for technical fix solutions is strongly under way.

To amplify the argument I want to turn to two very different types of materials: (1) some empirical data collected by a group of Massachusetts teachers and (2) some insights from the late French social theorist Michel Foucault.

The School as a Workplace

The material from the 1986 research study by the Boston Women's Teachers Group, *The Effect of Teaching on Teachers* (Freedman, Jackson, & Boles) provides a good starting point to look at the school as a workplace. The study was based on in-depth, 15-hour interviews of 25 women elementary school teachers over a two-year period. About half of them had taught for 15 years, the other half less. They were selected to match substantially the national teacher population in terms of socioeconomic and racial background, marital status, educational attainments, and father's occupation within the limitations of the small sample. They had taught in impoverished urban schools as well as in affluent systems.

Lengthy analyses of the data over many months led the teacher researchers to conclude that teachers' feelings with regard to burnout, isolation, job satisfaction, and sense of efficacy were rooted in the *working relations and institutional structures* of the schools. In their words, "Teacher stress is an institutionally derived problem, not a result of individual personality failures, as teachers have been led to believe" (Freedman, 1984, p. 25).

I can only sketch a profile of what they found. Since the study illustrates what I have called "crazy-making" and "violation of people," I shall make a rough sort according to these categories. They are not unrelated.

First, "crazy-making," referring to that which is crushed or fragmented or out of touch with reality. For the following passages from Freedman, Jackson, and Boles (1986), I will indicate whether each statement is a "commentary" by the researchers or a quotation from a teacher:

> *Researcher Commentary:* Teachers work in an institution which holds, in its rhetoric, that questioning and debating, risk and error develop one's thinking ability. But learning situations are structured to lead to one right answer, and both teachers and students are evaluated in ways that emphasize only quantifiable results.
>
> *Teacher:* The worst thing is that you get this printout and you're expected to find the profile of each individual child and then find material on those specific skills that they have to master . . . and then they take a multiple choice test where they have to choose a, b, or c. Well, the kids glance at the choices and figure out that one of those endings make a pretty good answer. They never read the whole sentence. They're used to a world of filling blanks without it meaning anything. I mean it's meaningless work.
>
> *Teacher:* This year my principal's evaluation said this: "Five kids looked up from their work and looked out of the window within a five-minute period. Now if you multiply five kids and five minutes in a period and you place it in an hour you get the percentage who are not doing their work and not involved." (pp. 11–20)

Massachusetts is not alone in imposing this style. Deborah Meier (1987), Director of the Central Park East High School in New York City and a critic of current educational reform, reports how evaluators prescribed hundreds of specific written goals. Example: "given teacher supervision, praise and positive reinforcement, the student will attend to difficult assignments for five minutes, three times out of four as recorded by teacher" (Meier, 1987, p. 546). Now, I ask, who's crazy?

And now some statements that point to "violation of persons" as *homo poeta.*

Researcher Commentary: Teachers were continually perplexed by the admonition to be *professional* while the area in which their expertise could be applied became narrower and narrower.

Teacher: The thing that aggravates me is that we as educators are not treated as adults. . . . They check up on you like you're children. . . . They walk into your room and you have to be within minutes of where your program card says.

Teacher: Every Tuesday is a half day for faculty meetings. . . . People sit there deadpan because they don't want to commit themselves, you know, get themselves into any kind of hot water. Most of the stuff comes down from the central office that is really separate from the actual core of teaching.

Teacher: One of the things that has bothered me about the hurried pace of teaching today is that a lot of the creativeness is taken away from you—the feeling that I'm going to think of a new, fresh way to do it. The curriculum gets reduced to: "Here is a book and teach it. You should be on page 200 by such and such a date." It has nothing to do with your kids and nothing to do with whatever ideas you might want to bring in.

Teacher: I think the merit evaluation is even worse than seniority. Oh, my God. In this particular school it has destroyed any type of relations. I mean you look at the person next door to you and you say, "Gee, I wonder how many points she has." So instead of encouraging teachers to be more open about what they're doing, there isn't one bit of sharing. When you're in competition for your job, you're pitting one person against another. I think in this business you can't do that. Because we tell the kids that everybody is unique.

Teacher: I started seeing myself not taking the risks I used to. I used to do all kinds of interesting things with my students—build things all over the classroom. But every once in a while someone would notice that classroom wasn't as neat as it should be . . . and since anything can be pointed to, you start to retrench. You feel a lack of growth and you look around. And I decided to leave. (Freedman, Jackson & Boles, 1986, pp. 11–20)

This teacher left. For those who stay there are heavy pressures to yield to the technocratic rationale.

Researcher Commentary: The teacher, under attack for failing to help children reach arbitrary grade level goals, accedes to the greater wisdom of the commercial test makers and the research academics. Once started on the road to quantification, the method becomes addictive. . . .

The new *objective* type *teacher* evaluations that have been introduced are examples of such quantitative methods. They take great pains to code and enumerate the type, number and direction of the interactions of the teacher with her pupils within the classroom.

The more quantitative measures and national exams that are used to evaluate the teacher, the more she will feel the need to use such quantitative methods to judge her students and other teachers. She is now the in-class representative of the national norms and country-wide bell curves. Once she has entered the child's progress in her book, both she and her pupils are assumed to be easily understood and evaluated. (Freedman, Jackson & Boles, 1986, pp. 11–20)

The same factors work on students. There is John Goodlad's (1984) famous observation that not even 1 percent of the instructional time in classes was devoted to discussion that "required some kind of open response involving reasoning or perhaps an opinion from students . . . the extraordinary degree of student passivity stands out" (pp. 239–240).

An example was furnished to me by Rita Roth from her observation journal:

Teacher: Why aren't you doing your work, Alphonse?
Alphonse: I though we were going to read today.
Teacher: That's what we did—you just had reading group.
Alphonse: But I thought we would read today.
Teacher: We just did, Alphonse. We looked for 's' sounds in your book, did two 's' sheets in your workbook and here is the worksheet you should be doing right now to find some more 's' words.
Alphonse: But I thought we would read today, you know *READ read*.
(Wirth, 1983, p. 133)

Deborah Meier's (1987) comment on the parallel experience of New York City teachers once more is relevant: "Predictable multiple-choice questions replace *conversation* about books. Reading scores went up, literacy collapsed. . . . Improved test scores, alas, are best achieved by ignoring real reading activity" (p. 544).

We need to note that something profoundly important is contained

in these statements of Alphonse and Deborah Meier. Hans-Georg Gadamer in *Reason in an Age of Science* (1981) reminded us that the right to
converse—to dialogue with texts and each other in reaching for understanding about the world and ourselves is *the* unique, distinctive characteristic of being human. It is what Alphonse was asking for in his request
to *"READ read."* To diminish the right to that kind of learning by
trivializing instruction is, I believe, a human rights violation of both
students and teachers.

I have talked with many teachers who have expressed a feeling of
helplessness about being able to articulate what is wrong with the model
being forced on them. It seems so reasonable. An applicant to a medieval
shoemakers' guild would be told: "You say you are a shoemaker—make a
shoe." In a twentieth century culture obsessed with bottom-line results, it
is assumed that reading teachers can be made accountable by simply
telling them to "show us your reading scores results." What can possibly
be wrong with that?

The issue, as Denis Goulet suggests in *The Uncertain Promise:
Value Conflicts in Technology Transfer* (1977), is not whether to be for or
against efficiency, but what kind of efficiency for human institutions.
Western engineering–type efficiency which worked wonders in closed
mechanical systems by simple measures of inputs to outputs can be
dangerous to well-being in nonmechanical human systems. What we
now need, says Goulet, is to explore ways of becoming integrally efficient:
how to produce efficiently, while optimizing social and human values.
Integral efficiency would tell us that if we are teaching so that scores are
going up and real reading is going down, we ought to stop it because it is
inefficient.

Toward Rational Efficiency

Now I want to refer briefly to what I learned from the French social
theorist Michel Foucault, who in *Discipline and Punish* (1979) helped
me to see why the rational efficiency assumptions seem so unassailable.
The great truth we must constantly hold before ourselves, said Foucault,
is the realization that the reason or rationality of the Enlightenment that
gave us the liberties also invented the disciplines.

Foucault showed that, from the seventeenth and eighteenth century
onward, there was a virtual takeoff in the increase of calculated power to

control people in state apparatuses like the army, prisons, tax administration, and so on.

A vivid example is the transformation of the rowdy soldiers of the late Middle Ages into the eighteenth-century redcoat-type soldiers who could be constructed into automatons by minute attention to detail in their training. As modern soldiers, they will be taught to remain motionless, never to look at the ground and to move on command with bold, uniform steps, later to become the goose step. "'Very good,' Grand Duke Mikhail remarked to a regiment, after having kept it for an hour presenting arms, 'Only they breathe'" (Foucault, 1979, p. 188).

We find the new controls also, says Foucault, in the fashioning of the late seventeenth century Christian Brothers Schools for the poor. Jean Baptiste de la Salle, the founder, said, "'How grave and dangerous is the task of teachers in the Christian Schools. . . . We must be concerned above all with the little things, the minute things in the lives of our students and their teachers. The little things lead to great results.'" Foucault adds, "The meticulousness of the regulations, the fussiness of inspections, the supervision of the smallest fragments of life and of the body will soon provide, in the context of the school, the barracks, the hospital or the work place a technical rationality for the mystical calculus of the infinitesimal" (Foucault, 1979, p. 140).

Foucault noted that Jeremy Bentham's panopticon proposals for prisons, factories, or schools in the early 1800s embodied the technically thought out disciplines required in the modern era. Panopticon comes from the Greek words *pan*, everything, and *opticon*, a place of sight. Thus, a place of sight to see everything. The general idea included a basic circular building, with cells for individual subjects around the inside of the circumference. In the center, facing the cells, is an Inspector's Tower with windows looking down on the cells. The observatory room at the top was constructed with a line of sight so that the Inspector could see all, while being invisible to the inmates below. Thus, the basic principle was that "the persons to be inspected should always feel themselves as if under inspection" (Bentham, 1962, p. 44). The person to be supervised must never know if at any moment he is actually being observed; at the same time he must constantly feel that he might be. "He is seen, but he does not see, he is the object of information, never a subject of communication" (Foucault, 1979, p. 200). The guiding concept, says Foucault, is the ideal of the Perfect Gaze: the Gaze that can see everything constantly. It employs three instrumentalities: (1) hierarchical surveillance—all of those intrusive Gazes from the central office, (2) normalizing judgment aimed at securing conformity, and (3) the examination. The gist of his argument is in his comments on the examination by which individuals may be measured, classified, and judged. In the examination, says Foucault, we can find a whole domain of knowledge and type of power:

1. Through techniques of the examination individuals are made *visible*—subject to "the gaze," and made into objects for measurement
2. By *documentation* individuals and groups are encoded in written reports and files—or they are organized into registers, classifications, and cumulative systems
3. By collecting documentary records on each individual, each is *individualized as a case* and becomes an object of knowledge and power

The examination is now pervasive in modern institutions and is notably present, said Foucault (1979), in the growth of larger, more systematized modern schools. The school has become, in fact, a sort of apparatus of uninterrupted examination, increasingly an arena for "a perpetual comparison of each and all that make it possible both to measure and judge" (p. 186). My New York state informants tell me that a regent's student will take 29 state-required examinations in 12 years. Only two years in the elementary school will be free of state-required examinations. The extension of the panopticon rationale throughout the society coincided, Foucault says, with the rise of the human sciences. In line with the ideal of the Gaze, quantitative test scores and record keeping created the conditions for a technical matrix which changed discourse about policy issues into the neutral language of science. In schools, for example, talk about problems is limited to the lexicon of technocratic ideology. Thus teachers are taught to think of classrooms as management systems, and to talk about their teaching in terms of performance objectives, system components, sequencing of instruction, and so on. When the terminology of technical experts takes over, teachers may feel mute in the face of it: "Who are we to question scientific expertise?" If the system breaks down and doesn't work, the only answer of panopticon technicians is to do more of the same.

The Resistance to Mindlessness

But retreat into acquiescence is not the only response. Resistance does break out: at work—in strikes, sabotage, and drug abuse; among teachers—as witnessed by the Massachusetts Women's Research Study; in a marvelous gadfly newspaper, *Rethinking Schools*; by Milwaukee teachers who are in rebellion against damaging, bureaucratic intrusions that harm their work; in Harold Berlak's newsletter *Democratic Schools*, providing a communication network for English, Canadian, and American teachers who resist the megamachine; and in George Woods' lively Institute for Democratic Education at Ohio University. Foucault would not be surprised. He predicts resistance because, he says, panopticon manipulation and domination violate our human needs for autonomy and freedom.

In industry there is a growing awareness that panopticon violation of people is impractical as well as immoral. There is, for example, the Office of Technology Assessment's (OTA) massive report, *Technology and the American Economic Transition* (U.S. Congress, 1988). The OTA says that we face a conjunction of two epochal events: (1) the acceleration of the electronic information revolution and (2) the fact that we now have to compete for economic survival in the one world market. The challenge is how to confront turbulent change—change which is rapid and unpredictable. Our greatest need and asset is for a well-educated, committed work force fully engaged in flexible interactions with high-tech equipment.

Since I began ten years ago, there has been a rapid expansion of awareness by some major corporations of the need to tap the brains of people at work—to move toward a democratic sociotechnical work design. There is, for example, the plan for the production of Saturn, G.M.'s "car of the future." The goal is to lay the groundwork for combining robotics with a new style of work relationships. The agreements worked out with the U.A.W. change the status of assembly-line workers from hourly laborers to salaried employees. Union workers in small production work units will be involved in decision-making processes that formerly were the prerogatives of management. They will perform their own quality control with electronic equipment (*New York Times*, 1985).

If you compare work places like this with accountability routinization in the schools, which drives creative teachers to despair, it doesn't take a genius to see who is out of step. A growing number of major leaders in industry and labor are becoming aware of the discrepancy. The 1985 statement *Investing in our Children* by the Committee for Economic Development (CED)—a statement I have argued with (Wirth, 1987)—is a case in point. CED members include executive officers from major American corporations that are being transformed by the rush of computer technology. They are forthright in declaring that a work force educated by "old school basics" will not be equipped for meeting challenges of turbulent change.

The report presents the case of Proctor and Gamble as a prototype. The strong trend now is for employees to perform a broad range of tasks, including operating and maintaining equipment; performing their own quality controls; and participating in goal setting, problem solving, and budgeting.

With this view of work in America, the report calls for "nothing less than a revolution in the role of the teacher and the management of schools" (CED, 1985, p. 60). High-tech firms, they say, are not served well by centralized rigid bureaucracies hostile to needed creativity. They stifle creativity because their goal is to keep control in the hands of centralized authority. The essential obligation of organizations in the new era is "to nurture creativity." School policy makers must learn the lesson of industry: Give employees a stake in the system by decentralizing decision making to the lowest possible level.

The interaction of teachers, students, and administrators in individual schools becomes the key arena for action. The report assumes that able people will not choose teaching, nor choose to remain in it, if they are stifled by bureaucratic regimentation, or shackled with "teacher-proof" materials. Teachers as creative actors will respond only if they are given a chance to exercise judgment and to reshape their own working environment. The authors of the report ask for a view of teachers as carriers of liberal culture with a responsibility to teach higher order learning—to think analytically, to cooperate as well as to compete, to assume responsibility, and to learn to learn.

They shy away from "merit plans" which often undermine collegial relations. Teachers working in a largely competitive environment, they say, will be less inclined to support the feeling of community that is essential for effective schools (CED, 1985).

Change in the corporate work world is widespread enough to lead to such recommendations. It would be a gross oversimplification, however, to assume that the issue about work in corporate life itself has been settled in this happy fashion.

Since many corporations continue the narrow scientific management traditions, the issue of whether we will choose to become architects rather than bees is very much in doubt. The Office of Technology Assessments says that a major challenge for both corporations and schools will be how they choose to make use of swiftly evolving computer technology.

Technology and the American Economic Transition (U.S. Congress, 1988) says that micro-electronic robotics and telecommunication technology, combined with democratic work styles, can provide an opportunity to revitalize the competitiveness of American industry. A work force with high morale linked to imaginatively designed technology can move us toward an economy of high-tech, high-skilled, high-wage industries. But don't bet the family savings on it. Our habits and the control needs of those in charge push us toward rational, bureaucratic management. With this bias, computer electronics can become a force to intensify hierarchical controls and surveillance.

A Ted Koppel program, "Surveillance on the Job" (ABC News, 1987), illustrated the new electronic monitoring of performance of airline representatives. One of the agents reported how she worked under a demerit system monitored by a computer. If she spends an average of more than 109 seconds talking to a customer about reservations or fares she gets one demerit. If she spends more than 11 seconds in between customers she gets two demerits. After 12 seconds a light flashes on the supervisor's board who comes in then with, "Anything wrong? May I help you?" Six demerits earns a warning; 36, dismissal. Another agent reported the monitoring of her time between calls. When she was heard saying a swear word to herself, it was evaluated as "evidence of a bad attitude."

Six million clerical workers are now being watched by the unblinking gaze. Another four million technical and managerial people are about to be electronically evaluated in the next few years. We come closer to what Gadamer (1986) saw as the ultimate nightmare—when science expands into a total technocracy.

We may take the road of deskilling and degrading work. The Office of Technology Assessment says that if we do, we ought to know its consequences. It not only downgrades American work and lowers our standard of living, but often includes sending hardware and software overseas to exploit the cheap labor and vulnerability of third-world women. It increases the gap between technical-managerial elites and a growing body of de-skilled workers, often nonwhite (U.S. Congress, 1988). As it exacerbates dualist divisions in the society and treats millions with disrespect, it violates the values of the democratic tradition.

But the OTA report says a comparable issue will appear in the near future in education. The evidence of serious inadequacies in the technical skills of basic literacy and numeracy of American students is clear. OTA recommends that we undertake a major research effort immediately to explore how the new potential of computer-enhanced instruction might help us with the stubborn problems of skill training and conceptual learning. It envisions two major policy choices. The first, which it warns against, is to aim for a uniform, national curriculum and examination system to which teachers everywhere will be made accountable. One of the major computer companies is now moving to what could become statewide or even nationwide mainframes through which uniform instructional materials could be piped. Electronic monitoring of scores could "keep book" on teachers and schools everywhere.

The other approach which OTA recommends is illustrated in an experiment by Apple Computer. In anticipating the near-universal availability of computers ten years from now, Apple has created "computer-saturated" classrooms in seven different school communities throughout the United States, including a black urban school in Memphis, a rural school in Minnesota, and a Cupertino, California school in Silicon Valley itself. Students and teachers are provided with individual Macintosh computers at home as well as at school. Apple operates on the assumptions that the culture of each school is different and that teachers in each setting should be free to experiment with usages to help meet their own broader educational goals. In those seven different schools, seven different strategies and designs are emerging. I could feel excitement and commitment by staff and students in the setting at West High School in Columbus, Ohio, which I visited. Here we see our capacity to create decentralized learning communities in which teachers can take initiatives in designing use of computer technology to meet their goals. Students, administrators, and parents join with teachers in the explorations. Each new use opens other possibilities. It feels freeing instead of controlling. In terms of our educational history, we could say that we need *both* the Thorndike skill-training and the Deweyan meaning-seeking parts of our tradition. We need the will to make the powerful tool of computer-assisted instruction subordinate to the Deweyan meaning-seeking needs of both teachers and students.

Conclusions

A title like "The Violation of People at Work in Schools" conveys an impression of anger. I am angry about teachers feeling hurt, worn down, and resentful, yet feeling unable to articulate what is wrong. One of our tasks as professors of education is to help with the articulation.

For me, those women teachers of Massachusetts conveyed a key insight. Their message was: It is not teachers' psyches that need massaging. The source of troubles is in the structure of the schools and its effects on teachers' working relations with each other, with administrators, with students, and with learning (Freedman, Jackson & Boles, 1986). Let us accept the working proposition that Deborah Meier (1987) articulated: "serious rooted change cannot happen unless the knowledge of those who do the job is tapped" (p. 549). That means putting teachers in charge by structural change that supports school-based initiative, inquiry, and decision making—changes that open time and space so that teachers are encouraged to converse and plan together.

I am also suggesting that we can get to the deeper issues about that structural problem and begin to use blunt language about what is going on. Michael Harrington (1983) in *The Politics at God's Funeral* helps. The crisis of our time, he says, is a crisis of the human spirit, and we have to give up the illusion that we can talk adequately about the real problem of our lives and our work by using only the bland value-free language of technocratic reform.

Foucault (1979) and Becker (1968) helped me see that the structure those caring teachers were pointing to as the source of their burnout was a manifestation of a much broader structural problem—the lifeless bureaucratic "Perfect Gaze": control systems that are killing our spirits in both late corporate capitalism and East Bloc communism.

Rationalized functionalism, with hierarchical surveillance, impoverishes the human spirit by denying people access to their dignity and personal enthusiasms. It is crazy-making.

Ernest Becker (1968) says that when these structures threaten the

core of who we are as *homo poeta*, we should call them what they are—
structures of evil.

The situation calls for resistance, and school people need allies to
resist. I was happy to find a greenshoot challenge to sterile scientific
management in the work world. The movement toward democratic
sociotechnical work explores how democratic values can be combined
with technological innovation—the same task that needs exploration in
the schools. Our reach must be for the ideal stated by Kant: We must try
to achieve maximum individuality with maximum community. Sterile
control models allow access to neither individuality nor community. We
are cheated of the strengths we need to meet the awesome challenges of
the coming twenty-first century.

Having taken such a lofty conceptual flight, I want to close this
chapter by returning to the reality of contemporary school life. The
choice between architect and bee is not fictional fantasy. It is being
played out in at least two major American school systems.

In my home town of St. Louis, a complex system of teacher evaluation has been introduced, based, in part, on student scores on standardized tests. The predictable charges of cheating occur with lurid
press headlines. A school board member responds by setting up his own
system of surveillance: a telephone hotline that encourages students,
teachers, or staff members to report to him anonymously suspicions of
teacher cheating. The plummeting of trust, morale, and care are "exter-
nalities," not counted in the evaluation equations. By equating examination scores with significant learning, this newest panopticon creates
a facade of "educational excellence" which cheats kids who can least
afford it.

Meanwhile, in Detroit, a very different and risky gamble is being
tried with major support from Detroit unions, corporations, and foundations. An effort is being launched to introduce into the schools the
philosophy and techniques of democratic sociotechnical work theory
from the level of classroom practice, through teacher and administrator
relationships, all the way up to the School Board/Teacher's Union Core
Committee. The project is directed by Neal Herrick, who has had a long
history of pioneering such efforts through the United Auto Workers and
the Union of Public Employees. I deliberately use the term "risky gamble" because we need to recognize how difficult it may be to learn new
habits after years of being bent by panopticon controls. Only the reality
of desperation has led to this effort to break out.

In these examples we can see the schizophrenia within reform: simultaneous moves toward uniform centralized control, and moves toward school-based autonomy with teacher participation and initiative. In both work and schools we confront the choice—architect or bee—the choice of who we want to be as a people for entering that third millennium.

References

ABC News. (1987, June 23). Surveillance on the job. [Transcript].

Adamany, D. (1975). Introduction. In E. E. Schattschneider, *The semisovereign people: A realist's view of democracy in America.* (Rev. ed.). Hinsdale, IL: Dryden Press.

American Association of School Administrators. (1980, January). Study attempts to explain superintendent "failure." *The School Administrator, 37* (1), 4–5.

American Freedom Library. (1971). Graphic story of American presidents (Vol. 1). Chicago: Encyclopedia Britannica Educational Corporation.

Apple Computer, Inc. *Apple classroom of tomorrow.* (Available from Apple Computer, Inc., Cupertino, CA 95014)

Atkin, J. M. (1973). Practice oriented inquiry: A third approach to research in education. *Educational Researcher, 2,* 3–4.

Ayres, L. (1909). *Laggards in our schools.* New York: Charities Publication Committee.

Bailyn, B. (1960). *Education in the forming of American society: Needs and opportunities for study.* New York: W. W. Norton.

Bates, R. (1986, March). *Theories of organizations: Theory of administration.* Paper presented at Division A of the American Educational Research Association, Chicago.

Beard, C. A. (1941). *An economic interpretation of the constitution of the United States.* New York: Macmillan.

Becker, C. L. (1935). *Everyman his own historian.* New York: Appleton-Century-Crofts.

Becker, E. (1968). *The structure of evil: An essay on the unification of science of man.* New York: The Free Press.

Becker, H., Geer, B., Hughes, E., & Strauss, A. (1961). *Boys in white.* Chicago: University of Chicago Press.

Bentham, J. (1962). *The works of Jeremy Bentham* (Vol. 4). New York: Russell and Russell.

Bernstein, R. (1978). *The restructuring of social and political theory.* Philadelphia: University of Pennsylvania Press.

Blumberg, A. (1985). *The school superintendent: Living with conflict*. New York: Teachers College Press.

Bobbitt, J. F. (1913). The supervision of city schools: Some general principles of management applied to the problems of city-school systems. In *National Society for the Study of Education Yearbook, Part 1* (pp. 7–96). Chicago: University of Chicago Press.

Bowen, C. D. (1959). *Adventures of a biographer*. Boston: Little, Brown.

Bowen, C. D. (1969). *Biography: The craft and the calling*. Boston: Little, Brown.

Bowen, C. D. (1970). *Family portrait*. Boston: Little, Brown.

Bredo, E., & Feinberg, W. (Eds.). (1982). *Knowledge and values in social and educational research*. Philadelphia: Temple University Press.

Bridges, E. M. (1982, Summer). Research on the school administrator: The state of the art, 1967–1980. *Educational Administration Quarterly, 18*, 12–33.

Brogan, D. W. (1949). Preface. In B. de Jouvenel (Ed.) & J. F. Huntington (Trans.), *Power: The natural history of its growth*. New York: Viking Press.

Burlingame, M. (1977). *An exploratory study of turnover and career mobility of public school district superintendents in the state of Illinois from 1960–1976*. Springfield, IL: Illinois Office of Education.

Burnham, W. D. (1970). *Critical elections and the mainsprings of American politics*. New York: W. W. Norton.

Burrup, P. E., & Bremley, V., Jr. (1986). *Financing education in a climate of change*. New York: Allyn & Bacon.

Button, H. W., & Provenzo, E. F., Jr. (1983). *History of education and culture in America*. Englewood Cliffs, NJ: Prentice-Hall.

Callahan, R. E. (1956). *An introduction to education in American society*. New York: Alfred A. Knopf.

Callahan, R. E. (1961). Leonard Ayres and the Educational Balance Sheet. *History of Educational Quarterly, 1*(1), 5–15.

Callahan, R. E. (1962). *Education and the cult of efficiency: A study of the social forces that have shaped the administration of the public schools*. Chicago: University of Chicago Press.

Callahan, R. E. (1964). *The changing conceptions of the superintendency in public education 1865–1964*. Cambridge, MA: The New England School Development Council.

Callahan, R. E. (1967). *The superintendent of schools: An historical analysis* (Final Report of Project S-212). Cooperative Research Branch, U.S.O.E., Department of Health, Education and Welfare.

Callahan, R. E. (1971). George S. Counts: Educational statesman. In R. J. Havinghurst (Ed.), *Leaders in American education* (pp. 177–87). Chicago: University of Chicago Press.

Callahan, R. E. (1975). The American board of education. In P. J. Cistone (Ed.), *Understanding school boards*. Lexington, MA: Lexington Books.

Callahan, R. E., & Button, H. W. (1964). Historical change of the role of the man in the organization: 1865–1950. In *National Society for the Study of Education Yearbook: 1964* (Section I, pp. 73–92). Chicago: University of Chicago Press.

Campbell, D. T. (1979). A tribal model of the social system vehicle carrying scientific knowledge. *Knowledge: Creation, Diffusion, Utilization, 1*, 181–202.

Candoli, I. C. Hack, W. G., Ray, J. R., & Stollar, D. H. (1986). *School business administration: A planning approach* (3rd ed.). New York: Allyn & Bacon.

Carlson, R. O. (1962). *Executive succession and organizational change.* Chicago: Interstate Printers and Publishers.

Carlson, R. O. (1972). *School superintendents: Careers and performance.* Columbus, OH: Charles E. Merrill Publishing Co.

Carney, M. (1912). *Community life and the country school.* Chicago: Row and Peterson.

Cartwright, N. H. (1963, March). Education and the cult of efficiency: A study of the social forces that have shaped the administration of the public schools. *The Mississippi Valley Historical Review, 49*, 722–733.

Castaldi, B. (1986). *Educational facilities: Planning, modernization, and management* (3rd ed.). New York: Allyn & Bacon.

Caswell, H. (1929). *City school surveys: An interpretation and appraisal* (Teachers College Contributions to Education No. 358). New York: Teachers College, Bureau of Publications.

Characteristics of public school superintendents. (1986). *ERS Spectrum, 4*, 28–31.

Charters, W. W., Jr. (1963). The social background of teaching. In N. L. Gage (Ed.), *Handbook for research in teaching* (pp. 715–813). Chicago: Rand McNally.

Chase, W. M. (1981). *Superintendent turnover: Antecedent conditions and subsequent organizational changes.* Unpublished doctoral dissertation, University of California, Santa Barbara.

Cochran, T. C. (1972). *Business in American life: A history.* New York: McGraw-Hill.

Collingwood, R. G. (1939). *Autobiography.* London: Oxford University Press.

Committee for Economic Development. (1985). *Investing in our children* [pamphlet]. Washington, DC: Author.

Conant, J. B. (1959). *The American high school today: A first report to interested citizens.* New York: McGraw-Hill.

Cooley, M. (1981). *Architect or bee?* Boston: South End Press.

Counts, G. (1927). *The social composition of boards of education.* Chicago: University of Chicago Press.

Counts, G. (1932). *Dare the school build a new social order?* New York: John Day.

Cremin, L. (1961). *The transformation of the school: Progressivism in American education, 1876–1957.* New York: Alfred A. Knopf.

Cremin, L. (1965). *The genius of American education.* Pittsburgh: University of Pittsburgh.

Cremin, L. (1967, Fall). The shaping of Teachers College. *Perspectives on Education,* p. 5.

Cronbach, L. (1975). Beyond the two disciplines of scientific psychology. *American Psychologist, 30,* 116–127.

Criswell, L. W., & Mitchell, D. E. (1980). Episodic instability in school district elections. *Urban Education, 15,* 189–213.

Cuban, L. (1974, December). Urban superintendents: Vulnerable experts. *Phi Delta Kappan,* pp. 279–285.

Cuban, L. (1976). *Urban school chiefs under fire.* Chicago: University of Chicago Press.

Cuban, L. (1979). Shrinking enrollment and consolidation: Political and organizational impacts in Arlington, Virginia 1973–1978. *Education and Urban Society, 11*(3), 367–395.

Cubberley, E. P. (1919). *Public education in the United States: A study and interpretation of American educational history.* Boston: Houghton-Mifflin.

Cubberley, E. P. (1916). *Public school administration.* Boston: Houghton-Mifflin.

Cubberley, E. P. (1922). *Public school administration.* (2nd ed.). Boston: Houghton-Mifflin.

Cubberley, E. P. (1929). *Public school administration.* (3rd ed.). Boston: Houghton-Mifflin.

Curti, M. (1935). *Social ideas of American educators.* New York: Charles Scribner.

Dahlke, H. O. (1958). *Values in culture and classroom.* New York: Harper and Brothers.

Danis, R. (1981). *Policy changes in local governance.* Unpublished doctoral dissertation, University of California, Santa Barbara.

Diesing, P. (1971). *Patterns of discovery in the social sciences.* Chicago: Aldine-Atherton.

DiMaggio, P., & Powell, W. (1982). The iron cage revisited: Institutional isomorphism and collective rationality in organizational fields. *American Sociological Review, 48,* 147–160.

Duffy, W. (1980, March). Director of Research in Work Innovation at General Motors. Unpublished presentation.

Eulau, H. (1972). Political science and education: The long view and the short. In M. W. Kirst (Ed.), *State, school, and politics.* Lexington, MA: D. C. Heath.

Fay, B. (1975). *Social theory and political practice.* London: George Allen and Unwin.

Festinger, L., Riecken, H., & Schachter, S. (1964). *When prophecy fails.* New York: Harper Torchbook. (Original work published 1956).

Festinger, L., Schachter, S., & Back, K., with Bauer, C., & Kennedy, R. W. (1950). *Social pressures in informal groups.* New York: Harper.

Fischer, D. H. (1970). *Historians' fallacies: Toward a logic of historical thought.* New York: Harper & Row.

Foucault, M. (1979). *Discipline and punish: The birth of the prison.* New York: Vintage Books.

Freedman, S. (1984, April 29). Classes help teachers understand burnout. *Boston Herald,* p. 25.

Freedman, S., Jackson, J., & Boles, K. (1986). *The effect of teaching on teachers.* Bismarck, ND: Center for Teaching and Learning, University of North Dakota.

Gadamer, H. G. (1981). *Reason in an age of science.* Cambridge, MA: Massachusetts Institute of Technology Press.

Gadamer, H. G. (1986). *Truth and method.* New York: Crossroad.

Geertz, C. (1973). *The interpretation of cultures.* New York: Basic Books.

Geertz, C. (1983). *Local knowledge.* New York: Basic Books.

Goodlad, J. (1984). *A place called school.* New York: McGraw-Hill.

Gore, S. J. (1962). *The economy of time movement in elementary education.* Unpublished doctoral dissertation, Washington University, St. Louis, MO.

Gough, D., & Jemison, S. (Eds.). (1986, Fall). Characteristics of public school superintendents. *ERS Spectrum, 4*(4), 28–31.

Goulet, D. (1977). *The uncertain promise.* New York: IDOC/North America.

Griffiths, D. E. (1964). The nature and meaning of change theory. In D. E. Griffiths (Ed.), *Behavioral science and educational administration: Sixty-third yearbook of the NSSE, Part II.* Chicago: University of Chicago Press.

Griffiths, D. E. (1966). *The school superintendent.* New York: Center for Applied Research in Education.

Grodzins, M. (1966). *The American system: A new view of government in the United States.* Chicago: Rand McNally.

Gross, N., Mason, W. S., & McEachern, A. W. (1958). *Explorations in role analysis: Studies of the school superintendency role.* New York: Wiley.

Gunnell, J. G. (1975). *Philosophy, science, and political inquiry.* Morristown, NJ: General Learning Press.

Hamilton, D. (1981). Generalization in the educational sciences: problems and purposes. In T. Popkewitz & R. Tabachnick (Eds.), *The study of schooling: Field based methodologies in educational research.* New York: Praeger.

Harrington, M. (1983). *Politics at God's funeral.* New York: Holt, Rinehart and Winston.

Hartz, L. (1955). *The liberal tradition in America.* New York: Harcourt, Brace and World.

Hays, S. P. (1964, October). The politics of reform in municipal government in the progressive era. *Pacific Northwest Quarterly,* 157–169.

Hays, S. P. (1965, Spring). Social analysis of American political history, 1880–1920. *Political Science Quarterly, 80,* 373–394.

Henderson, H. (1977). A new economics. In D. Vermilye (Ed.), *Relating work and education* (pp. 227-235). San Francisco: Jossey-Bass, Current Issues in Higher Education.

Hexter, J. H. (1971). *The history primer.* New York: Basic Books.

Hofstadter, R. (1959). *Social Darwinism in American thought.* New York: Braziller.

Hogan, D. J. (1985). *Class and reform: School and society in Chicago, 1880–1930.* Philadelphia: University of Pennsylvania Press.

Holusha, J. (1985, August 4). Saturn Division finds a home in the heartland. *New York Times,* p. E4.

Iannaccone, L. (1966). The future of state politics of education. In F. W. Lutz & J. J. Assarelli (Eds.), *Struggle for power in education* (pp. 49–66). New York: Center for Applied Research in Education.

Iannaccone, L. (1967). *Politics in education.* New York: Center for Applied Research in Education.

Iannaccone, L. (1977). Three views of change in educational politics. In J. D. Scribner (Ed.), *The politics of education.* Chicago: University of Chicago Press.

Iannaccone, L. (1981). The Reagan presidency. *Journal of Learning Disabilities, 14,* 55–59.

Iannaccone, L. (1987). From equity to excellence: Political context and dynamics. In W. L. Boyd & C. T. Kerchner (Eds.), *The politics of excellence and choice in education.* New York: Falmer Press.

Iannaccone, L., & Cistone, P. J. (1974). *The politics of education.* Eugene, OR: ERIC Clearinghouse on Educational Management.

Iannaccone, L., & Lutz, F. W. (1967). The changing politics of education. *American Association of University Women Journal, 60* (May 1967), 160–162.

Iannaccone, L., & Lutz, F. W. (1970). *Politics, power and policy: The governing of local school districts.* Columbus, OH: C. E. Merrill.

Iannaccone, L., & Wiles, D. K. (1971). The changing politics of urban education. *Education and Urban Society, 3,* 255–264.

Jackson, P. (1968). *Life in classrooms.* New York: Henry Holt.

Jackson, P. (1981). The promise of educational psychology. In F. Farley (Ed.), *Psychology and Education: The state of the union.* Berkeley, CA: McCutchan.

Jorgenson, L. P. (1964, Summer). Essay review: The cult of efficiency in school administration. *School Review,* pp. 230–235.

Kammerer, G., Farris, C., Degrave, J., & Clubok, A. (1962). *City managers in politics.* Gainesville, FL: University of Florida Press.

Kammerer, G., Farris, C., Degrave, J., & Clubok, A. (1963). *The urban political community.* Boston: Houghton-Mifflin.

Kanter, R. M. (1977). *Men and women of the corporation*. New York: Basic Books.

Katz, M. B. (1968). *The irony of early school reform: Educational innovation in mid-nineteenth century Massachusetts*. Boston: Beacon Press.

Katz, M. B. (1971). *Class bureaucracy and schools: The illusion of educational change in America*. New York: Praeger.

Kaufman, H. (1955). Emerging conflicts in the doctrine of public administration. *American Political Science Review, 50*, 1057–1073.

Key, V. O., Jr. (1955). A theory of critical elections. *Journal of Politics, 17*, 3–18.

Knezevich, S. J. (Ed.). (1971). *The American school superintendency*. Washington, DC: American Association of School Administrators.

Kuhn, T. S. (1970). *The structure of scientific revolutions* (2nd ed.). Chicago: University of Chicago Press.

Leacock, S. (1946). *The Leacock roundabout*. New York: Dodd, Mead.

Lewis, O. (1961). *The children of Sanchez*. New York: Random House.

Lieberman, M. (1956). *Education as a profession*. Englewood Cliffs, New Jersey: Prentice-Hall.

Lindblom, C. E. (1968). *The policy-making process*. Englewood Cliffs, NJ: Prentice-Hall.

Loomis, C. P. (1960). *Social systems: Essays on their persistence and change*. New York: D. Van Nostrand.

Lortie, D. (1964). The teacher and team teaching: Suggestions for long-range research. In J. Shaplin & H. Olds (Eds.), *Team teaching* (pp. 270–305). New York: Harper & Row.

Lortie, D. (1975). *Schoolteacher*. Chicago: University of Chicago Press.

Lowi, T. J. (1964). *At the pleasure of the mayor*. New York: Free Press.

Lutz, F. W. (1971, April). Educational accountability: A social science critique. *Planning and Changing, 2*(1), 24–30.

Lutz, F. W., & Iannaccone, L. (Eds.). (1978). *Public participation in local school districts*. Lexington, MA: Lexington Books.

Lutz, F. W., & Lutz, S. B. (1985, November). *A Connecticut Yankee in Sam Houston's schools*. Paper presented at the annual meeting of the American Anthropological Association, Washington, D.C.

MacIver, R. (1937). *Society: A textbook of sociology*. New York: Farrar and Rinehart.

MacRae, D., Jr., & Meldrum, J. A. (1960). Critical elections in Illinois: 1888–1958. *The American Political Science Review, 54*(3), 669–683.

March, J., & Simon, H. (1958). *Organizations*. New York: Wiley.

Maxwell, W. (1890). City school systems. *NEA Proceedings: Department of Superintendence*, pp. 447–460.

Meier, D. (1987, Fall). Good schools are still possible. *Dissent*, p. 546.

Merton, R., Reader, G. K., & Kendall, P. (1957). *The student physician*. Cambridge, MA: Harvard University Press.

Meyer, J., & Rowan, B. (1977). Institutionalized organizations: Formal structure as myth and ceremony. *American Journal of Sociology, 83,* 840–863.

Mills, C. W. (1959). *The sociological imagination.* London: Oxford University Press.

Mintzberg, H. (1973). *The nature of managerial work.* New York: Harper & Row.

Mitchell, D. E., & Iannaccone, L. (1980). *The impact of legislative policy on the performance of public school organization.* Berkeley: University of California Institute of Governmental Studies.

Murray, H. A. (1951). Some basic psychological assumptions and conceptions. *Dialectica, 5,* 266–292.

National Commission on Excellence in Education. (1983). *A nation at risk.* Washington, DC: Government Printing Office.

NEA *Proceedings* (1884).

NEA *Proceedings* (1890).

NEA *Proceedings* (1925).

O'Connor, E. (1956). *The last hurrah.* Boston: Little & Brown.

P. W. (1962, December 15). Editor's bookshelf. *Saturday Review of Literature, 45,* 60.

Peppel, M. J. (1986). *Educational excellence: A function of school board and executive succession.* Unpublished doctoral dissertation, University of California, Santa Barbara.

Peterson, P. E. (1976). *School politics Chicago style.* Chicago: University of Chicago Press.

Peterson, P. E. (1985). *The politics of school reform 1870–1940.* Chicago: University of Chicago Press.

Phenix, P. (1964). *Realms of meaning.* New York: McGraw-Hill.

Plank, D. N. (1986, Summer). The ayes of Texas: Rhetoric, reality, and school reform. *Politics of Education, 13*(2), 13–16.

Rasmussen, K. (1967). *A journey to the Arctic.* Cambridge, MA: Education Development Center. [adapted from *The Netsilik Eskimos,* 1931]

Raverat, G. (1952). *Period piece.* London: Faber and Faber.

Research and Policy Committee of the Committee for Economic Development. *Investing in our schools: Business and the public schools.* (Available from Committee for Economic Development, 447 Madison Ave., New York, NY 10022).

Russell, J. E. (1937). *Founding Teachers College.* New York: Teachers College, Bureau of Publications.

Ryan, K. (1970). *Don't smile until Christmas.* Chicago: University of Chicago Press.

Schaefer, R. J. (1967). *The school as a center of inquiry.* New York: Harper & Row.

Schattschneider, E. E. (1960). *The semisovereign people.* New York: Holt, Rinehart and Winston.

Schattschneider, E. E. (1975). *The semisovereign people*. (Rev. ed.). Hinsdale, IL: Dryden Press.

Sellers, C. (1965). The equilibrium cycle in two-party politics. *The Public Opinion Quarterly, 29*(1), 16–38.

Slater, P. (1977). *Origin and significance of the Frankfurt school: A Marxist perspective*. London: Routledge & Kegan Paul.

Smith, L. M. (1979). An evolving logic of participant observation, educational ethnography, and other case studies. In L. Shulman (Ed.), *Review of research in education 6* (pp. 316–377). Chicago: Peacock Press.

Smith, L. M. (1980). *Archival case records: Issues and illustrations*. Unpublished manuscript. Exemplary Case Records Conference, York, England.

Smith, L. M. (1981). Accidents, serendipity, and making the commonplace problematic: The origin and evolution of the field study problem. In T. Popkewitz & B. R. Tabachnick (Eds.), *The study of schooling* (pp. 69–111). New York: Praeger.

Smith, L. M. (1982). Ethnography. In H. Mitzel (Ed.), *Encyclopedia of educational research* (pp. 587–591). Chicago: Rand McNally.

Smith, L. M. (1987). *The voyage of the Beagle: Field work lessons from Charles Darwin*. Paper presented at the meeting of the American Educational Research Association, San Francisco.

Smith, L. M., Dwyer, D. C., Prunty, J. J., & Kleine, P. F. (1988). *Innovation and change in schooling: History, politics, and agency*. London: Falmer Press.

Smith, L. M., & Geoffrey, W. (1968). *The complexities of an urban classroom*. New York: Holt.

Smith, L. M., & Keith, P. (1971). *Anatomy of educational innovation*. New York: Wiley.

Smith, L. M., Kleine, P. F., Prunty, J. J., & Dwyer, D. C. (1986). *Educational innovators: Then and now*. London: Falmer Press.

Smith, L. M., Prunty, J., Dwyer, D., & Kleine, P. (1983). *Kensington revisited: A fifteen year follow-up of an innovative school and its faculty* (Vols. 1–6). Washington, DC: National Institute of Education.

Smith, L. M., Prunty, J. J., Dwyer, D. C., & Kleine, P. F. (1987). *The fate of an innovative school: The history and present status of the Kensington School*. London: Falmer Press.

Smith, L. M., Prunty, J. J., Dwyer, D. C., & Kleine, P. F. (1988). *Innovation and change in schooling: History, politics, and agency*. London: Falmer Press.

Sorokin, P. (1947). *Society, culture, and personality, their structure and dynamics*. New York: Harper.

Spaulding, F. E. (1952). *One school administrator's philosophy: Its development*. New York: Exposition Press.

Spaulding, F. E. (1955). *School superintendent in action in five cities*. Rindge, NH: R. R. Smith.

Stein, J. W. (1962, October 1). Book review digest 1963. *Library Journal*, 87, 3445.

Stephenson, R. W. (1884). City and town supervision of schools. *NEA Proceedings: Department of Superintendence*, pp. 283–292.

Stone, L. (1981). *The past and the present*. Boston: Routledge & Kegan Paul.

Strayer, G. (1905). *City school expenditures*. New York: Teachers College, Bureau of Publications.

Strayer, G., & Engelhardt, N. (1925). *Problems in educational administration*. New York: Teachers College, Bureau of Publications.

Strayer, G., Engelhardt, N., & Hart, F. (1917). *School building survey of the public schools in Omaha, Nebraska*. New York: Teachers College, Bureau of Publications.

Study attempts to explain school failure. (1980). *The School Administrator, 37*(1), 3, 5.

Tolchin, M. (1985, August 4). When the justice system is put under contract. *New York Times*, p. E5.

Tönnies, F. (1963). *Community and society* (E. Loomis, Trans. and Ed.). New York: Harper & Row.

Toulmin, S. (1972). *Human Understanding*. Princeton, N.J.: Princeton University Press.

Townsen, R. (1970). *Up the organization*. New York: Alfred A. Knopf.

Tyack, D. (1964, March). Pilgrim's progress: Toward a social history of the school superintendency, 1860–1960. *History of Education Quarterly*, 4, 76–77.

Tyack, D. B. (1974). *The one best system*. Cambridge, MA: Harvard University Press.

Tyack, D. B., & Cummings, R. (1977). Leadership in American schools before 1954: Historical configurations and conjectures. In L. Cunningham, W. G. Hack, & R. O. Nystrand (Eds.), *Educational administration: The developing decades* (pp. 46–66). Berkeley, CA: McCutchan Publishing.

U.S. Congress, Office of Technology Assessment. (1988). *Technology and the American economic transition: Choices for the future*. Washington, DC: Government Printing Office.

Waldo, D. (1963). *The study of public administration*. New York: Random House.

Waller, W. (1961). *The sociology of teaching*. New York: Wiley.

Warner, W. L., & Lunt, P. S. (1941). *The Social Life of a Modern Community*. New Haven: Yale University Press.

Warner, W. L., & Lunt, P. S. (1942). *The Status System of a Modern Community*. New Haven: Yale University Press.

Warner, W. L., Meaker, M., & Eells, K. (1960). *Social class in America; a manual of procedure for the measurement of social status*. New York: Harper.

Whyte, W. (1956). *Organization man*. New York: Simon and Schuster.

Wildavsky, A. (1985). Federalism means inequality. *Society, 22*, 42–49.

Willower, D. (1986, March). *Marxist Critical Theory in Educational Adminis-tration: Pros and Cons.* Paper presented at Division A of the American Educational Research Association, Chicago.

Wilson, W. (1887). The study of administration. *Political Science Quarterly.* As cited in E. D. Cronin (Ed.), *The political thoughts of Woodrow Wilson.* New York: Bobbs-Merrill.

Wirth, A. G. (1983). *Productive work in industry and schools: Becoming persons again.* Lanham, MD: University Press of America.

Wirth, A. G. (1987). Contemporary work and the quality of life. In *National Society for the Study of Education Yearbook: 1987, Part 2, Society as educator in an age of transition,* Kenneth D. Benne and Steven Tozer (eds.), 54–87.

Wise, A. E. (1979). *Legislated learning.* Berkeley: University of California Press.

Wolfe, T. (1979). *The right stuff.* New York: Farrar, Strauss, and Giroux.

Yengo, C. A. (1964). John Dewey and the cult of efficiency. *Harvard Educational Review,* 33–53.

Ziegler, H., Jennings, M. K., & Peak, G. W. (1974). *Governing American schools: Political interaction in local school districts.* North Scituate, MA: Duxbury Press.

Ziegler, H., Kehoe, E., & Reisman, J. (1985). *City managers and school superin-tendents: Response to community conflict.* New York: Praeger.

Ziman, J. (1968). *Public knowledge.* Cambridge: Cambridge University Press.

Ziman, J. (1976). *The force of knowledge.* Cambridge: Cambridge University Press.

About the Contributors

H. WARREN BUTTON completed his Ph. D. studies at Washington University in 1961. That same year he joined the faculty at the State University of New York at Buffalo, where he continues to teach in the area of the history of education and edit the journal, *Urban Education*.

Professor Button's initial interest in the history of school administration has broadened to encompass a wide range of topics and interests within the field of educational history and bibliography. He is the coauthor, with Eugene F. Provenzo, of *Hisotry of Education and Culture in America* (Prentice-Hall), which is dedicated to Raymond Callahan.

WILLIAM E. EATON received the Ph. D. in Education from Washington University in St. Louis in 1971 with a specialty in the history and philosophy of education. He joined the faculty at Southern Illinois University in Carbondale the same year. With the exception of a two-year period as an assistant to the Academic Vice-President and Provost, he has served as a faculty member. In 1985, the Department of Educational Administration and Higher Education was formed, with Eaton as its first chair.

Professor Eaton's research interests are in the history of American education, especially in regard to teacher unionism, social reconstructionism, and the history of school administration. He is the author of *The American Federation of Teachers, 1916–1961; A History of the Movement* and, with Lawrence J. Dennis, coedited *George S. Counts: Educator for a New Age*. Both books were published by SIU Press.

LAURENCE IANNACCONE earned his Ed. D. in educational administration from Teachers College, Columbia University in 1958. In 1959, he took a faculty position at the Graduate Institute of Education at Washington University, St. Louis. He moved to Claremont in 1964, New York University in 1966, Harvard University in 1968, Ontario Institute for Studies in Education in 1969, the University of California at Riverside in 1971, and into his present position as professor of education at the

University of California at Santa Barbara in 1975. He has, since 1973, also served as a senior lecturer for Nova University's doctoral program.

Professor Iannaccone's research interests are in educational administration with a special focus on the politics of education. His major books include: *Politics in Education* (Center for Applied Research in Education, 1967); *Understanding Educational Organizations*, with F. Lutz (Merrill, 1969); *Politics, Power and Policy: The Governing of Local School Districts*, with F. Lutz (Merrill, 1970); *Organizing and Governing Education: A Report to the New York State Commission on the Quality, Cost, and Financing of Elementary and Secondary Education*, with J. Cronin (Harvard Graduate School of Education, 1971); *Problems of Financing Inner-City Schools* (Ohio State Research Foundation, 1971). He has published numerous chapters and articles.

FRANK W. LUTZ received the Ed. D. from Washington University in St. Louis in 1962 with a specialty in educational administration. After a year with the New Mexico State Department of Education, he joined the faculty at New York University. In 1968, Lutz became the director of the Division of Education Policy Studies at the Pennsylvania State University. He became the dean of the College of Education at Eastern Illinois University in 1980. In 1983, he assumed his current position as Director of the Center for Policy Studies and Research in Elementary and Secondary Education at East Texas State University.

Professor Lutz has published extensively in the area of educational administration, especially in the politics of education. With Laurence Iannaccone, he published *Public Participation in Local School Districts: The Dissatisfaction Theory of American Democracy* (Lexington Books, 1978); *Understanding Educational Organizations: A Field Study Approach* (Merrill, 1969); and *Politics, Power and Policy: The Governing of Local School Districts* (Merrill, 1970). He has also written *Toward Improved Urban Education* (Charles E. Jones, 1970); *Grievances and Their Resolution*, with Lou Kleinman and Seymour Evans (Interstate Publishers, 1967); and *The Struggle for Power in Education*, with Joseph Azzarelli (Center for Applied Research, 1966).

EUGENE F. PROVENZO, JR. completed his Ph. D. from Washington University in 1976 and took a position in the School of Education at the University of Miami. He has served as an associate dean of the School of Education, and is now a professor teaching the history, philosophy, and sociology of American education.

Professor Provenzo has diverse interests. In addition to writing two textbooks and several other monographs from the social foundations perspective, he has interests in the foundational aspects of curriculum and worked with a team of co-researchers in the replication of Dan Lortie's work on school teachers. His most recent book is *Beyond the Guttenberg Galaxy: Microcomputers and the Emergence of Post-Typographic Culture* (Teachers College Press, 1986).

ROBERT J. SCHAEFER earned his Ph. D. from Teachers College, Columbia University in 1951. He served as a faculty member and assistant dean at Harvard's Graduate School of Education before being invited to lead the Department of Education at Washington University in St. Louis. He organized the Graduate Institute of Education in 1956 and served as its director until 1963. In 1963, he was selected to be dean at Teachers College, Columbia.

Professor Schaefer is best known as author of the book, *The School as a Center of Inquiry* (Harper, 1957) which received national recognition. Schaefer has been retired from Teachers College for the last ten years.

LOUIS M. SMITH graduated from the University of Minnesota in 1955 with a Ph. D. in Educational Psychology. He joined the faculty at Washington University in St. Louis that same year. He has served at this institution since that time.

Professor Smith's research interests have moved over the years from psychology to social psychology, applied anthropology, and classroom ethnography. His major books include: *Educational Psychology: An Application of Social and Behavioral Theory*, with Bryce B. Hudgins (Knopf, 1964); *The Complexities of an Urban Classroom*, with W. Geoffrey (Holt, Rinehart and Winston, 1968); and *Anatomy of Educational Innovation*, with P. M. Keith (Wiley, 1971). Most recently, Smith had published a trilogy written with David C. Dwyer, John J. Prunty, and Paul F. Kleine. These books, published by Falmer Press, include: *Educational Innovators: Then and Now* (1986); *The Fate of an Innovative School: The History and Present Status of the Kensington School* (1987); and *Innovation and Change in Schooling: History, Politics, and Agency* (1988). Chapters written by Professor Smith appear in several books.

ARTHUR G. WIRTH earned his doctorate in 1949 from Ohio State University, where he had been working as a social studies instructor in its laboratory school. From 1949 until 1961 he taught history and philosophy of education at Brooklyn College. He continued to teach these subjects when he joined the faculty at Washington University in 1961.

Professor Wirth has been very active in philosophy and the history of ideas. His book, *John Dewey as Educator* (1966), and his several other books and articles on work and vocationalism have been widely reviewed and broadly recognized for their creative insights. Professor Wirth retired from Washington University in 1986.

Index

ABC News, 177
Adamany, D., 139
Adams, John, 98–100
Adams, Randolph, 99–100
Administrative doctrine, municipal reform
    and, 149–153
Adventures of a Biographer (Bowen), 85,
    94–101
Alger, Horatio, 163
American Association of School
    Administrators (AASA), 25–27, 31–32,
    112
American Freedom Library, 122–123
American Historical Association, 21, 101
American School Board Journal, 12, 113
Apple Computer, Inc., 178
Archival Case Records Conference,
    104–105
Associations, efforts to establish
    professionalism by, 34
Atkin, J. M., 102
Autobiography (Collingwood), 105
Autobiography (James), 105
Ayres, Leonard, 70, 75

Bagley, William, 50–51
Bailyn, Bernard, 4–7, 9, 21
Ball, Stephen, 106
Barlow, Nora, 84, 90, 94, 96–98, 100, 108
Barnard, Henry, 12–13
Bates, R., 133
Bateson, William, 84
Beard, Charles A., 39, 60
Becker, Carl L., 105
Becker, Ernest, 165–166, 179–180
Becker, H., 43
Bell, Daniel, 74

Bentham, Jeremy, 173
Berlak, Harold, 175
Berlin, University of, 72
Bernstein, R., 94
Biography, biographers
    craft insights into, 94–97
    as ethnographers, 100–101
    as human beings, 98–100
    as more fundamental perspective,
        97–98
    as research method, 82–85,
        94–101
Biography: The Craft and the Calling
    (Bowen), 85
Blow, Susan A., 51
Blumberg, A., 25
Boards of education
    conflicts between superintendents and,
        17
    cultivating members of, 32–33
    elections for, 15, 20–21
    members of, 31
    and professionalism of superintendents,
        34
    superintendents as agents of, 12–16
    and vulnerability of superintendents,
        12–22, 24–27, 29–35, 77
Bobbitt, J. Franklin, 19, 46, 48, 76, 126
Boles, K., 168–171, 179
Book Review Digest, 2
Boston Women's Teachers Group, 168
Bowen, Catherine Drinker, 84–85, 94–101
Boys in White (Becker, Geer, Hughes, &
    Strauss), 43
Brandeis, Louis D., 76, 97
Bredo, E., 94
Bremley, V., Jr., 126

Briggs, Thomas, 65
Brogan, D. W., 153
Bryce, James, 116
Burlingame, Martin, 29
Burnham, W. D., 137, 139–140
Burrup, P. E., 126
Business ethic, 35
  capitulating to, 37, 64
  conquest of, 145–146
  democratic values vs., 144–153
  emergence of new public creeds and,
    148–149
  and municipal reform and
    administrative doctrine, 149–153
  public school education influenced by,
    12, 16, 18
  relationship between government policy
    and, 161–163
  social conflicts and, 146–148
Business management, 27
Business manager model, 13–15, 18–19,
  114
Busing, 28
Butler, Nicholas Murray, 48–49
Button, H. Warren, 5–6, 12, 67–78, 139,
  150

Callahan, Helen, 74
Callahan, Raymond E., 1–10
  on educational reform, 111–116, 120,
    122, 124–126, 131, 133
  on history of public school education,
    3–4, 6–9
  new paradigm demonstrated by, 9
  and training of superintendents, 36–50,
    53, 55–60, 65
  U.S. realignment politics and, 135–164
  on vulnerability of superintendents,
    11–12, 15–16, 18–19, 21–28, 30–33,
    35, 37, 42
  and writing on history of education,
    67–78
Campbell, D. T., 103, 107
Candoli, I. C., 126
Cappon, Lester J., 4–5
Career-oriented superintendents, 28
Carlson, Richard O., 22, 28, 40
Cartwright, N. H., 2–3

Castaldi, B., 126
Caswell, Hollis, 52
Center for Applied Research, 104
Change, vulnerability increased by, 28
"Changing Conceptions of the
    Superintendency in Public Education
    1865–1964, The" (Callahan), 46–48
"Characteristics of Public School
    Superintendents," 26
Charters, W. W., Jr., 73
Chase, W. M., 142
Chicago, University of, 37, 46
Children of Sanchez, The (Lewis), 94
Childs, John, 60
Cistone, P. J., 140, 154
City managers, superintendents compared
    to, 17
City School Expenditures (Strayer), 52
Civil rights, 16, 28
Class Bureaucracy and Schools: The
    Illusions of Educational Change in
    America (Katz), 9
Cochran, T. C., 151, 155, 164
Collingwood, R. G., 95, 105
Combined role model, 13–15
Committee for Economic Development
    (CED), 176
Community, vulnerability of
    superintendents and, 21–22, 32
Conant, James B., 1–2, 117, 124
Conant Study, 124
Congress, U.S., 175, 177–178
Connor, William, 82
Conservativism, 121–123
Contract cycles, 20–21
Cooley, Mike, 165
Coolidge, Calvin, 120, 122–123, 158
Countesthorpe School, 106
Counts, George S., 1, 3, 9–12, 40, 60, 69,
    72–73, 75, 146
Crary, Ryland, 73
Cremin, Lawrence A., 3, 9, 21, 40–42
  Teachers College and, 48, 50, 54,
    62–64
Criswell, L. W., 140, 142
Critical election theory, 137–144
Critical theory, educational reform and,
    131–133

Cronbach, L., 107
Cuban, Larry, 16, 24–25, 28, 77
Cuban missile crisis, 10
Cubberley, Ellwood P., 3–9, 13, 19, 46, 49, 70, 126
  on cultivating school board members, 33
  and vulnerability of superintendents, 23, 33
Cult reform, 123–124, 126
Cummings, Robert, 38–40, 46
Curti, Merle, 24, 40

Danis, R., 140, 142
Dare the School Build a New Social Order? (Counts), 40
Darwin, Charles, 84, 97, 100
DeCharms, Richard, 73
Defense Department, U.S., 118
Democratic Schools, 175
Democratic socialism, 11–12
Desegregation, 16, 28
Dewey, John, 41, 57–58, 60, 132, 178–179
Diesing, P., 92
DiMaggio, P., 129
Discipline, 28
Discipline and Punish: The Birth of the Prison (Foucault), 172
Dissatisfaction theory of American democracy, 114, 133
Don't Smile Until Christmas (Ryan), 44
Dow, Arthur Wesley, 50
Draper, Andrew, 19
Dreiser, Theodore, 74
Drugs, 28
Duffy, W., 167
Dwyer, David C., 45, 79, 82–84, 86, 89, 92, 94, 102, 104–106

Eaton, William Edward, 11–35
Economic Interpretation of the Constitution of the United States, An (Beard), 39
Educational Administration as Social Policy (Newlon), 60–61
Educational Innovators: Then and Now (Smith, Kleine, Prunty, & Dwyer), 82–83, 86, 106
Educational Research Service (ERS), 26

Educational Review, 48
Education and the Cult of Efficiency: A Study of the Social Forces That Have Shaped the Administration of Public Schools (Callahan), 1–10
  on capitulating to business ideology, 37
  contribution of, 3–8
  on educational reform, 111–116, 120, 122, 124–126, 131, 133
  genesis of, 1–2
  original title of, 74
  prescription of, 9–10
  and shifting historical paradigm, 8–9
  success of, 2–3
  and training of superintendents, 37–42, 45–46, 48–49, 55, 59, 65
  U.S. realignment politics and, 135–164
  on vulnerability of superintendents, 11–12, 15–16, 18–19, 21–28, 30–33, 35, 37
  and writing on history of education, 67–77
Education as a Profession (Lieberman), 33
Education in the Forming of American Society: Needs and Opportunities for Study (Bailyn), 4–6, 21
Eells, K., 39
Effect of Teaching on Teachers, The (Freedman, Jackson, & Boles), 168–171, 179
Einstein, Albert, 8
Eisenhower, Dwight D., 121–123
Elementary and Secondary Education Act (ESEA), 106, 121
Elliot, Edward, 46
Encyclopedia Britannica, 122
Englehardt, N., 52
Ethnography, 100–101
Eulau, Heinz, 149
Evendon, Sam, 55
Explorations in Role Analysis: Studies of the School Superintendency Role (Gross, Mason, & McEachern), 25–26

Fate of an Innovative School: The History and Present Status of the Kensington School, The (Smith, Prunty, Dwyer, & Kleine), 83

Fay, B., 94
Federalism
  characteristics of developing paradigm
    in, 157–158
  hierarchical control in, 156
  redefining of, 158–160
  in the twentieth century, 153–160
Federal reform, 114–115
Feinberg, W., 94
Festinger, Leon, 80
Fischer, D. H., 67
Ford, Gerald, 121
Ford Foundation, 62
Formative period of American
  superintendency, 12–15
Foucault, Michel, 168, 172–174, 179
Frankfurt School, 131–132
Frankfurt University, 131
Freedman, S., 168–171, 179

Gadamer, Hans-Georg, 172, 177
Gage, Nathaniel, 52–53
Gary Plan, 41–42, 76
Geer, B., 43
Geertz, C., 92
Gemeinschaft to Gesellschaft trend,
  110–111, 123–125, 127
Generalization, vulnerability as, 18–19
General Motors (GM), 167
Genius of American Education, The
  (Cremin), 62–63
Geoffrey, William, 45, 88
Gerhard, Dietrich, 69, 72, 75
Goettingen University, 72
Goodlad, John, 171
Goodson, Ivor, 105–106
Gore, S. Joseph, 73
Goulet, Denis, 172
Gove, Aaron, 15, 33
Governing American Schools: Political
  Interaction in Local School
  Districts (Ziegler, Jennings, & Peak),
  24
Great Depression, 28, 61
Griffiths, D. E., 110
Grodzins, Morton, 136
Gross, Neal, 25–26
Gunnell, J. G., 130–131

Hamilton, Alexander, 159
Hamilton, D., 92
Handicapped children, 16
Hanus, Paul, 46
Harding, Warren G., 122
Harrington, Michael, 179
Harris, William Torrey, 19, 47, 50
Harrison, Benjamin, 122
Hart, F., 52
Hartz, Louis, 162–163
Harvard Educational Review, 24
Harvard University, 37, 46, 49, 72
Hays, S. P., 151
Henderson, Hazel, 165
Herrick, Neal, 180
Hexter, Jack H., 84–88, 105
Hierarchical control, 156
Hill, Patty Smith, 50–51
Hiring and promotions, favoritism and
  nepotism in, 16
"Historical Change of the Role of
  the Man in the Organization:
  1865–1950" (Callahan & Button),
  12
Historical method of research,
  82–89
Historical paradigms, 8–9
History
  Kuhn on, 9
  processive, 85–88
  vulnerability thesis and, 23
History of education
  Bailyn on, 4–7, 9, 21
  Callahan on, 3–4, 6–9
  Cubberley on, 3–9, 23
  as history of formal instruction, 5
  need for rewriting of, 5
  research on, 79–109
  writing of, 67–109
History Primer, The (Hexter),
  85–88, 105
Hofstadter, Richard, 40
Hogan, David John, 77
Holmes, Oliver Wendell, Jr., 95–97
Hoover, Herbert, 122, 163
Hudgins, Bryce, 73
Hughes, Charles E., 97
Hughes, E., 43

Iannaccone, Laurence, 30, 35, 73, 77, 114, 133, 135–164
Ianni, Francis A., 63–64
Illinois, University of, 19
Industrial efficiency, models of. *See* Taylor, Frederick W.; Taylorism
Innovation and Change in Schooling: History, Politics, and Agency (Smith, Dwyer, Prunty & Kleine), 83–84
Institute for Democratic Education, 175
Interstate Commerce Commission, 70, 76
Introduction to Education in American Society, An (Callahan), 42, 69, 72–73
Investing in Our Children, 176
Irony of Early School Reform: Educational Innovation in Mid-Nineteenth Century Massachusetts, The (Katz), 9

Jackson, Andrew, 149–150, 157, 159
Jackson, J., 168–171, 179
Jackson, Phillip, 44–45, 107
James, Henry, 105
James, William, 49
Jefferson, Thomas, 159
Jennings, M. K., 24
Johnson, Henry, 50
Johnson, Lyndon, 106, 121–122
Jorgenson, Lloyd P., 22–23

Kammerer, G., 140
Kant, Immanuel, 180
Kanter, R. M., 43
Katz, Michael B., 9
Kaufman, H., 148–149, 164
Kehoe, E., 17
Keith, P., 45, 82
Kellogg Foundation, 62
Kendall, Patricia, 44
Kennedy, John F., 10, 123
Kensington Revisited: A Fifteen Year Follow-Up of an Innovative School and Its Faculty (Smith, Prunty, Dwyer, & Kleine), 82, 89, 92, 94, 102, 104
Kensington School, 82–83, 85–86, 89–92, 94, 106
Key, V. O., Jr., 137–138, 141

Kilpatrick, William, 50–51
Kleine, Paul F., 45, 79, 82–84, 86, 89, 92, 94, 102, 104–106
Knopf, Alfred A., 42, 74
Koppel, Ted, 177
Kuhn, Thomas S., 8–9, 103, 107

Laggards in Our Schools (Ayres), 70, 75
Land Grant Act, 117
La Salle, Jean Baptiste, 173
Last Hurrah, The (O'Connor), 115
Leacock, Stephen, 71
Lenin, Vladimir Ilyich, 111, 133
"Leonard Ayres and the Educational Balance Sheet" (Callahan), 75
Lewin, Kurt, 61
Lewis, Oscar, 94
Library Journal, 2
Lieberman, Myron, 33
Life in Classrooms (Jackson), 45
Lindblom, C. E., 144
Linn, Henry, 55
Local reform, 114–115
Lodge, Gonzalez, 50
Logical positivism, 130–131
Loomis, C. P., 132–133
Lortie, Dan, 44
Lowi, T. J., 140
Lunt, P. S., 39
Lutz, Frank W., 30, 35, 110–134, 137, 140, 153
Lutz, S. B., 124

McEachern, Alexander W., 25–26
MacIver, Robert, 43
McKinley, William, 139, 158
McMurry, Frank, 50
MacRae, D., Jr., 137, 140
Macro-issues, vulnerability to, 15–16, 35
MacVannel, John A., 50
Majority rule, myth of, 138–139
Malinowski, Bronislaw, 100
Mann, Horace, 12–13, 114
March, J., 17
Marx, Karl, 36
Marxism, 23, 130–132
Mason, Ward S., 25–26

Massachusetts Institute of Technology (MIT), 80
Massachusetts Women's Research Study, 175
Maxwell, William H., 14–15, 19, 47–48, 50
Meaker, M., 39
Medical schools, schools of education vs., 65
Meier, Alphonse, 172
Meier, Deborah, 169, 171–172, 179
Meldrum, J. A., 137, 140
Men and Women of the Corporation (Kanter), 43
Merton, Robert, 43–44
Meyer, J., 129
Micro-issues, vulnerability to, 16–17
Milford School District, 83, 90–92, 94
Mills, C. Wright, 101–103
Mintzberg, Henry, 44
Mississippi Valley Historical Review, 2–3
Mitchell, D. E., 137, 140, 142
Monroe, Paul, 50
Mort, Paul, 65
Mosca, Gaetano, 137
Municipal reform, administrative doctrine and, 149–153
Murray, Henry A., 73, 81

National Commission on Excellence in Education, 118–119
National Defense Education Act (NDEA), 117, 124
National Education Association (NEA), 6, 59–60
  Department of Superintendence of, 13–14, 112
  Proceedings of, 14, 70–71
National Governor's Conference, 118
National Society for the Study of Education, 12, 76
Nation at Risk, A, 118–121
Nature of Managerial Work, The (Mintzberg), 44
New Deal, 163
New Harmony, 36–37
Newlon, Jesse H., 59–64, 146
Newton, Isaac, 8, 166

New York Times, 175
"Nora Barlow and the Darwin Legacy" (Smith), 84, 90, 94
Norton, John, 65

O'Connor, E., 115
Office of Education, 56, 62, 71
Office of Technology Assessment (OTA), 175, 177–178
Organization Man (Whyte), 43
Origin of Species, The (Darwin), 84
Owen, Robert Dale, 36

Paradigms
  historical, 8–9
  of political science, 24
  reforming of, 133–134
  scientific, 8
  twentieth century consolidation of, 157–158
Past and the Present, The (Stone), 85, 88–104
Peak, G. W., 24
Peppel, M. J., 142
Perfect gaze, ideal of, 173–174, 179
Peterson, P. E., 128–129, 140
Phenix, Philip, 46
Place-bound superintendents, 28
Plank, D. N., 128–129
Platoon schools, 41–42, 76
Policy manuals, 34
Political epochs, features of, 141–144
Political Ideas of the American Revolution (Adams), 99
Political science, paradigm of, 24
Politics
  business values and governmental policy in, 161–163
  Callahan's contribution in context of U.S. realignments in, 135–164
  characteristics of developing paradigm in, 157–158
  and competition of business and democratic values in reform context, 144–153
  conquest of business ideology in, 145–146

conservativism in, 121–123
critical election theory in, 137–144
crucial decades of conflict in, 139–140
cyclical patterns in, 140–141
educational reform and, 110–115,
121–123, 144–153
emergence of new public creeds and,
148–149
hierarchical control in, 156
innovation and reform in, 163–164
and municipal reform and
administrative doctrine, 149–153
myth of majority rule and, 138–139
redefining federalism in, 158–160
social conflicts and, 146–148
stressful coexistence of public vs.
private matters in, 160–164
twentieth-century federalism and,
153–160
Politics, Power and Policy: The Governing
of Local School Districts (Iannaccone
& Lutz), 30
Politics at God's Funeral, The
(Harrington), 179
Powell, W., 129
Principals, vulnerability of
superintendents and, 25
Processive history, 85–88
Productive Work in Industry and Schools:
Becoming Persons Again (Wirth), 167
Professionalism, development of, 33–34
Professional schools, 56–59
Program-planning-budgeting systems,
118
Progressive education movement, 41
Prosopography, 88–94
Provenzo, Eugene F., Jr., 1–10, 21, 25, 77
Prunty, John J., 45, 79, 82–84, 86, 89, 92,
94, 102, 104–106
Public Knowledge, An Essay Concerning
the Social Dimensions of Science
(Ziman), 103
Public Law, 94–142, 121–122
Public School Administration
(Cubberley), 6–7, 33
Public school education
application of efficiency and scientific
management to, 76–77

as continuation of European heritage
and early Colonial experience, 4–5
growth and development of, 3–9, 13,
21–23
history of. See History of education
influence of business ethic on, 12, 16,
18
reforming of. See Reforming education
scientific management in, 24

Rapp, George, 36
Rasmussen, Karl, 80
Raverat, Gwen, 98
Reader, G. K., 43–44
Reagan, Ronald, 118–120, 123, 156
Realms of Meaning (Phenix), 46
Reason in an Age of Science (Gadamer),
172
Reforming education, 110–134
Callahan on, 111–116, 120, 122,
124–126, 131, 133
common elements from 1900 to 1980s
in, 121–125
common models of, 126
competition of business values and
democratic values in context of,
144–153
conquest of business ideology in,
145–146
conservative federal politics and,
121–123
cost of, 127
critical theory and, 131–133
cult of, 123–124, 126
and dissatisfaction model of American
democracy, 114, 133
in early 1900s, 115–117
emergence of new public creeds and,
148–149
Gemeinschaft to Gesellschaft trend in,
110–111, 123–125, 127
Gesellschaft, secular, and bureaucratic
aspects of, 123–125
local, state, and federal, 114–115
logical positivism and, 130–131
municipal, 149–153
Nation at Risk, as impetus behind,
118–121

Reforming education (*continued*)
  from 1900 to 1930, 122
  political process of, 110–115, 121–123,
    144–153
  at present, 123–125
  and reforming of paradigms, 133–134
  rhetoric vs. reality in, 128–130
  social conflicts and, 146–148
  Sputnik as impetus behind, 117–118,
    122–124, 127
  tyranny of methodology in, 130–134
Reisman, J., 17
Research
  biographical method in, 82–85, 94–101
  classical statements as models for,
    85–101
  craft of, 101–103
  familiarity with single method in, 81
  genres of modalities in, 81–82
  getting methodology straight in,
    107–109
  historical method in, 82–89
  problem, method, and personal style in,
    80
  processive history in, 85–88
  prosopography in, 88–94
  series of beliefs and assumptions in,
    79–82
  sociology of, 103–109
  use of multiple modalities in, 80–81
Rethinking Schools, 175
Revisionist movement, 9, 23, 67
Rice, Joseph M., 150
Riecken, H., 80
Roosevelt, Franklin D., 122–123, 157–158,
    163
Roosevelt, Theodore, 122
Roth, Rita, 171
Rowan, B., 129
Russell, James Earl, 46, 48, 50–52, 54–56,
    58–59, 64–65
Ryan, Kevin, 44

Sachs, Julius, 50
St. Hilda's Conferences, 105–107
Saturday Review, 3
Schachter, S., 80
Schaefer, Robert J., 27, 36–66, 73, 134

Schattschneider, E. E., 136–139, 141, 147,
    154, 161–162, 164
School as a Center of Inquiry, The
    (Schaefer), 45
School Board/Teacher's Union Core
    Committee, 180
School districts, sizes of, 31–32
School inspector model, 13–15, 18–19
School Review, 22–23
Schools
  crowding and substandard nature of,
    16, 28
  limitations of, 8
  medical vs. education, 65
  professional, 56–59
  toward rational efficiency in, 172–179
  resistance to mindlessness in, 175–179
  as social institutions, 44
  violation of people in, 165–181
  and vulnerability of superintendents,
    22–23
  as workplaces, 168–172, 179
Schoolteacher (Lortie), 44
Schwab, Joseph, 52–53
Schwimmer, Rosika, 97–98
Scientific management, 24, 76
Scientific paradigms, 8
Scientific revolutions, 8
Sellers, C., 141
Semisovereign People, The
    (Schattschneider), 136, 154
"Shaping of Teachers College, The"
    (Cremin), 48
Shedd, Mark, 25
Simon, H., 17
Single-cause theories, 23
Slater, P., 131–133
Smith, David Eugene, 50
Smith, Louis M., 45, 73, 79–109
*Social Composition of Boards of
    Education, The* (Counts), 40
Social conflicts, 146–148
Social Darwinism, 152
Social Darwinism in American Thought
    (Hofstadter), 40
Social Ideas of American Educators
    (Curti), 40
Social origins tradition, 39–40

Social Science Citation Index, 2
Society: A Textbook of Sociology (MacIver), 43
Sociology
of research, 103–109
of work tradition, 42–44
Sociology of Teaching, The (Waller),
21–22, 44
Sorokin, Pitirim, 43, 45
Spaulding, Frank E., 19, 46, 48, 74, 126
Special education, 28
Special Education bill (PL 94–142),
121–122
Spectrum, 26
Spencer, Herbert, 152
Sputnik reform, 117–118, 122–124, 127
Stanford University, 37, 46
State reform, 114–115
Stein, J. W., 2
Stenhouse, Lawrence, 85, 105
Stephenson, R. W., 13–14
Stevens, Henry, 99
Stone, Harlan F., 97
Stone, Lawrence, 84–85, 88–94
Strauss, A., 43
Strayer, George, 46–47, 49, 51–53, 55–56,
59, 61–62, 64–65, 126
Strodtbeck, Fred, 102
*Structure of Evil: An Essay on the
Unification of Science of Man, The*
(Becker), 166
Structure of Scientific Revolutions, The
(Kuhn), 8–9
*Student Physician: Introductory Studies
in the Sociology of Medical
Education, The* (Merton, Reader, &
Kendall), 44
Students, schools as workplaces for, 171
Study of Public Administration, The
(Waldo), 148
*Superintendent of Schools: An Historical
Analysis, The* (Callahan), 145–146
Superintendents, superintendency
as agents of boards of education, 12–16
as business administrators, 3, 48
characteristics of, 26
city managers compared to, 17
conflicts between boards of education
and, 17

as distinct from teachers, 6
as educational statesmen, 18–19
failure rate among, 26
formative period of, 12–15
horizontal mobility of, 29
involuntary turnovers among, 29, 32, 35
models for, 13–14, 18–19
perils of, 24–25
professionalism of, 34
reasons for turnovers among,
28–30, 35
salaries of, 26, 31
training of. *See* Training
vulnerability of. *See* Vulnerability;
Vulnerability thesis
Supreme Court Justices, 15. *See also
specific Supreme Court Justices*
"Surveillance on the Job," 177

Taft, William Howard, 122
Tarbell, H. S., 15
Taylor, Frederick W., 7, 70, 75–76, 115,
148, 151, 156, 159
Taylorism, 41–42
Tchaikovsky, Peter Ilyich, 95
Teachers, teaching
as distinct from superintendents, 6
salaries of, 12, 26
schools as workplaces for, 168, 179
and training of superintendents, 44–45
and vulnerability of superintendents, 19
Teachers College (TC), Columbia
University, 3, 11, 69, 72–73
Cooperative Program in Educational
Administration at, 62
courses vs. programs in educational
administration at, 50–51
Cremin and, 48, 50, 54, 62–64
departmental system at, 58–59
Department of Administration at,
54–56, 59, 61, 63–64
Department of Social and
Philosophical Foundations at, 61
Division of History, Philosophy, and
Social Science of Education at, 63
Division of Instruction at, 58–59
early training programs in educational
administration at, 46–59

Teachers College (TC), Columbia
  University (*continued*)
  Institute for Field Studies at, 52–53
  Newlon at, 59–64
  Program for Educational Leadership at,
    62–64
  study of practice as source of
    professional knowledge at, 51–56
  subsidization of, 54–56
  and superintendents as administrators-
    philosophers-scholars-statesmen,
    47–50
  superintendent training at, 36–38, 40,
    46–65
*Technology and the American Economic
  Transition*, 175, 177
Theory movement, 118
Theory of Relativity (Einstein), 8
Thorndike, Edward L., 50, 58
Thorndike, Robert L., 68
Time for Results, 118
Tom, Alan, 53
Tönnies, F., 123
Toulmin, Stephen, 87–88
Townsen, R., 43
Training, 65
  capitulating to business ideology and,
    64
  conflicting perspectives on influence of,
    37–64
  and cultural and intellectual factors as
    historical determinants, 40–46
  and job of school administrator, 45
  and job of school teaching, 44–45
  Newlon and, 59–64
  social origins tradition in, 39–40
  and sociology of work tradition, 42–44
  at Teachers College. *See* Teachers
    College
  and vulnerability of superintendents,
    17, 27, 30, 32
*Transformation of the Schools:
  Progressivism in American
  Education, 1876–1957, The*
  (Cremin), 3, 21, 40–42
Truman, Harry, 163
Tyack, David B., 16–17, 38–40, 46, 77,
  149

*Uncertain Promise: Value Conflicts in
  Technology Transfers, The* (Goulet),
  172
Union of Public Employees, 180
United Auto Workers, 180
University of Chicago Press, 42, 74
Up the Organization (Townsen), 43
"Urban Superintendents: Vulnerable
  Experts" (Cuban), 24–25

Veblen, Thorstein, 43, 45
"Voyage of the *Beagle*: Field Work
  Lessons from Charles Darwin, The"
  (Smith), 84
Vulnerability
  change in increase in, 28
  and cultivating school board members,
    32–33
  and development of professionalism,
    33–34
  and formative period of American
    superintendency, 12
  as generalization, 18–19
  to macro-issues, 15–16, 35
  to micro-issues, 16–17
  perception vs. reality of, 17
  of superintendents, 1, 7–8, 11–35, 37,
    42, 73, 77
  in terms of intraorganizational and
    extraorganizational factors, 17
Vulnerability thesis, 19–34
  contemporary data on, 25–27
  and effect of school district size,
    31–32
  history and, 23
  possible refinements to, 30–34
  reaction to, 21–25
  reconsideration of, 25–30

Waldo, Dwight, 138, 148, 152, 164
Waller, Willard, 21–22, 44–46
Warner, W. Lloyd, 39
Washington University, 3, 42, 68–69,
  72
  Graduate Institute of Education (GIE)
    at, 73–74, 114, 134
  Graduate School of Arts and Sciences
    at, 57

Weber, Max, 150
When Prophecy Fails (Festinger, Riecken, & Schachter), 80
Whyte, William, 43
Wildavsky, Aaron, 158–159
Wiles, D. K., 140
Willower, D., 133
Wilson, Woodrow, 111, 113, 122
Wirt, William A., 41–42
Wirth, Arthur G., 82, 165–181
Wisconsin, University of, 46
Wise, A. E., 75
Wolfe, Tom, 81
Woods, George, 175

Workplaces
    toward rational efficiency in, 172–179
    resistance to mindlessness in, 175–179
    schools as, 168–172, 179
    violation of people in, 165–181
Work tradition, sociology of, 42–44

Yale University, 47
Yearbook of the National Society for the Study of Education, 12
Yengo, Carmine A., 24

Ziegler, H., 17, 24, 35, 113
Ziman, J., 72, 103